AROUND THE WEIRD
IN 80 DAYS

RICH SMITH

BANTAM PRESS

LONDON · TORONTO · SYDNEY · AUCKLAND · JOHANNESBURG

TRANSWORLD PUBLISHERS
61–63 Uxbridge Road, London W5 5SA
A Random House Group Company
www.rbooks.co.uk

First published in Great Britain
in 2008 by Bantam Press
an imprint of Transworld Publishers

A CIP catalogue record for this book
is available from the British Library.

ISBN 9780593059425

Addresses for Random House Group Ltd companies outside the UK
can be found at: www.randomhouse.co.uk
The Random House Group Ltd Reg. No. 954009

The Random House Group Limited supports The Forest Stewardship
Council (FSC), the leading international forest-certification organization.
All our titles that are printed on Greenpeace-approved FSC-certified
paper carry the FSC logo.
Our paper procurement policy can be found at
www.rbooks.co.uk/environment

Typeset in 11.5/15pt Palatino by
Falcon Oast Graphic Art Ltd.
Printed and bound in Great Britain by
Clays Ltd, Bungay, Suffolk

2 4 6 8 10 9 7 5 3 1

Mixed Sources
Product group from well-managed
forests and other controlled sources
www.fsc.org Cert no. TT-COC-2139
© 1996 Forest Stewardship Council

FSC

To Montgomery Brown,
beloved hamster,
who saw me through every moment
of the writing process

Introduction

As I fell to the ground, following an attack by a Native
American who had just leapt from his horse and
pummelled me into the ground before sinking a spear
into my stomach, I knew that this latest trip to the States
was to be far from the standard sightseeing tour
experienced by other tourists. At least I had my candy.
With this safely stored away, I was sure that I could keep
my trousers on and leave the battlefield in one piece.

Perhaps I should explain why on earth I was lying in
a field in central Montana after having been killed for
the second time in two days. My past experiences in
America are not unconnected.

In 2005 my accomplice Luke Bateman and I travelled
14,000 miles across America in an attempt to break
obscure, outdated and outlandish laws. A frivolous
crime spree, if you will. It was a thoroughly pleasurable
experience and, ever since our arrival back in the UK, I
had been yearning for an excuse to return.

The crime spree was a different type of road trip. In theory, although it was I who ultimately decided which direction we took, the location of the laws determined the path our cross-country venture would follow. It dictated where we would end up and whom we would meet. And I liked that. I enjoy small-town America, its people, history and peculiarities. They are communities in which the presence of a couple of Englishmen is something of interest.

In January 2007, I happened to stumble across a video clip on a very well-known video-sharing website documenting an event in Georgia known as the 'Redneck Games'. Hundreds of people in dungarees yelling and screaming whilst jumping in pits of mud was enough to get my undivided attention. From then on, I scoured every festival and events guide on the internet as well as all fifty states' tourism websites, and with a calendar, map and reams of scrap paper, I began to make a note of my favourites. I had found my excuse – a trip that would surely be as amusing as my last and, so far as I could tell, entirely legal.

With the crime spree, plotting a path was simple as I could turn up on any day of the week and break the law. This new itinerary was far more difficult, as although I wanted to stay out for an entire year, I couldn't afford to, meaning that the festivals that were held outside of my budgeted three-month summer were out of the question. Sadly, 'Mike the Headless Chicken Day' was an early casualty. Also, most events were staged over weekends and inevitably some coincided with others, meaning I had to pick and choose. The 'Mission Mountain Testicle Festival' in Montana did not make the cut, for example.

It wouldn't be much of a road trip either: although a hire car needed to be used at all times, reaching the far-flung locations would demand several domestic flights.

The only festival I decided to attend outside of the summer months was the 'World's Largest Machine Gun Shoot', in Louisville, Kentucky, which was to be held in April. I had heard it was a convention for gun enthusiasts and Nazi sympathizers, which sounded . . . interesting. Bateman and I would spend a few days there before returning to the UK to await the beginning of our major excursion in June.

A week before we were due to leave, Bateman sent me a text. It read simply: 'Don't think I can go'. He had broken his ankle playing rugby after a heavy night's drinking. I began a two-month campaign to have my flight money refunded because of his injury. A month later, Bateman pulled the plug on his entire involvement with the project, saying that he wanted to spend the summer 'getting a proper job'. Is 'professional sidekick' no longer considered a job these days?

Not wanting to travel alone, I enlisted the help of another friend, 22-year-old Antony, who naturally jumped at the chance of embarking on a free three-month holiday. He was a perfect choice. He was funny, light-hearted and, at that point, the best kind of student at Cheltenham University: one who had already failed (twice) and was simply enjoying the life of a dosser too much to return home to Cornwall.

With no late surprises, Antony was about to embark on his first trip to America and I had finally been granted what I had wished for two years ago: my chance to return.

1

Cowboys & Indians

I have always found entering America to be a bizarre experience. In 2005 I visited Niagara Falls, spent all of thirty minutes on the Canadian side of the river, then spent an hour in a queue to return to the United States. Fifty cents and a quick flash of your passport will allow you safe passage into the US's northern neighbour; whereas an iris scan, finger printing, and answers to a litany of questions including 'Have you eaten anything whilst in Canada?' were expected of me by Uncle Sam. Still, I was luckier than the woman and her baby taken to an office adjacent to me and subjected to half an hour of shouting by an immigration officer. Goodness knows what she must have eaten.

Past experiences, such as my Niagara nightmare, mean that the thought of entering the US fills me with dread. But worst of all is the fact that the entry procedure begins when you're 30,000 feet above sea level.

In order to be approved and accepted, and as long as

you are a citizen of one of the twenty-seven eligible nations, you are expected to complete what is known as an I-94W Nonimmigrant Visa Waiver Arrival/Departure Form. This, completed successfully and to the satisfaction of the terribly rude and sociopathic passport control officer, will allow you to spend ninety days in the Land of Opportunity. Along with the obvious and compulsory inclusion of your name, address and nationality, Part 10 requests you complete the address at which you are staying: pretty pointless if you plan to trek from coast to coast in an improvised and impromptu style. It isn't even that easy to fabricate an American address either: house numbering stateside can be anything from 1 to 50,000.

Still, the real fun doesn't begin until you realize there are more questions awaiting you on the form's reverse – and these really have me perplexed.

'Do any of the following apply to you?' it begins, and then lists a series of statements to which you simply tick the box marked 'yes' or 'no'.

Do I have a communicable disease or am I a drug addict? Nope. Mind you, how do British rock bands manage to sly their way past that one?

Am I a criminal or have I spent five years in prison? No.

Have I ever been deported from the US or previously removed from the United States? No.

Have I ever detained, retained or withheld custody of a child from a US citizen granted custody of the child? Well, let's have a think about that one. There was that time I withheld custody of a child back home, and that time I did it again after a night out in Prague . . .

Neither of those involved a US citizen, so that's a 'No'.

The form also includes the mother of all statements, one to which I'm sure the 'Yes' box has never been ticked since the form's introduction in 1986. And this one is so good I copied it on to my mobile phone word-for-word.

'C. Have you ever been or are you now involved in espionage or sabotage; or in terrorist activities; or in genocide; or between 1933 and 1945 were involved, in any way, in persecutions associated with Nazi Germany or its allies?'

Who in their right mind would even contemplate gracing the 'Yes' box with ink? Even Rudolph Hess, who was still alive when the form was first compiled, would simply have ridden his luck and hoped he wasn't recognized.

Once completed and signed, the form only then warns you that if you have answered 'yes' to any of the statements, you should contact the American Embassy before travelling to the United States, since you may be refused admission. Considering that by now the plane is making its final descent into Newark International Airport, it's just a little late to ask the pilot to turn around so you can plead with the ambassador in Grosvenor Square that you have already served your time for crimes against humanity following the Nuremburg Trials.

Anyway, having been born in 1981 and denied my chance of meeting anyone even loosely affiliated with Nazism by Bateman and his broken ankle, I made my way to passport control ready to face whatever impudent and graceless officer Newark airport had chosen to place on the day's rota.

'Hey, number fourteen, NOW!' he shouted.

Antony and I shuffled ourselves towards his allotted booth before he really lost his temper.

'Been here before?' he asked in a stentorian voice. I gathered he meant the US and not booth 14.

'I have, Antony hasn't,' I replied simply. The iris and finger scans followed before he examined our passports meticulously, every so often staring down at the picture before locking eyes with us in a way which suggested we had each replaced our official photo with a candid image of the two of us in bed with his wife.

Having finally passed security, Antony and I were free to leave the airport and catch a shuttle bus to New York City to begin our American adventure. Unfortunately, our first port of call was 2,000 miles west in the vast plains of Montana. The Manhattan skyline, which had glistened and shone below the cumbersome wing of our plane as she descended on to American soil, was to be as elusive as our collection of luggage at the carousel. While our fellow passengers departed through the terminal's automatic doors to hail a cab or collect a hire car, we made our way to the check-in desks and produced our documents once again in order to board a six-hour flight to Salt Lake City.

Ever since I first visited in 2005, I've liked Salt Lake City. Sure, the Mormons may have ruined it slightly by decreeing that all beer sold in the state should have an alcohol content of less than 3.2 %. And yes, the Great Salt Lake itself smells of sulphur, and is home to nothing more than billions of flies that cling to the shoreline and move in massive swathes like the rippling effect of water whenever anything comes near; but, generally, Utah's largest city and capital is a pleasant place to be. The city stands at the foot of the spectacularly beautiful Wasatch mountains, many of which are snow-capped even when the thermometers have pushed the mercury past 100 °F (which is a regular occurrence in the summer). Its downtown area is well laid out and unflashy, while eight-lane inner-city roads mean that traffic jams are rare.

Still, there was no time to hang around and sample the city's many architectural delights such as the Salt Lake Temple and the ultra-modern public library, nor was there enough respite for a quick bathe in our motel's outdoor pool. Today was Tuesday. Because I was too frugal to buy an expensive flight there, we were left with an eight-hour drive through three states in order to arrive in Hardin, Montana for the beginning of Antony's and my acting career.

The state of Montana has the nickname 'Big Sky Country', which I'm sure has as much to do with the region's beautiful blue atmosphere as it does with the fact that there isn't anything of great interest on the ground. When you take into account that the state – the fourth largest in the Union – is three times the size of England but home to just a fiftieth of its population, it's little wonder that the region appears to be totally deserted. Thankfully, once we arrived the town of Hardin seemed open for business and so Antony and I made our way to the Chamber of Commerce. We wanted to learn more about the town's weekend extravaganza, Big Horn Days, and to see if we could become active cast members for the highlight of the weekend: the 'Custer's Last Stand Reenactment'.

The Hardin Chamber of Commerce is situated in the

town's old train depot and, although there were many displays and purchasable goods pertaining to the Battle of Little Bighorn, Antony and I headed straight for the back office and to the three elderly ladies who operated the chamber's business.

'Hello. Is it possible to speak to Dorothy or Betty?' I asked, thinking it was best to speak to one of the ladies with whom I had exchanged emails about the reenactment.

'I'm Betty and she's Dorothy,' replied the lady closest to me. 'How can I help you?'

'Um, we've exchanged emails if you remember?'

'Oh, yes,' she replied, proving she was either very good at putting a name to a face, or that she didn't receive emails from the UK too often.

'Still possible for us to take part in the reenactment, is it?' I asked rather timidly. A look of worry shrouded Betty's face as she rose from her seat in order to fetch a large book from the shelf behind her desk.

In her emails, Betty had assured me that the show was always in need of fort soldiers, and that if we brought a navy jacket and a pair of navy trousers with a yellow stripe down the seam, we would be more than welcome to take part. I had both – albeit with some masking tape acting as the yellow stripe.

'You could be a pioneer,' suggested Betty as she ran her finger down one of the book's pages. Antony and I glanced at each other in disappointment.

Imagine, if you will, the situation. I had driven from my Cornish home to Gatwick Airport, flown to New York, waited three hours for a connection, caught another flight to Salt Lake City, then driven 600 miles to a small town in the middle of nowhere, just so an elderly woman could tell me that I could be a pioneer! Someone who dresses like a character from *Little House on the Prairie*, whose only action throughout the entire production was simply to walk from one side of the battlefield to the other. I was going to have to be just a tad more insistent.

'Any chance we could be fort soldiers? You said that they are always on the lookout for them. We've brought the navy jacket and trousers you asked for. I would have brought the gun too, but they didn't sell them at the army surplus store where I bought the clothes, and I doubt I would have managed to smuggle it through customs anyway.'

Betty looked up and slid her glasses from the front to the bridge of her nose. 'Pioneer?' she repeated doubtfully.

In the end, however, Betty acceded to our request and Antony and I were despatched from the chamber with identical application forms to complete in the town's main street on one of the tables that were positioned on the sidewalk. It was at this point that I turned to my new travelling partner and decided to explain why I love 'small-town America'.

'Ant, isn't this wonderful? We are in a place with a population of just over three thousand; there are nothing but fields once you leave the town limit, and the closest settlement of any reasonable size is almost fifty miles away. We must be the only British people in the entire county.'

This was a serious point on which to ponder, and made us both aware of the importance of our role in the weekend's reenactment. Any smugness we were tempted to feel was swiftly doused when we sat ourselves down with a can of cold drink and began to fill in the application form. We realized that of the four people sitting at the only other occupied table, one was an Englishman and another his Scottish friend. What made matters worse was the fact that with neither an American social security number nor a work visa, there was no way we would be paid the seventy-five dollars for our amateur dramatics.

After returning the forms (which had more disclaimers and places to sign than my mortgage agreement) to Betty at the chamber, and confirming our place as fort soldiers by deflecting yet another one of Betty's attempts to encourage us to take on the role of pioneers, we decided that we would each treat ourselves and purchase a kepi (a style of hat similar to those worn by the French gendarmes) to complete our makeshift nineteenth-century regimental outfits.

Due to the popularity of Big Horn Days, Hardin's three motels were booked solid for the three-day event, and so Antony and I based ourselves in Billings, Montana's largest city, conveniently located just 50 miles west of Hardin along I-90. It was here that Antony and I experienced our first decent night's sleep since leaving the UK.

The next day, Antony and I found ourselves in Hardin a couple of hours before the rehearsal was scheduled to begin, so we decided that it would be a sensible idea to visit the local museum to see if we could garner any more information about the battle. Before this point, I simply knew that the official name of the conflict was the

Battle of Little Bighorn, Custer's first name was George, it was probably the most famous Indian victory ever, and that Custer's men not only suffered a humiliating defeat but were totally annihilated. I was pretty sure that this knowledge wouldn't stand us in great stead when we met up with our fellow reenactors who presumably had years of experience, and would frown upon any faux pas made by two bungling Englishmen who had applied for a part in the festivities simply as a holiday jolly. You'll be impressed with what we managed to discover in a short amount of time.

What first struck me about the museum was the panoramic picture of the town taken in 1921 that adorned one of the building's walls. By simply changing the cars for their modern counterparts, the photo could easily pass as a black and white picture taken now. The museum's toilet was one of the most aesthetically pleasing places in which I have ever had the fortune to excrete. It was similar to a bathroom you'd find in your grandmother's house, with the added bonus of a moose head and Indian artefacts which you could study while business was being taken care of downstairs. Antony and I entered hoping to learn more about the Battle of Little Bighorn and left the museum safe in the knowledge that the town hasn't changed greatly in the past eighty years, the toilet was lovely, and that even though Montana's dress code (especially for the over forties) appeared to be denim dungarees and chequered shirt with oily baseball cap, and some sort of overgrown beard, not a single one of Hardin's previous twenty-four mayors had facial hair. That was going to impress the lads on the battlefield.

The site of the reenactment is five miles to the west of Hardin and fifteen miles directly north-west of where the actual battle took place, just outside the rather ridiculously named town of Crow Agency. A large, shabby-looking sign with the words 'CUSTER RE-ENACTMENT SITE' directed us from the main road and on to a dirt track. Travelling anything above ten miles an hour shot rocks and emitted huge clouds of dust from the rear tyres of the car, shrouding whatever had the misfortune to be behind you in a visually impenetrable plume of dirt which seemed to take forever to settle. After 500 yards, the track reached the brow of a hill, the road became much firmer, giving way to grass, and the higher ground revealed something I was certainly not expecting. There, in the middle of a flat plain amongst the rolling hills of Montana's Big Horn County, standing proudly before an assortment of corrals and camper vans like some modern-day refugee camp, stood a grandstand large enough to accommodate thousands of people. I had expected people who had paid sixteen dollars to see the show to sit on a bank or jostle for position to get a good view of the battlefield. Yet here was an arched stand known as bleachers (a wooden, roofless and inexpensive section of seating) that stood perfectly positioned in front of the 'stage' complete with fifty flags: one to represent each state in the union.

Once parked, Antony and I looked around for anyone who looked as if they knew what two aspiring re-enactors from England should be doing. Luckily, by the steps leading to the commentary box, beneath the flag of Idaho, we found Dave Riley, the show's director, and the Reenactment Committee chairperson Barbara Fickle.

(Before you start thinking that I have a brilliant and slightly disturbing knowledge of the state flags, I should point out that this particular state's ensign has the words 'State of Idaho' emblazoned on it . . . twice).

'Excuse me, but we're fort soldiers,' I said proudly. 'Just wondering if you knew what we should be doing.'

After discovering that we were an hour early for the rehearsal, Dave introduced himself and Barbara, and informed us of our very complicated duties during each one of the weekend's four shows.

'Basically, you come out of the fort and die,' said Dave bluntly, before Barbara added the killer line: 'And you just lie there until the show ends and the national anthem is played.'

Antony and I looked at each other, wiping sweat from our foreheads, imagining how hot it would be lying 'dead' in the middle of a field for the duration of the show. Antony then asked what both of us were thinking. 'How long do we have to stay there for? The entire show?'

'Oh, no,' Barbara replied. 'You only come out of the fort at the very end for the final battle. You'll only be on the ground for about five or ten minutes.'

So instead of having to lie on the ground for over an hour, mine and Antony's basic duties as fort soldiers were far more exciting: we were to stand in the fort for almost an hour, hidden away from the audience, before falling to the floor and staying there for a bit.

Simple.

Barbara remained talking to us as Dave made his way into the commentary box which stood in the centre of the stand, and gave us her number-one tip for reenactment debutants: 'Bring bags of candy with you.'

'Pardon?' I asked, not because I didn't know it was the stupid American word for sweets, but because the advice just sounded so peculiar. 'What do we need candy for?'

'For the Indian kids. When you die, they run across the field and try and get whatever they can from you. If you don't have candy you could be in a bit of trouble. One guy lost his pants one year!'

'We are in the right place, aren't we?' asked Antony. 'We haven't stepped into some sort of sordid outdoor orgy?'

With a lot of organizing to be getting on with, Barbara told us the best place to buy sweets, before making her apologies and leaving us to assemble the tables where the reenactors would sit for lunch following the rehearsal. At one thirty, an announcement thundered out of the site's public-address system to inform us that the rehearsal was just fifteen minutes away, and if the actors weren't already in costume, now was the time to change and meet their respective stage manager. It wasn't difficult for us to locate our supervisor: it didn't take a genius to work out that if we were fort soldiers, we should walk in the direction of the fort – a wooden structure made from thin tree trunks bound together, approximately 20 feet high, with a 200-foot perimeter and two gigantic plywood gates.

The inside was pretty basic: a seating area which appeared to have been constructed by me (or someone else with equally terrible DIY skills), a portaloo and a large wooden desk, on which we were promised two water tanks would be placed for tomorrow's opening show. Other than that, the fort – which was only three-sided to allow the cavalry easy access from the rear when their presence was not required on the battlefield – was pretty spacious, probably owing to the lack of soldiers who had bothered to attend the rehearsal.

In all there were just five of us, and the first thing Antony and I noticed was that their perfectly itemized and historically accurate outfits put our half-assed efforts to shame. Our inept attempt at clothing ourselves didn't seem to bother our stage manager, Pat, however, who clipped his walkie-talkie on to the waistline of his trousers and came over to greet us.

'You two fort soldiers then?' he enquired.

'Apparently so,' I replied self-deprecatingly, in an attempt to make a subtle apology for our attire, or lack thereof. 'What do you want us to do?'

'Well, Bob needs two people to open the gates . . .'

'We can do that,' I replied enthusiastically, sensing an instant promotion from fort soldiers to the more important-sounding 'fort soldier / gate operative', or perhaps 'defenders of the gate'; maybe even 'threshold protectors'. Yes, the title of 'threshold protectors' would fit Antony and me quite nicely.

Bob Port was a rather burly fellow in his early forties, with a grey biker-style moustache and a friendly and youthful face. He explained how to open the gates – a difficult procedure which involved removing the rope from around the handles and then pulling sharply towards the inside of the fort – before changing the conversation to something far more British. 'Oh, man. I love your Britcoms. My wife and I watch them all the time.'

Thinking Bob would list some of Britain's most recent finest, he began to recite the British situation comedies that American public television decides to broadcast.

'We love *'Allo 'Allo, Waiting For God* and ... what's that one where the guy lives off the land?'

'*The Good Life!*' I supplied in complete and utter shock.

'They're about twenty years old!' added Antony. 'What about *Only Fools and Horses* and *The Office*?' Bob stood dumbfounded and a puzzled look appeared on his face.

'We like *Fawlty Towers* too,' he added.

All was forgiven.

By now, the rehearsal was well under way, and because Antony and I had nothing to do apart from open a gate and die, we remained talking to Bob until a voice from above our heads introduced himself. Looking down from a rickety-looking platform to the right-hand side of the gates stood a man whose outfit not only looked exquisite, but made Antony and me look less like military figures and more like Compo from *Last of the Summer Wine*. According to his business card, which he dropped from his 10-foot vantage point – it landed between a clump of long grass and a dead rabbit – his name was Rod Beattie and he was portraying 1st Sergeant James Butler, allegedly the 'Last Man Standing at Custer's Last Stand'.

'Those World War Two RAF jackets?' he asked.

'Um ... yeah,' I replied unconvincingly. I didn't actually know what they were.

Rod was a rather dapper-looking fellow sporting what we were beginning to notice was the prerequisite reenactor moustache – this time of a thick, drooping handlebar and chin puff-style design. It transpired, once he'd managed to navigate his way down the ladder, past two rungs which were broken and not to be stepped upon, that he was an avid collector of military paraphernalia. He stood before us and studied our outfits, in the same way a headmaster would look disapprovingly at a pupil who had been made to stand outside his office. And he was right to do so, really. I was wearing Nike trainers (circa 2005, not 1885); navy trousers from when I worked for Haven Holidays, where I was employed to serve outrageously overpriced alcohol to over-aggressive northerners; and the navy jacket, which may have looked good on the previous owner but stopped short a few inches above my wrist. Unfortunately, there wasn't much time for any formal introduction as Pat was giving us our first orders.

'Open the doors!' he bellowed, as Custer's cavalry lined up for some sort of charge. A minute or so later the same call was made, and Antony and I welcomed both the cavalry and the pioneers' wagons into the fort. As the dust settled and the horses made their way to the back of the enclosure, Rod shook our hands and made an instant gesture of friendship.

'If you want, I can kit you boys out properly,' he suggested. 'Just come round to my camp.'

'Which one's yours?' Antony replied.

'Over there,' he said, pointing to what could have been one of five or six caravans and camper vehicles. 'It has four flags, a tented area between the van and my outdoor kitchen, and there's a giant buzzard sat on my camp's sign—'

I interjected quickly. 'We're not really gonna miss it are we, Rod?'

'No, I suppose not.'

The next stage of the reenactment was the meeting of the peace treaty council. Here, representatives of the Indians and the United States Army draft out and sign a deal in the very centre of the battlefield before each faction returns to their respective camp. The treaty, in the show's timeframe at least, lasts about ten minutes. The two opposing sides exchange signatures and hand-shakes for spears and hand-to-hand combat in the show's finale.

'Wanna go down as part of the treaty party, you two?' asked Pat. You didn't have to ask us twice.

'Yeah, sure. We can handle that. What do we have to do?'

'Just stand there.'

'Brilliant.'

Out of the fort and into the direct sunlight and intolerable heat, military promotions were arriving with increasing regularity. We began as badly dressed extras. Now we were badly dressed 'treaty party/threshold protectors'. At this rate by Saturday one of us would be asked to be Custer.

In actual fact, on a blisteringly hot day, the job of US treaty party was not a glamorous one. Antony, Pat, a few pioneers and I stood in a straight line directly facing the actors portraying Red Cloud and General Philip Sheridan, who led the negotiations for their respective sides. In the centre of the battlefield, on the only bit of raised land, stood a small table and beside it, a tribal translator gestured the words of the Indian leader whilst the actual speech was read out by a narrator for the benefit of the audience. In reply, Sheridan also moved his hands as if explaining something and a different (and clearer) announcer voiced *his* words. The whole inter-action was pretty effective and very well orchestrated, but for me, the best part of the scene was our retreating march back to the fort, my return to my position by the gate and the shade it produced.

The rehearsal for the final battle itself was more or less a non-starter. The main aim today was to check that people knew where to be, that the sound system worked and the narrators were in fine voice. Because it wasn't an official show, the cavalry units for both sides were nowhere near full strength and so Antony and I simply ran out of the fort when we were instructed to do so and fell to the ground when everybody else did. As we made our way back to the fort and then in the direction of our free lunch, Bob and Rod assured us that the real show's battle would be a completely different experience and that we should prepare ourselves for a 'proper attack'. We were going to be fine – Barbara had told us where the best sweet shop was and I was planning on buying enough to feed the entire tribe.

After a standard, but ultimately satisfying, lunch, which included Sloppy Joes (a burger bap filled with shredded minced meat in a seasoned tomato sauce), some cookies and a side of potato salad, Antony and I talked to our new friends some more about their role as reenactors. It turned out that both Rod and Bob were Custer's Last Stand veterans. This year, 2007, was Rod's ninth year at the reenactment and Bob's fourth. Both loved taking part and their involvement was something that obviously meant a great deal – especially to Rod, who lives eighty miles from Hardin and uses his annual holiday to make his yearly appearance at the show.

Our loud and resonant voices and English accents grabbed the attention of a fellow reenactor – the only one without whom the show couldn't continue. General George Armstrong Custer – or Mr Rick Williams when not at such events – was an amateur reenactor who had begun his career in Civil War reenactments in 1999. Because of his obvious physical resemblance to Custer, Rick had found himself playing the role for the past four years at Civil War reenactments over America. Like us, he had come to Hardin for the first time this year – all the way from Ohio. But as he said: 'I've been doing this for a few years now and you don't turn down an offer like this.' He said he felt like an actor who has been chosen to star in a film alongside his childhood hero.

Rick was quickly whisked away for interviews with newspapers, and to meet and greet fellow riders. Nevertheless, Rod invited him to his camp whenever he was free, and also asked if Antony and I would like to join him for some post-rehearsal refreshments.

Rod had described his camp perfectly. There was indeed a stuffed buzzard that sat atop a homemade wooden sign with the words 'Camp Wishah-Kudah-WunWun' on the top plank, and 'COMPANY L MESS', '1ST SERGEANT JAMES BUTLER', and 'ORDERLY SERGEANT' written beneath.

'Wishah-Kudah-WunWun?' I asked as Rod sat down to loosen his boots.

'Yeah,' he chuckled. 'I wish I coulda won one. It's just a joke.'

As Rod stepped into his camper van to look for clothes which would befit two fort soldiers better than our efforts, we were introduced to Rod's wife June. June looked to be in her fifties, with long brown hair which reached her lower back. Oddly, she looked more at home in her nineteenth-century pioneer outfit than in her everyday attire.

'Here it is,' shouted Rod as the door of his camper swung open. 'My toy box.'

A wooden crate was placed on the ground and the cover removed. It was like no toy box I had ever seen. Instead of coloured building blocks and miniature cars, Rod's box contained a collection of knives, holsters, belts and bullet shells, which he had amassed over his years as a military enthusiast. And, boy, he takes enthusiasm to a whole new level. As well as holding down a steady job as an electrical supervisor, he and June run a second-hand collectibles and historical memorabilia store. Rod is the founder and curator of a memorial museum; and including his saddle (which he used before he retired as a member of the reenactment's cavalry), his complete outfit was worth over three thousand dollars.

Antony and I sat down as Rod rummaged around for things to make our costumes more fort-soldiery (apparently it's a word) and gave us an insight into his own military background. He had only served for seven years in the United States Army, but had risen to the rank of sergeant and his CV read like G. I. Joe's. He was a paratrooper, a qualified armourer and survival expert, jumpmaster and gunner on the Redeye Air Defense Missile; he had served in divisions of the infantry, armoury and air cavalry units; and was a fully trained commando.

I know all this because Rod loves to talk. Mention any conflict and Rod has a fact, anecdote, or, if you're really lucky, a detailed account of the combatants and the weapons used around that time. Boring as this may sound, listening to the human military encyclopaedia was an absolute joy. His infectious enthusiasm and brilliant storytelling ability would endear him to anyone; children would hang on his every word.

In the two hours we spent at the camp, we learnt that at Rorke's Drift the Zulus never did commend the Brits' gallant defence of the outpost as the Michael Caine film would have you believe. We also discovered that Rod's father was a friend of Ernest Hemingway, and that one of the camp's flags – a star in the centre of a white rectangle on a red background – meant that Rod and June had a son overseas in the US military. Thankfully, the star was blue and not golden. Gold would have meant that their son had been killed whilst serving in Afghanistan.

At five o'clock, Antony and I decided it was time we should be leaving. We felt we had overstayed our welcome, but Rod and June didn't agree.

'We've been known to feed everyone on this site,' shouted June as she pottered away in the kitchen. 'You're welcome back any time.'

'We have to get some candy anyway, Rod,' we replied. 'Better go now before the shop closes.'

We said our goodbyes and were instructed by Rod to visit Fort Custer General Store where we could not only buy some sweets, but the correct insignia for our five-dollar kepis.

Fort Custer General Store was like no other shop I had ever entered. It was a strange mix of souvenirs, tacky play items and food essentials. To make the experience a little stranger, a small boy followed us around the store, hiding behind the end of each aisle and staring at us unflinchingly.

At the checkout, we found the correct insignia for our hats. Forty or so different types of sweets were available, ranging from the usual sours and liquorice to flavours based on soft drinks like root beer and Dr Pepper.

'Don't get the root beer ones, mate, it tastes like the stuff you get at the dentist,' I warned Antony.

The sweets were served to us by Christian, the child who had been hiding from us. We opted for a selection, so the Indian children would definitely find something they liked, which would hopefully allow us to keep both our trousers and our dignity.

'Why don't you ask them?' said the woman behind the counter to Christian after he had whispered something into her ear. 'He wants to know where you're from,' she said.

'England,' we replied.

'He thought you were from Australia.'

'Australia!' We were astonished, not so much because he was so wildly out, but because the way he looked at us suggested he believed us to be from another planet.

We left the shop and, strangely enough, so did Christian, picking up a motorized scooter from the shop next door to the store.

'I got this for my birthday,' he explained.

'Um . . . that's nice,' replied Antony. 'You like it?'

'Yep.'

'Right.'

'Bit lazy don't you think? You don't even have to use your feet,' I added.

'Yep.'

As Christian shot off back in the direction of the store, Antony and I made our escape. Once we'd reached our car, we could see Christian in the distance. By this time he had turned his scooter around, eager to catch a last glimpse of us. As we made our way out of Hardin, I could see in my rear-view mirror Christian leaning further and further out from behind a street corner for a better view of the aliens and their spaceship.

The following day, Antony and I arrived at Rodney's camp complete with two toy cap guns we had bought from Toys 'R' Us in Billings. Thinking Rod could supply us with a small holster in which to hold our plastic firearms, I asked if his 'toy box' contained such helpful items. Unfortunately, asking a man like Rod for a holster for your pathetic toy gun is like joining a group of Hell's Angels and arriving for your initiation on a moped. But instead of asking us if we were actually serious about our choice of weaponry, Rod looked up and said something we definitely were not expecting.

'Who's the best arm wrestler?'

Believing he was about to clear his camp table and get June to officiate, embarrassing me in front of Bob and Rick, who were a matter of feet away and already in costume, I decided I would allow Antony to take up Rod's challenge. Antony, however, was already pointing in my direction.

'He is.'

This would be my first ever international arm wrestle. Rod turned away and instead of clearing a space for the battle, headed into his camper van and came out holding some sort of rifle.

'Rich, have you ever seen an 1866 Sharps Carbine Conversion?' he asked.

'I think we both know the answer to that, Rodney,' I replied. I assumed he was referring to the rifle – unless he had taken to constructing his sentences by selecting words from the dictionary entirely at random.

'It's quite heavy, so you'd better have it,' said Rod as he handed me the rifle and the shoulder strap to which it was attached.

As well as the rifle, Rod had laid out entirely new outfits for Antony and me, and we were asked to enter Rod's camper van so we could change.

I shall now attempt to explain what we were wearing and use the appropriate name, followed by a standard explanation for those of you whose knowledge of historical military uniforms is not in the same league as Rod's. Accompanying my original trainers and navy trousers were a model 1866 Conversion Sharps Carbine (a rifle), a model 1855 carbine sling (a belt to which the rifle was attached), a prairie belt (a belt in which rifle shells were kept), a kepi/forage cap with cavalry sabres and regimental number (my hat with correct insignia), and a Bowie knife (a Crocodile Dundee 'That's not a knife, *that's a knife*' kind of knife). Rod had also provided me with a thick white shirt and a navy waist jacket. This made me glad I had the rifle. Without it, my costume made me look as if I was more likely to ask you for your train ticket than defend a fort from some Native Americans.

Antony's kit had more of a Wild West feel to it. It

consisted of a model 1858 Remington Percussion Revolver (a gun), a model 1860 flap holster (a holster), a buckskin jacket with fringe (a coat with frilly bits on the pockets and seams), a campaign hat (similar to a cowboy hat) and another Crocodile Dundee special. Antony was also given a pair of boots which rounded off his outfit perfectly. Unfortunately, no such boots were available in a size 14 for me to wear.

As the five of us made our way to the fort, Bob explained that the director had decided to change the show's ending so the battle took place directly in front of the audience instead of several hundred yards away on the hillside. As well as that, the show's committee had managed to persuade a descendant of one of the battle's Indian chiefs to open the show and speak on behalf of his people. To be honest, when he picked up the microphone and began to speak to the two thousand-strong crowd, I wasn't sure if he was speaking English or some sort of Native American dialect. To Antony and me it sounded more like the drunken ramblings of a man at chucking-out time. Unfortunately, these were not the only changes that had been made.

Blasting out of the stand's speakers was a song which I had never heard before even though it was originally released in 1984. It was with great dismay that Antony and I learnt we were to be subjected to it at least three more times if we were to fulfil our duties and take part in all four shows. Lee Greenwood's 'God Bless the USA' is a genuinely patriotic song, designed to stir the raw emotions of every proud American and kindle their passion for the virtues of the flag. And, in my opinion, it is complete and utter tripe. And that's not because it makes everyone within earshot stand still from jingoism (as if the rules of Musical Statues had been reversed), but because of the song's ghastly and laughable lyrics. If you wish to find out how truly terrible the song is, can you please make sure you obtain the single by some sort of illegal means. I wouldn't be able to sleep at night if I knew I was responsible for adding a single penny to one of Mr Greenwood's royalty cheques.

Following the ear-wrenching 'music' Bob released a fearsome shot from a cannon which stood outside the fort's gates – shocking the audience and scaring the hell out of Antony and me as it wasn't used in rehearsal. The show followed the same pattern as the rehearsal with the exception that Antony and I had been relieved of our treaty party responsibilities, and that all the fort soldiers who hadn't bothered to turn up for the previous day's practice run were now present. With Bob's wife Jill now alongside Rod in the lookout post, the fort was at full strength.

Soon the time came for the attack. Rod helped me load my rifle as well as handing Antony five blanks to store in his six-barrel revolver. In each show, the fort soldiers have two chances to use their firearms: once when Custer makes his initial charge to save the pioneers, and once in the final battle. As we opened the gates to allow Custer's cavalry unit through, I dropped to one knee and fired off a shot. Antony's gun simply clicked after he managed to find its only empty chamber.

When the cavalry returned, and the treaty scene had finished, Custer and his men made their way to the nearby hillside from where the final attack is launched. As Pat informed us, we had a matter of minutes until we too had to descend on to the field of battle. Bob loaded his revolver and talked us through what he thought we should know.

'You ready?' he asked. 'Be careful out there.'

'I've got some candy. It's all good, Bob,' I replied rather smugly.

'I'm not talking about the kids. I'm talking about the rattlesnakes.'

'The what!?' Antony and I shouted in horror.

'Rattlesnakes. Some were spotted earlier out there.'

'Just remember they can strike a distance equal to a third of its length,' added Rod.

'Thanks,' I replied sarcastically. 'But I'll be too busy running to get a ruler out and make sure I'm a safe distance away.'

'Yeah, if these people think I'm going to be lying still whilst a snake is trying to bite me, they can piss off,' added Antony.

Rod and Bob chuckled to themselves, apparently dismissing our serious concerns as simple pre-battle banter.

'Oh, and you'd better keep hold of all that stuff. Those kids'll take anything,' Rod warned.

'Get ready, people!' shouted Pat as we made our way to the side of the fort. 'Custer's attacking!'

'Pat?' I asked. 'What happens if no Indian actually kills me? Do I just walk around for a bit?'

'If no one kills you, commit suicide.'

Antony and I were both nervous. In the centre of the battlefield were dozens of horses which had created a whirling of dust and smoke from the blanks being fired. And it was into the mêlée of ferocious activity that we were expected to run.

'CHARGE!' bellowed Pat as he sprinted past me, before falling to the ground just yards from the fort.

'I'm following you, Bob,' I shouted as we darted across the plain and into the fray. After a jog of about a hundred yards I aimed my rifle high into the sky, as I was advised, and released my one and only shot before coming to the realization that Antony and I were the only remaining soldiers yet to be killed. Just then, totally unexpectedly, an Indian on horseback raised an axe above his head, wielding it at mine. He obviously missed on purpose so as to not kill me in reality, but I knew this was my time to 'die'. Having previously decided how I was going to act out my death, I slowly fell to my knees before slumping face first into the ground, making sure I landed on top of Rod's rifle. Antony, however, didn't have the same luxury of choosing his own fall: he was unceremoniously introduced to the soil by a dump tackle of which Jonah Lomu would have been proud.

When all the army units had met their fate, the Indians gathered Custer's flag and returned to the centre of the battlefield where the announcers explained more of the story and the repercussions of the war. This was the signal for the Indian children to leave their camps and begin their pillage. All of the warnings I had been given about the ferocity and ruthlessness of the children's plundering were greatly exaggerated.

'Do you have any candy?' a young girl who had approached me on her own asked politely.

'Yes. You can have the whole bag if you want,' I replied kindly, before realizing what a horrible and foolish mistake I had made.

I had two pockets on the front of my waist jacket in which I could have stored the sweets. I could have even strapped the bags to the back of my belt or rifle strap. Instead, I was stupid enough to place them inside my right-trouser pocket – a place where it was surely morally and ethically wrong to invite a young girl's hand.

Although we had been instructed to stay perfectly still once we had been killed, I decided it would be wise to employ a bit of posthumous nerve twitching – the kind that loosens the position of a bag of sweets from out of your pocket and on to the ground.

Finally, after the American national anthem is played, all troops rise from the dead and the audience are allowed to walk on to the battlefield and converse with members of the cast. This is where Rod is in his element. It's the part of the show you can tell he has waited a year for.

Antony and I simply skulked around hoping no one would ask us anything and uncover our pitiful lack of knowledge about everything we were wearing and doing.

Ten minutes after the end of the performance, Ant and I made our way back to Rod's camp, shortly followed by June and Bob. It was about half an hour before Rod and Rick joined the group.

'You love it, don't you, Rodney?' asked Antony.

'I do indeed,' he replied. 'Absolutely love it.'

After just one performance, however, it appeared as if Rick wasn't too enamoured of his role as Custer. He had only fifteen minutes at our camp before he had to take part in newspaper and television interviews, and he was appearing in Hardin's street parade the following day. Custer was a wanted man on the battlefield, and off it everyone wanted a piece of Rick.

Rod wasn't too happy either. At the rehearsal, we had been asked to remain 'dead' during the national anthem, and resurrect ourselves after it had finished. Rod and many of the fellow reenactors were not in favour of this. 'I want to stand for the anthem,' he declared. 'I've had a word with Pat and he says they are going to play "Taps" (a bugle song similar to the "Last Post") tomorrow and then we rise for the anthem.'

All in all, the show went very well and was only marred by two helicopters passing overhead, ruining the authentic nineteenth-century Montana feel. What was strange, however, was that in our mock battle, not a single Native American ended the performance on the ground. Surely that couldn't be right? To find out, and because two performances were booked for the following day, Antony and I decided that now was the best time to visit the actual site of the battle. We wanted to discover just how accurate our reenactment was compared to what really took place in 1876, 131 years ago. Rod and June were kind enough to invite us to eat with them in the evening and told us that the battlefield was well worth a visit.

'It's very good, Rich,' stated Rod. 'Best of all, I think it's free.'

For a mere ten dollars, the public are allowed to explore the grounds of Little Bighorn Battlefield National Monument, and, at over 750 acres, the area's vastness is overwhelming. Along the luscious and undulating hills, white marble markers pinpoint where both soldiers and Indians fell on 25 June 1876. They are peppered everywhere, too numerous to count. Historical estimates put the battle's length at less than thirty minutes, in which time over 400 men lost their lives and 200 more were wounded. On the brow of the hill where Custer and his men drew their final breaths, and where the concentration of markers is at its most dense, an obelisk commemorates the fallen soldiers. Only 500 yards away is Custer National Cemetery, home to the remains of almost 5,000 people: not only the battle's 7th Cavalry unit but also the dead of more modern conflicts. Despite the cemetery's name, General George Armstrong Custer's body was exhumed and taken to be buried 1,500 miles west in New York.

The park's visitor centre and museum contained a great deal of interesting information about the battle as well as some rather strange exhibits, not least the glass cabinet that contained a razor and bar of soap once used by Custer. Snippets that caught my eye included the fact that many of the Indians actually used better rifles in the battle than their adversaries; Custer and Crazy Horse were both aged thirty-six at the time of the Little Bighorn; and five months after their defeat, the American army won the rather interestingly named Dull Knife Fight. Before we made our way back to Hardin, I noticed another display that depicted what nations were represented in Custer's unit. Of the 793 enlisted men, 473 were born in America, 129 were Irish, and 127 were Germans. The remaining 64 were drawn from 14 other countries including the United Kingdom and 2 who were simply categorized as 'at sea'.

Back at Camp Rodney, June and her husband were

busy preparing the evening's meal and we learnt that the committee weren't best pleased with Antony – or, as they put it, 'the idiot with the cowboy hat'. The reason for this was that when Antony 'died' and the Indian children had approached his 'corpse' for candy, they had also asked for any shells or military souvenirs. In attempting to inform them that what they were after didn't belong to him, Antony had found himself lying on his side, gesticulating and casually conversing with the kids as if he were lying on a towel and chatting to friends at the beach.

In the evening, June and Rod's antelope steak was the obvious cause of the camp's sudden increase in popularity. We were joined by most of the fort crew including Bob, his wife, and Randy, one of the cavalry members. We all tried our best to keep Rod from dominating the conversation but he loved talking too much. His that-reminds-me-of-another-story finger was in constant use. The only dull moments came when, for nearly half an hour, Rod attempted to explain his pay and pension structure to us. He went on so long that I think he even confused himself. Antony and I diverted him by telling our favourite jokes. After an hour or so, it became apparent that Montanans use North Dakotans and Texans as the English use the Irish as their subject of ridicule, and that Randy would only find a joke funny if there was a rude word in the punchline. Several hours passed before we decided to leave, and because Rod was such a good storyteller, no one noticed the sun had set below the rural horizon and his distinctive face had become a mere silhouette in front of a gas camplight.

*

The weather report had predicted temperatures as high as 102 °F, so it was with great relief to find as we arrived at Rod's camp that the overcast conditions had lowered the temperature to the high eighties.

'Glad you could make it,' said Rod sarcastically.

'Plenty of time, Rodney,' replied Antony, as we made our way into the camper van to get changed. We had less than an hour before the first of the day's two shows.

Back in the fort, normal service was resumed. Lee Greenwood made everyone stand perfectly still, the Indian descendant continued his ramblings, and Bob shocked everyone with his cannon fire – quite literally scaring the shit out of Antony who was in the portaloo at the time. Instead of helicopters ruining the historic authenticity, this show had to deal with a passing train: it took almost ten minutes for its four forbidding diesel engines to pull its eighty carriages past. Trains are supposed to stop for performances, and as many in the fort complained about it, I busied myself picking bits of spiky thorns out of my leg. Because I was wearing trainers and not boots, they had managed to attach themselves to my sock. I removed my shoes and Bob noticed me plucking them from my sock.

'Fuck tale?' he shouted.

'I beg your pardon, Bob?' I asked, thinking he hated them more than I did.

'Foxtails. They're called foxtails.'

It quickly became apparent to Antony and me that Rod wasn't Pat's biggest fan, took no notice of the stage manager when an order was shouted. I may not be a brilliant lip reader but I've watched enough football matches to know when someone is mouthing the words

'Fuck off, Pat'. I later learnt that Rod had been asked to be the stage manager in only his second year, a job he'd accepted before deciding to step down because it took the fun out of the reenactment.

Minutes before the final battle, everyone prepared themselves with the exception of Jill who decided she would remain in the fort. Antony, still smarting from the previous day's warning from the committee and the spear tackle he received from his 'killer', played things safe by quickly taking a shot and falling to the floor just yards into his battle sprint. I, on the other hand, managed to attract the attention of a warrior who leapt from his horse, and tackled me to the ground before taking a knife from his pocket and pretending to thrust it into my stomach.

With a change to the ending in place, all soldiers remained on the floor for 'Taps' but rose to observe the national anthem. Before Antony and I could escape the post-show interaction with the audience, a member of the crowd and his son approached me and pointed at my rifle.

'What kind of gun is that?' he asked.

'It's a 1970 ... no ... hang on,' I replied, trying to remember its name. 'Rod! What's this called again?'

As he was only standing a matter of feet from me, Rod came to my rescue and informed the father and son that it was an 1866 Sharps Carbine Conversion. I needed to remember that.

Back at the camp, post-show conversations always began with how you died, and Rick, playing the much coveted part of Custer, always had the best stories.

'I was attacked by a young guy at first,' he told us. 'So

as I pinned him down and pretended to punch him, his big brother spotted me and hit me with such force that I was thrown to the floor. I think I'm getting too old for this.'

The two-hour break between the end of the matinee and the beginning of the evening show gave Rod more time to tell stories and, this time, complain about the state of journalism in the country. With a degree in journalism myself, I thought I'd best keep quiet. Because the reenactment featured within its pages, Rick had a copy of the local newspaper in his hand, and Rod's point was instantly proven. Not only had the *Billings Gazette* used the word 'losingest' in one of its front page headlines, but they highlighted the reenactment's international appeal by including a quote from 63-year-old John Jeffries, an Englishman who was in the audience! All he'd done was sit in the stand. There wasn't even a mention for the two threshold protectors who hailed from that fair nation, and who had already died for someone else's country twice.

In the second of the day's shows, I was invited to join the treaty party and, with Rod leading the march, I walked out of the fort. Rod took this role very seriously and you could tell he had once had military experience. He would shout things like 'About turn!' and 'About face!', and because I didn't know what either of them meant, I simply did whatever everyone else under his command did.

After the battle – in which I had to commit suicide as I couldn't find a single person to kill me – I saw some members of the audience making their way towards me. I grasped my rifle, constantly reminding myself of its name so as not to make the same mistake as I had earlier in the afternoon. *1866 Sharps Carbine Conversion. 1866 Sharps Carbine Conversion.*

'Hey,' remarked one of two burly-looking men in baseball caps. 'What type do you call that?'

With an air of smugness about me, I pulled the gun down from my shoulder and lay it across my two open hands. I may not have had a single line in the show, but this was my cue. My time to deliver. 'This . . .' I said with a smile on my face, 'is an 1866 Sharps Carbine Conversion.'

'Oh yeah?' the other replied. 'What calibre?'

Shit.

It was surprising that after three shows in two days, it took until the Saturday night for Rick, Bob and Rod to make Antony and me try our hand at shooting some guns. After all, we were in Montana, a state which, according to Rod and Bob, had no rules, and even the speed limit was just 'a suggestion'. To begin with, Bob showed Antony that a blank could easily dent a can from close range. Bob then produced an 1860 Henry Rifle and an 1873 Colt Peacemaker (which I've always thought to be a stupid name for a gun) which he had used in the reenactment, and asked Antony and me to try them out.

'Where should I aim?' asked Antony.

'Anywhere towards that hill,' Bob replied.

Antony and I blasted holes in the hillside for some time before we noticed that owing to the kick of the gun most of our shots were missing the bank completely and continuing over the brow of the hill.

'What's over there?' enquired Antony as he turned to Bob with gun in hand, making him duck with fear.

'Nothing much,' he replied. 'Only the freeway.'

Rod, who by this time must have been incensed by no one listening to him, decided to teach me a lesson by handing me my 1866 Sharps Carbine Conversion and a real bullet for it, instead of the blanks I'd had all day.

'Try this out,' he said.

'Sure,' I replied, insouciantly, well aware by now what little impact a blank had when shot from the rifle.

Unbeknownst to me, however, Rod had handed me a full-bore shell instead of the regular shell. Apparently, this was a trick played on new recruits when entertainment was hard to come by on Western posts. The change made a lot of difference.

Holding the gun up to my shoulder and aiming at nothing in particular so long as it was green and unpopulated, I squeezed the trigger gently. An almighty blast produced smoke from the barrel, another shot sped towards the freeway, and an instant and undesirable pain ignited in my right shoulder. I turned around clutching my collarbone, which was already beginning to bruise, to see the rest of the camp laughing at my misfortune, revelling at the sight of a Brit biting off more than he could chew.

On the night-time drive back to Billings, Antony and I witnessed our first piece of major road kill: a dead deer in the middle of the road. As quickly as it appeared in our headlights, it was under the wheels of our 4-wheel-drive Suzuki, sending us a foot or so out of our seats. As I regained control of the car, we complained to each other about people who would leave such a large animal carcass in the middle of the road. It wasn't until we returned to the motel that it dawned on us. With our erratic and inaccurate gunfire earlier in the evening, it may well have been us who killed it.

When we arrived for the final day's reenactment, we found Rod and Rick standing side by side and Rod began to read from a piece of paper in his hand.

'Private Richard Smith, having distinguished himself by his perseverance and dedication to his duty, while serving as a trooper in Company L, 7th US Cavalry during the 2007 reenactment of the Battle of Little Bighorn, is hereby awarded the rank of Honorary Corporal, and is entitled to all the privileges therein, and to expound at great length on his exploits, without censure. Given this twenty-sixth day of June 2007.'

Both he and Rick shook my hand before handing me the certificate. Antony then received the same treatment.

'Um . . . thanks, Rod.' What else *do* you say to that?

The final show was the best yet, with the exception of a car alarm resonating through some of the early parts. As Antony and I ran into battle, you could tell that neither of us wanted it to end. By the look of it neither did the Indians, as I had to shout at a passing warrior to get him to kill me.

Back at the camp, Antony and I handed out presents to Bob, June and Rick. Because of his love of British sit-coms, we gave Bob and Jill something equally British: a croquet set. To June we presented a decorative glass paraffin lamp. And to Rod, a man who not only bought military clothing but made his own, we presented a British Bulldog belt buckle (complete with British flag reverse) that we had purchased from the Fort Custer General Store. He promised to wear it – or at least make a belt that would accommodate such an item – when he returned home.

Bob and Jill decided that beating the Native Americans and the horse boxes out on to the road was the best bet and after a parting handshake, hit the road, leaving Antony and me with Rod and June.

'Thanks for everything, June, you've been great,' I said, as I extended my right hand. June ignored it and gave both Antony and me a hug.

'It's been great having you. A real pleasure,' she replied.

Rod gave each of us a firm handshake, which I couldn't help but convert into a quick hug and pat on the back. And why not? Rod and June had been perfect hosts, and had extended the arm of friendship with unquestioning generosity: for the past four days, Antony and I had been dressed and fed magnificently by them. Now, in the middle of a field amongst the clamour of people packing up, horses refusing to enter their boxes and the constant drone of departing vehicles, it was time to say goodbye. The reenactment had been a wonderful start to our American trip, and we hoped that meeting such pleasant and welcoming people would fast become a trend. It may have been a fake battle, but Bob and Rod were true companions-in-arms, and there were no other people that we would rather have had by our side.

2

Basquing in the Sun

We were in no particular rush to get to Salt Lake City when we left Billings, so we decided that instead of driving back to Utah using interstates, we would travel south and enter the north-west region of Wyoming. A major factor in this decision was that this particular route would take us through Yellowstone National Park.

The last time I was in Wyoming was with Bateman in 2005. He was given a $220 speeding fine for travelling at 97 mph in a 75 mph zone. He later admitted that it was a good job the State Trooper hadn't stopped him ten minutes before, when he was doing 120. Instead of paying the outrageously high fine or appearing in court as his ticket instructed, Bateman and I had flown home. I suspect that there still remains a warrant out for his arrest. I was in the passenger seat at the time but, confident that 'accomplice to speeding' isn't a crime, assumed that I wouldn't see myself on Wyoming's Most Wanted list.

We entered Wyoming on a standard road which twisted and carved its way through a surrounding mountain range in the Shoshone National Forest. The only way we could drive was upwards. It wasn't until we had reached a lookout point at 8,000 feet that I noticed the hire car was dangerously low on fuel. We had enough petrol to take us ten more miles, and even that was being generous. Having already driven through it, I knew that Red Lodge was at least twenty miles behind us and so I turned to Antony, who had the map in his hand, and asked how far it was to the next town.

'Um . . .' he said, running his fingers between the map's mileage scale and the road we were on, '. . . about eight miles, mate.'

'Thank God for that,' I exhaled. 'Thought we were gonna have to walk for miles then.'

'Oh, no. Hang on,' he added. 'Make that about thirty-eight miles. I didn't know where we were.'

'Great.'

For the next ten minutes, my eyes spent less time focusing on the road and more on the car's digital fuel economy readout and the fuel tank display. Hard as it was to not over-rev the engine and save fuel, the job was made increasingly difficult by the fact that the summit appeared to be nowhere in sight. We passed 9,000 feet, then 10,000 feet with snow by the sides of the road and an outdoor temperature that had plummeted from 92 °F to 41 °F.

Thankfully, at 11,700 feet we reached a flat snow-covered plateau and the road began to descend. I put the car into neutral and coasted downhill, changing my miles per gallon readout from 26 to 99. After several miles, the road began to level out and gears were required once again, thrusting us back into despair. As we entered a forested area, a small building with several cars parked outside came into view. The entrance sign to what was a 'last-chance type store' informed us it sold food, drinks, souvenirs ... and gas. I pulled up by its 1950s-style pump and entered the shop to enquire how much it was.

At almost seven dollars a gallon they really were cashing in on idiots like me who were in desperate need of fuel. Even though most people in the shop gasped at the prospect of paying such an absurd amount of money for a gallon of petrol, I was only too happy to part with my cash. Although Americans relentlessly complain about the price of fuel in their country, seven dollars a gallon was still less than I paid back in the UK, so as far as I was concerned, I was getting a bargain. It was enough fuel to get us to Silver Gate, where we could fill up before entering Yellowstone National Park.

On 1 March 1872, Yellowstone became the world's first national park. It is best known for its geothermal activity, including the well-known geyser Old Faithful. Unfortunately, it's also the temporary home to a mass of tourists who hold up queues of traffic in order to take photographs of squirrels sitting by the side of the road. Covering 3,472 square miles, Yellowstone is impossible to see in just one day, and so Antony and I decided we would simply do the 'touristy thing' and see the 'good stuff'. Our first challenge was locating a parking space along the roadside beside the Mammoth Hot Springs. The springs are a series of fractured limestone rock terraces through which hot water can reach the earth's surface. Past volcanic activity has left the terraces a technicolour visual feast, and created shapes that even the greatest artistic mind couldn't conjure up.

The region in which you find Old Faithful is dotted with hundreds of other geysers, giving you the distinct impression that the earth is not only wild but most definitely alive. From a distance, it looks as if a steam locomotive is coming around every corner as steam fills the air at random intervals and from arbitrary positions across the barren expanse.

Old Faithful is the most popular of all of Yellowstone's geothermic treats and, since this is America, is located near several shops, car parks and hotels. The geyser itself is surrounded by enough seating to accommodate several hundred people and erupts every ninety minutes. By the look of the number of people who had already assembled around the hole in the ground, it appeared as if Antony and I would not have to wait too long for the action to begin. Little jets of water that shot several yards into the air teased the audience before everyone felt the ground rumble beneath their feet. Just twelve minutes after we had arrived, Old Faithful let rip. A wall of water was discharged over a hundred feet into the afternoon sky. It was obvious why people had waited so long for the spectacle, and explained why the seated area is situated a clear 200 yards from the geyser. At the end of the eruption, after 5,000 gallons of water had been ejected from the earth's crust, the crowd departed quickly, rushing to their cars for a quick get-away in order to beat the traffic. As Antony and I scrambled through the mob, it was perversely pleasing to know that the people we passed walking in the direction of the geyser unknowingly had an hour and a half to wait for Old Faithful's next performance.

We arrived back in Salt Lake City late the next day and because our next festival was a long drive instead of a flight away, we decided to check into a Best Western in the south of the city. We had some days to spare, which gave me enough time to meet an old friend. And we were in luck – owing to some severe sunburn, he was off work for the remainder of the week.

Lee James and I have been friends ever since he lived in Cornwall, and in 2005 he and his girlfriend Jen helped Bateman and me hunt for whales in a local Utah reservoir. With a quick phone call and the internet for directions, we were knocking on his front door in under twenty minutes. By now it was late afternoon, so I invited Lee for some dinner to catch up. And, because I'd met up with one old friend, it was about time I re-acquainted myself with another.

Hooters of Salt Lake City is certainly not the best of the restaurant's chain. The waitresses aren't in the same league as some of the Hooters girls I've seen before, and they don't accept UK driving licences as proof of age because 'they aren't in the big book of IDs' (apparently). Their attempt at fish and chips was pretty awful too, but Antony and I ploughed through our meal, while Lee was on his phone, trying to organize some sort of party for the evening. As he was talking, I discovered that Hooters waitresses are paid less than two dollars an hour (and these ones wouldn't make a great deal in tips). Lee was on his fifth or sixth phone call and, by the sounds of it, the party arrangements weren't going particularly well.

As the sun went down, Lee made one final attempt at

organizing some sort of shindig and took us to his cousin's flat just outside the downtown area. Here we met the cousin and his flatmate, neither of whom were in any mood for a knees-up. Lee, who refused to admit defeat, tried one last contact and rang another cousin. And so it was that Antony, Lee, his cousin and I listened to quiet music playing from my laptop as we sat in our motel room drinking low-alcohol lager. Hardly a contender for party of the year.

The following morning – on a day which saw Tony Blair's ten-year reign as Prime Minister come to an end after stepping down to make way for his Chancellor, my email inbox showed a startling coincidence concerning Lee. In the top toolbar it suggested a 'word of the day', and that particular day's word was factious (adj.): *inclined to forming parties.*

Still, Antony and I weren't in much of a party mood anyway. We had to save our energy for the 200-mile journey to Elko, Nevada for the 44th National Basque Festival.

The trouble with Salt Lake City is that once you have left the city limits, the radio fails to pick up any radio station, and there is pretty much nothing of any interest out of any of the windows. This makes for a terribly boring game of I-Spy. Once you have exhausted 'road', 'sky', 'desert' and 'road' again (which you used because your opponent would never think the answer would be the same twice), there isn't much to do apart from set the car's cruise control to ten above the speed limit, and sit back in perfect silence. That is until you notice something totally out of the ordinary; and in our situation this could be anything.

'Look at that dog!' Antony yelled in amazement before bursting into hysterics. I took a closer look at the vehicle we had overtaken.

On the back of a pick-up, which was pulling a bundle of underground piping, sat two dogs. Because the trailer's attachment had taken up so much room in the van's cargo area, the dogs had been placed atop a metal box which wasn't especially spacious and was higher than the sides of the vehicle. One sharp turn or a paw out of place would have sent one or both of the dogs tumbling to the road below. This didn't seem to bother the driver, however, who continued his drive at a safe 70 miles per hour. In order to get another glimpse at the 'wonder dogs', and to calm Antony down (who by this time was like a hysterical child, twisting around between our car's mirrors and back window for a better view), I decided to pull into a rest area so that we could get behind the pick-up and then pass it once more. As we veered off the road, unfortunately so did the pick-up, we were going to have to wait for him to leave before we could follow. Instead of talking to the dogs' owner, however, I was more interested in where, by complete chance, we had arrived.

The Bonneville Salt Flats form one of the most extraordinary features in America. This enormous tabular expanse is a remnant of Lake Bonneville from glacial times; but the plains are now more famous for being the place to set automotive speed records. Ever since Malcolm Campbell managed to reach 301 mph in 1935, the plains have been the venue for all but three of the subsequent twenty world-record-breaking runs. With the salt as deep as 6 feet in places, the entire 30,000-acre landscape looks like snow heavily sprinkled on frozen water, and it isn't surprising to learn that, owing to the curvature of the earth, it is impossible to see from one end to the other.

We studied the plains, then returned to our car to find that the pick-up guy had set his own land speed record. We had spent only five minutes at the rest area, but he and his dogs were nowhere to be seen.

Elko, Nevada is a rather odd place and is even more in the middle of nowhere than Salt Lake City. The town is no metropolis, but it is home to more than seventeen thousand people and, being a Nevadan town, many casinos and places in which to gamble. It is also of interest that because of Nevada law, which states that any town with a population of less than four hundred thousand may have licensed brothels, Elko has four bordellos: Mona Lisa's Ranch, Inez's, Sue's Fantasy Club, and the rather unimaginatively named Sharon's Brothel. What's more surprising is that the town – well over 5,000 miles away from the Spanish autonomous region – plays host to an annual Basque Festival . . . and, oddly enough, has a shop that sells Cornish pasties.

When mining became the principal source of income in the region, thousands of people descended on the area, including people from the Basque region of Spain and my home county of Cornwall. Today, mining is still the main industry in Elko and employs over a third of the town's male workforce. It was because of the emigrating Cornish contingent that Antony and I had found ourselves in a town centre bakery contemplating which type of pasty to buy.

On the menu, five pasties were listed: beef, onion and potato; beef and cabbage; chicken and rice; cheese and vegetable; and a breakfast pasty with egg and sausage. Even though I had explained that only one of the five was a true Cornish pasty, the shop assistant allowed us to sample one of each. The last time I tried an American attempt at a pasty was in another town steeped in mining history, Mineral Point in Wisconsin. That had been pretty devastating. The pasty looked more like a deflated scone, it was presented in a polystyrene box, and, for some unknown reason, came with chilli sauce. As we sampled the array of oggies on offer, we began chatting to the shop assistant and asked him what we should expect from the weekend's Basque Festival.

'Oh, is it Basque weekend?' he asked breezily.

'Didn't you know?' I replied in amazement. 'It starts tonight just a few streets from here.'

'Yeah, but I've never been. I don't know a great deal about it, to be honest. How are the pasties?'

Unable to garner much information other than we had arrived several months too early for the town's Cowboy Poetry Gathering Festival in January, and two weeks late for Elko's Motorbike Jamboree, we bought a couple of pasties (proper ones) and headed in the direction of the Chamber of Commerce to learn more about the Basque Festival.

The Elko Chamber of Commerce is set inside a log-cabin-type building and has hundreds of pamphlets and brochures about local attractions. There not a single piece of literature on the Basque Festival. I was beginning to think the festival may have been cancelled and we had driven for over three hours for nothing when the chamber's clerk asked if we were in need of any help. In return we asked her for any information she had on the Basque Festival. She turned to her assistant, who handed her something. On a badly photocopied piece of paper no bigger than a postcard was the schedule of events for the festival.

'That's all we've got,' she said as we left the chamber.

The festival is a celebration of everything Basque, including traditional Basque dancing, a parade, an entire day of athletic 'old country' games, and, the most traditional of all, a running of the bulls. According to the schedule, the Bull Run was to take place twice over the weekend's festivities, and so we decided we would watch the idiotic men attempting to evade a skewering from the herd in this evening's run. Then, even though I had promised my girlfriend I wouldn't take part, in tomorrow's run, two of those idiots would be us.

Outside Stockmen's, one of Elko's largest and oldest casinos, a lonely refreshment stand and sign-up desk stood between a series of bleachers and a menacing-looking array of metal fencing which lined the 200-yard course into which the bulls and their 'victims' would be released.

By six p.m., a display of traditional Basque dancing had begun and the bleachers surrounding the run had already started to fill. The course, whose path followed two sides of the casino, certainly didn't look safe and wasn't particularly well organized. It was by a segment of fencing next to what we presumed to be the start line that we met John, a travelling American who had arrived in Elko earlier that day, and had taken one of the last remaining motel rooms in the town.

'I've been to the fiesta in Spain before,' he said, 'and this place may not look much like it, but they do have a lot of the Spanish feel to it when the festival is on.'

'Like what?' I enquired.

'The dancers are authentic, the clothes are very good, and the restaurants make fantastic food. Everything you'd expect to find in the Basque region is here,' he continued.

I looked up with a concerned look on my face. 'Let's just hope ETA aren't here too!'

Elko's version of Pamplona's Running of the Bulls is known by what I believe to be the more accurate name of Running *from* the Bulls. At seven p.m., it was time for the event to begin, and the crowd sat tense and eager, expecting at least a few injuries. A dozen or so competitors in white T-shirts, some in a traditional red scarf (or *paliacate*), waited. It soon became apparent that the stars of the show weren't present. By seven thirty, the bulls still hadn't made their appearance. As the sun began to set, word was circulating that they wouldn't make it in time for the evening's run. At eight o'clock, the run was called off and a wood-chopping and weight-lifting display took its place. Because the crowd had come to see panic-stricken competitors and hilariously comical injuries, it wasn't long before the stands were vacated, leaving Antony and me with nothing to do but lose some money at a nearby casino's blackjack table.

The next day began in the same style that my Saturdays do at home: with a pasty. My weekends, however, don't usually begin with a Basque Parade. Antony and I managed to find an adequate location to watch the morning's cavalcade beside a woman who thought we were Australian and a dozen children with carrier bags. The reason for the carrier bags soon became apparent when the occupants of the procession's first car – a not-very-Basque-looking pair of men dressed as crash test dummies – threw sweets in the direction of the waiting kids. The cars and floats that followed, from what I can remember, were a mix of local groups and businesses ranging from members of the local church and Miss Elko County to a carpet-cleaning company, cowboys on horseback and a loudmouth radio DJ from the town's Mix 96.7 in a golf buggy. Remembering now what passed us that morning is as difficult as the final round on *The Generation Game* (mind you, there was a cuddly toy in the form of a giant polar bear used to promote the casino who had taken our money the previous night). After almost an hour the procession was nearing its end and the road had become somewhat littered. The children found locating the sweets among the piles of horse excrement a near impossible task.

The afternoon's Basque Games were to take place at Elko's County Fairground, and because we didn't know where that was (and the pasty shop assistant's directions were incredibly difficult to understand), we simply followed the parade route. Fortunately this led us straight to the fairground. From what I could make out from the showground, it was much more used to holding livestock sales and horse racing than Basque dancing, weight-carrying and a tug-of-war. On a day where the temperature reached 95 °F in the shade, things didn't begin very well. For starters, the sign by the front gates read 'ENTRENCE'. Perhaps that's the Basque translation. Then we took our positions in the stand and, this being America, were asked to rise straight away for their national anthem. At this stage, I wasn't really sure which song I hated more: Lee Greenwood's atrocities or the national anthem, which going by what I'd seen, was probably played before any true American even sat down for a meal. There was, however, an instant third contender as the 'Oinkari' dancers from Boise, Idaho began a routine to the 'Birdie Song'. They were soon joined by the local 'Arinkak' group, whose dancers would perform to the crowd before the games began. Three-quarters of an hour later, Antony and I had sat through eleven separate dances and weren't exactly convinced by what the games classed as entertainment. And when one of the commentators informed the crowd that 'there are over four hundred and forty traditional Basque dances', we knew we were in for a long afternoon.

By two o'clock, the games were finally under way. The first contest was the Bucksaw competition. Basically, the event consists of teams of two able-bodied men sharing the job of making three cuts through an 18-inch diameter log with a giant saw. After the contestants were intro-duced, I spotted a missed opportunity to make up for our casino losses the previous night. A hundred and fifty dollars were awarded for first place; the runners-up would pocket a hundred, with third taking home a respectable fifty bucks. With only two teams, and an entry fee of five dollars, Antony and I could have used a spoon and finished while the interval dancers were leav-ing and we would still have made a tidy sum.

The remainder of the games, with the exception of the high-school tug-of-war, seemed more like a display of

101 things you can do with a piece of wood. They would stand on it and chop away at the piece from above, carry it around for a bit, and even lift a log above their heads. Incidentally, the latter event was won by a guy who looked exactly like a traditional weightlifter you would expect to see in a nineteenth-century travelling circus, complete with leotard and outlandish moustache. As the dancing recommenced, Antony and I visited a nearby stall which sold items of Basque clothing so that we could kit ourselves out for the evening's run. We each bought a red scarf and I purchased a white T-shirt featuring the Basque flag for myself and a shirt depicting sheep for Antony. I cleverly planned on giving the sheep T-shirt to my girlfriend once Antony had used it as a sorry-I-broke-my-promise-and-ran-with-the-bulls kind of present.

After we returned to our seats to witness yet another traditional Basque dance (which made Morris Dancers look as graceful and dignified as Torvill and Dean), we decided we should stay for just one more event. Forty minutes of bell-ringing and stick-striking later, the junior weight-carrying contest began. Anyone under sixteen whose parents had signed a release form (or anyone they plucked from the audience, such was the desperation for entrants) had to carry two 75-pound weights across a 100-foot course. The person who covered the greatest distance was deemed the winner. A local fifteen-year-old named Casey won the event, having lugged his burden more than 500 feet, narrowly beating a girl named Kelly who embarrassed her gender by coming a cropper before finishing a single length. Still, it *was* hot. Out of the corner of my eye I could see more dancers preparing to fill the gap between this and the next event, and so before Casey was crowned, Antony and I left hastily before they got the chance to bore us once more.

I mean, why allow dancers to bore us to death when the bulls in tonight's run could take care of that quite nicely?

We had been told at the sign-up desk that if we wished to run with the bulls that evening, we had to find the members of the Elko Basque Club outside Stockmen's. Because no one knew how many of the previous day's entrants would take part, it was not yet clear how many spaces would be made available for the evening's run. Nevertheless, Antony and I sat outside the casino for nearly an hour as our fellow runners joined us, sharing stories of the run and what lay in store for us. The rumour circulating amongst the crowd was that yesterday's cancellation was due to an accident in which one of the bulls had lost a horn. In the beast's fit of rage, he had put one of his handlers in hospital. Not the kind of thing you want to hear when you plan to be within a few feet of such animals.

As more and more people arrived to sign up, with still no sign of a Basque Club representative, we began talking to two young guys, Jonathan and Sam, who had travelled from California to take part in the run. Unfortunately, this is also where we met Mike. I didn't mean to be instantly judgemental, but when a man in his forties arrives wearing long shorts and a T-shirt with 'Lifeguard' emblazoned across it, you just know he's going to turn out to be a bit of a twat. Next to him stood Geoff, his neighbour, whose only form of communication was to grunt whenever Mike felt the need to pause for breath.

'Hey, I'm Mike,' he shouted enthusiastically as he out-stretched his arm to shake all of our hands.

'Hi, Mike. Are you taking part in the run?' I enquired.

'Damn, right. Fourteenth year in a row!' he bellowed. 'Woo!' He held an open hand aloft and was 'high-fived' by the two young Californians. Antony and I simply looked at each other wishing we were somewhere else. Having a drink at the bar . . . losing money in the casino . . . watching more traditional Basque dancing . . . being gored by a vicious bull . . . anywhere but talking to Mike. For a moment I felt trapped. We couldn't leave the queue and lose our place, and yet the line was the last place on earth I wanted to be. I wasn't sure how we were going to handle the situation.

'So what brings two Brits out to Elko?' he asked, as if standing in a queue to sign up for a bull run wasn't obvious enough.

'We came to see you, Mike,' replied Antony sarcastically.

Sarcasm, good old British sarcasm. *That* was how we were going to handle the situation. Like Osama Bin Laden to American intelligence, the use of sarcasm in the US is undetectable.

Even though it was pretty obvious that we didn't want to know, Mike used the next ten minutes to bombard us with trivial information about his life. For instance, I know his house was 3,000 square feet, that his Samoan wife (yes, he was married) worked for an airline and was sitting in the crowd, and that he'd always wanted to do the famous bull run in Barcelona.

'Barcelona?' I said. 'Don't you mean Pamplona?'

'No, man. The most famous Spanish bull run is in Barcelona.'

'I think you'll find it's Pamplona, Mike.'

'Oh, Pamplona,' he teased in an aristocratic English accent. '*Pamplona.*'

'Well, I could have said it in some ghastly American accent but I think it sounds better that way,' I replied. I wasn't sure if it was the heat or the possibility of being killed by a cow that was making me dislike a total stranger. Perhaps it was the constant dancing earlier in the afternoon.

No . . . it was Mike, I thought. He really was a pompous twat.

After informing us that U2's Bono and the Edge were of different religions and that his favourite film was *Braveheart*, he spotted my digital watch, which had a compass and thermometer built in.

'Well, *that's* a watch,' he said. 'What can that do?'

I paused for a moment, then decided to inform him of the miracles the little device could achieve. 'It tells me what the time is.'

Further blunt answers to his idle questions followed. Eventually Mike either realized that we didn't want to speak to him, or decided to go and annoy the hell out of somebody else. As he sauntered off around the corner of Stockmen's with Geoff in tow, I think he may have called something along the lines of 'Keep my place' or 'Hold my spot'. Whatever he said, I chose to ignore it.

Just as he disappeared from sight, the Basque Club representative appeared accompanied by two of her colleagues, one of whom was checking the entry forms of yesterday's runners and working out how many newcomers they could sign up. Luckily for us (or unluckily, depending on your way of looking at it) there were twelve spaces available and we were fourth and fifth in the queue. Mike and Geoff reappeared just as the final spot had been allocated, and so a disgruntled Mike and just plain grunting Geoff had no choice but to watch the action from the stands.

Thank God.

As it was already an hour behind schedule, the run, we were informed, was to start almost immediately, so Antony and I made our way to the car to retrieve our red scarves. Upon returning to the enclosed run, it was clear that out of the twenty or so competitors – who by now were stretching, running on the spot and preparing for the run of their lives – only four of us were wearing scarves. We might as well have just painted red targets on the back of our T-shirts. Antony had a look of determination on his face.

'I'm really ready for this. I can't wait,' he shouted eagerly. 'Aren't you really looking forward to this?'

'Yeah,' I lied, unconvincingly.

Fortunately for me, I had a slight advantage over the other runners. A couple of years ago, I visited Pamplona where the annual Running of the Bulls takes place every day for a week during the festival of San Fermín. I had experience of taking to the cobbled and curving streets of the Plaza del Ayuntamiento and the Calle de la Estafeta, and what was best was that I had made it unharmed to the finish at the gateway of the town's bull ring. Unfortunately, that was in November – a full four months after the bull run had taken place and where the only thing that chased me down the narrow streets was the breeze. Still, it should count for something.

To be honest, I wasn't looking forward to the Elko run at all. There was something ominous about the evening. An orangey-red sun hung in the sky, the temperature had dropped suddenly, and there wasn't a breath of wind. Everything was still. The tortures we had suffered at the hands of Mike and the Basque Club dancers had passed, and we seemed to be entering the eye of the storm before rage and fury would besiege the streets once again.

'I heard these beasts are worse than the ones in Spain,' shrieked one guy excitedly.

'They are,' shouted his friend. 'I've seen so many injuries here!' he added, before the two engaged in an impromptu high-five.

As the sun began to drop, rumours reached us that the bulls weren't anywhere near the town and had been held up on their way down to Elko. Although I didn't show it, turning my back to everyone and shrugging my shoulders disappointedly, this was music to my ears. I didn't mind taking part in the run, I definitely wasn't going to pull out, but I would certainly not complain or leave a despondent and dejected man if the bulls repeated their previous day's no-show. In fact, that would be the best result. I could claim I wanted to run with them but my dreams had been shattered when the bulls didn't turn up. Perfect excuse.

Unfortunately, the shrieks from the crowd and the incessant reversing alarm of two huge lorries confirmed my worst fears. The rumours, it turned out, were just that, and as the vehicles moved into position, the monotonous reverse warning siren was beginning to sound more like a death toll. The tremendous thudding on the inside walls of the trucks, as loud as a tribal drum preceding a sacrifice, filled the crowd with elation, my fellow bull runners with obvious excitement, and my heart with dread. I still had over nine weeks in America remaining and didn't want to see the country through the window of a hospital room.

As we jostled for position at the start, all around I could hear my co-runners discussing tactics. Some were planning on jogging close to the horns of the bulls and a few had even decided to run backwards to taunt the beasts. My plan, however, was much simpler: run and reach the end with all limbs intact.

There was no more time for thinking or contemplating what injuries may befall us. The runners were ready, the six terrifying bulls were certainly ready, and the crowd had been waiting for this moment since the last massacre in 2006. It was time.

No starter's pistol or horn sounded the start of the run, just a man who rather nonchalantly shouted 'Go!' completely out of the blue (no 'On your marks' or even a 'Get set'). A throng of people passed me as my timing off the line wasn't the best, and I could tell by the reaction of the crowd without even looking over my shoulder that the bulls had joined the party. Because the course had been watered just an hour before the run had begun, building up a great speed was a bad idea: treading carefully and precisely was definitely the order of the day.

From the crashing against the barriers and the yells from the crowd, it was obvious that the bulls hadn't enjoyed the long drive down to Elko and were loving their new-found freedom. Antony was now by my side and we were sprinting around the corner of Stockmen's, neither of us knowing that by taking the inside route we would be crossing the path of a charging bull. I looked back. Just yards behind me was one of the Californian lads, who had a definite look of concern on his face, and a rather angry-looking animal just a matter of feet from his heels.

'Watch out, Rich!' Jonathan shouted as he quickly swerved to dart straight up the rungs and to the top of a nearby fence, seconds before the bull's onslaught would have sent him through it. I didn't need to be warned, I was nearing the end of the run anyway, and Antony was yards in front, fast approaching the pen into which only an idiot would run. I leapt on to the fence and clung on for my life. It was only then that I realized how close the bull had been. I lifted my feet just a few more inches before it charged below my shoes.

Antony wasn't so lucky.

Slipping on the first rung of the fence with the bull closing the gap with exceptional speed, Antony stood no chance of evading the charge. As I began to climb to the top of the fence into the safety of the crowd, I could only look on with horror.

At first it appeared as if the bull had slipped, but as the beast lifted its head, Antony rose with it, rocketing into the air, flaccid as a rag doll. The T-shirt was ripped from his body by the bull's right horn and his body struck the ground with considerable force, landing shoulder first on to the concrete. The crowd wailed and applauded seconds before a sudden silence descended as it became obvious that something had gone horribly wrong. Blood poured from Antony's back and he remained on the ground. Organizers and medics waited impatiently by the fencing, bracing themselves for a sprint to the wounded as soon as all the bulls were in their pen. Antony looked OK though, and I have to admit that my first thought was that I couldn't give the T-shirt to my girlfriend now. With the exception of a big cut below his shoulder, it seemed as if no permanent damage had been done. Antony managed to scramble along the floor, and the audience sighed with relief.

Occasionally, Antony would sit up slightly to check for bulls and shield himself from any further attack. A single bull remained on the loose. Every runner was now vacating the run via the fencing. The mammal seemed to be running straight into the pen, avoiding Antony by a number of yards. At the last second, whilst Antony was protecting the sides of his head with each of his forearms, linking the fingers of his hands around the back of his head, the bull changed direction. Whether an organizer behind the pen had caused the animal to swerve, or Antony's red scarf proved too much for the bull to resist, the animal trampled on Antony's lower back and, most horrifically, his neck.

Antony lay motionless.

Medics and organizers swarmed around him as everyone looked on in disbelief. I raced toward the mêlée, quicker than I had done when over a ton of angry bovine was bearing down on me. As I stepped aside to allow a paramedic through with a stretcher, it was obvious that Antony was no longer OK.

'His name's Antony!' I yelled to him as he passed.

We were all told to stand well back to give Antony

plenty of room. The crowd stood in deathly silence.

'He's breathing, but he's in a bad way!' yelled the medic who was first on the scene, before he asked for a brace to be applied to Antony's neck. As they lifted him on to the stretcher, I was grabbed by Jonathan, who asked me what exactly had happened. I wasn't sure quite what to say.

'Is anyone with him?' shouted the medic.

'He is!' shouted Jonathan as he pushed me towards the crew.

As the door shut behind us, the mood in the ambulance was sombre. I realized that I was to blame for his condition. As I looked down at Antony's battered and bruised frame, I slumped into the corner of the vehicle and wept for my friend.

Well, all of that *could* have happened.

The bulls didn't turn up again.

In reality, we paraded through the course and were applauded by an appreciative crowd for simply wearing a white T-shirt and saying we were *going* to run. I may not have run with the bulls, but at the very least I had unwittingly kept a promise.

Shortly after the 'event', Jonathan bought us a beer and Mike and Geoff came from nowhere to complain about the queue and their exclusion from the 'run'. (Well, Mike complained, Geoff simply stood in the background staring at the floor.)

'Where are you guys staying tonight?' he asked.

'Um, in our motel, I guess,' I replied, trying not to give the name of it away.

'You should come back to mine. The wife won't mind.'

'Yeah, we just might do that,' I said convincingly enough for him to believe me.

'We'll meet you in a bit,' Antony added. We both knew this was our one and only chance to escape.

As we darted around the corner of the casino with Mike and Geoff in pursuit, a day we thought might end in injuries from wild animals resulted instead in our attempting to outpace a man and a different kind of grunting beast. Instead of running from the bulls we were running from the fools.

3

Birthday Greetings

Upon returning to Salt Lake City, Antony and I were faced with a tough decision. Our next festival was still six days away and between then and now was 4 July: Independence Day. The problem was deciding where to spend America's birthday. I'd never spent the Fourth of July in the US, and as it's the biggest annual party in the country, I wanted to see it in properly; and that meant finding the appropriate city. Neither Antony nor I thought we should spend the day in Salt Lake City, owing to the state's ridiculous alcohol laws, and any other town was an unnecessarily long drive away. To do it properly, we needed to be on the east coast of the country: an area that was steeped in history, heavily populated, and was definitely going to be much cooler.

In the end, it boiled down to two contenders: Washington DC and Boston, one because it was the capital, and therefore the political heart of the country, and the other because of its cosmopolitan feel and pleasant surroundings. Luckily, I'd been to both cities on a previous trip to the States, and knew what I thought of the two places.

It was a simple decision to make: one I think you'd agree with once you balanced the pros and cons. Boston is the cultural capital of New England, is situated on the coast, has a mild climate, and is the type of city where pedestrians are more likely to be hit by a jogger than a car. Washington, on the other hand, is the nation's capital city and its only drawback is that it's a horrible, filthy, stinking, odious, abhorrent, beastly, detestable, ghastly, repellent, disgusting litter-strewn dump, where shops and bars are replaced with monuments and museums.

Can you guess which one we chose?

Our early morning flight to Boston would take us via Chicago, and when we boarded our connecting flight we realized that for once on the plane's radio it wasn't just the usual mix of jazz, spoken voice and cheesy pop channels. This time, there was a station through which you could listen in to our captain's conversations with air traffic control. I thought it was rather good; Antony disagreed. He thought it was nerdy and boring. Ignoring him, I slipped my headphones on and listened in.

'This is United 536,' came the voice from the cockpit. To be honest, the rest was foxtrots, tangos and other exotic dances and words used in the NATO phonetic alphabet. Then it suddenly got a bit interesting.

The flight in front of ours was apparently losing some sort of fluid out of the right side of its fuselage as we taxied our way to Juliet Foxtrot Left (good, hey?). This delayed our take-off by quite some time, and the captain's voice came through on the plane's internal public-address system to clarify the situation.

After the full yet rather vague explanation, most people slumped in their seats to show their disappointment. I looked quite smug, removed my earphones and turned to face Antony.

'I knew that.'

At 30,000 feet, the boredom of listening to air traffic control twittering on about golfs, sierras and whiskeys – along with something about irreparable damage to one of the wings of our plane (well, I may have made that one up) – kicked in. Antony and I discovered that we had forgotten a fundamental travel accessory for those times when you find yourself on an aeroplane where there isn't a television screen mounted to the back of the seat in front of you: a book. With any luck, we could solve that problem in Boston. With a metropolitan population of over four million, I was sure they would have a book shop.

Boston is a lovely city: liberal, cultured and full of history, with a mild temperature to boot. Sitting at the mouth of the Charles River as it washes into a crystal-clear Atlantic, many claims have been made about Massachusetts's capital, each summed up by one of its many nicknames: City on the Hill, the Hub of the Universe. For me, though, there is only one moniker that truly reflects Boston's relationship to the country as a whole: the Cradle of Modern America.

Colonists first settled there in 1630, naming it after a small town in Lincolnshire. The city was the home of America's first public school and university and, most famously, was the scene of the Boston Tea Party, where America's Revolutionary War against the British first ignited. Its many landmarks include Boston Common, the statue of Benjamin Franklin, Old State House and the USS *Constitution*. They can all be located on a 2-mile-long brick path known as the Freedom Trail, which has earned Boston the title of a 'walking city'. If there was going to be a truly patriotic and cultured Fourth of July, then surely Boston was the city to host it.

Our arrival in the city could not have been more badly timed. Not only did we arrive during Boston's rush hour, but the subway train to our hotel was crammed with an exceptional number of people in baseball caps – even for America. As Antony and I wondered why so many had chosen to wear a similar style of hat, a young girl who was sitting quietly reading a book looked up at us and noticed our puzzlement.

'There's a game on tonight,' she said helpfully.

'Oh, I see,' I replied.

Noticing our accents, she turned the book over on to her thigh. 'Oh my, you're from England,' she said. Top marks so far for not thinking we were Australian. Perhaps I now had a chance to show Antony what intelligent, enlightened and informed people Bostonians really were.

'We are indeed,' I replied.

'That's so cool.' Nice bit of colonial appreciation. 'I've always wanted to go to England,' she added.

'You should do, it's really nice,' Antony quipped, before she really went for gold.

'Have you met the princes?'

Never mind. There were plenty of other people in Boston.

We checked into our hotel on Beacon Street, west of the historic Kenmore Square, where every other building is a coffee house, restaurant, or a Dunkin' Donuts. Instead of giving the rooms numbers, the hotel used famous names from Boston's history. Both the John Quincy Adams and the Mayflower Room were available but we opted for the lesser known Paul Revere (a local silversmith and patriot during the American Revolution); a perfect choice for Independence Day.

The next day, a package arrived for me. I opened it immediately, like a child on Christmas Day. It was from Rod. I had emailed him the details of where we were staying in Boston and he had been kind enough to return my sunglasses which I had left behind in his camper van. And that wasn't all he sent. Accompanying my glasses were my kepi (which I had also left behind), a CD each with pictures Rod had taken, posters advertising the Custer's Last Stand Reenactment, some sew-on stripes, certificates and the prerequisite bag of sweets. It was more like a goody bag from a children's television game show than a stash of military memorabilia. A rather touching letter from Rod and June was also included in the package. They thanked us for our presence in their camp and Rod explained why he had included more than just a 'cheap pair of sunglasses' in the box. They both wished us good luck for the remainder of the trip and apologized for the brevity of the letter as Rod had to hurry in order to put the parcel in the 'post' and then paint his flag pole ready for Independence Day.

AROUND THE WEIRD IN 80 DAYS

The first thing we did on stepping out of the hotel for our first full day in Boston was to take a subway train to see the setting for what would be the biggest party of the year, on this, the eve of America's 231st birthday.

We made our way to the banks of the Charles River and a monolithic hatch shell stage surrounded by hundreds of seats. Because there is a concert (without fireworks) on the 3rd as well as the 4th, and entry is free on a first-come, first-served basis, people were already beginning to queue for a show which was still over seven hours away. As we weren't really in the mood to queue for a party on the wrong day, we made our way to Cambridge, the area of Boston that is home to Harvard University, not for a coffee or to breathe in the academic air, but to find a place where Antony could go to the toilet.

Once Antony returned from a nearby café after abusing their facilities, we came across a man who seemed to own some sort of outdoor bookstore. Remembering we were in need of something to read on future plane journeys, Antony began to peruse the three shelves and adjacent tables for something suitable as I began talking to the 'shop assistant'.

'So how did all of this come about?' I asked, making small talk.

While he was informing me that he had had to fight the government and various city courts for over two years in order to be allowed to pitch up on the pavement, Antony approached us and proudly made his purchase. The book was called *Sexual Reproduction*, clearly a good read, and the inclusion of pictures only elated him further. (It wasn't a pop-up book though, unfortunately.) As I half listened to the salesman babble on about local bureaucracy and red tape, a book caught my eye. If the content was half as ridiculous as the title, I was in for a treat.

The Humor of Jesus by Father Henry Cormier, C.J.M. (a member of the Congregation of Jesus and Mary, if you wanted to know) is a study of the Bible and, as the title suggests, the sense of humour enjoyed by Our Lord. If the hilarious title wasn't enough of an incentive to quickly swipe it off the shelf before anyone else got their hands on it, the two-dollar price tag and alluring psychedelic yellow and blue front cover certainly sealed the deal. First published in 1977 in Montreal as *L'Humour de Jésus*, this English translation had chapters with titles such as 'Jesus, the number-one journalist' and 'Jesus, the number-one caricaturist'. It certainly had me laughing, and I don't believe that they were the jokes that Jesus had cracked either. For a thirty-year-old paperback, it was in quite good condition, and, as an added bonus, many of the pages had passages highlighted by one of the book's previous owners.

Before making our way back to our hotel, we thought it would be a good idea to settle down with a quick pint and make a nice start on our books. This, however, seemed to be an impossible task because in each of the three bars we attempted to be served, we were turned away because neither of us had our American state driving licence on us at the time.

Funny that. No matter how hard I looked in my wallet and trouser pockets, I just couldn't seem to find my Massachusetts driver's licence anywhere. I suppose it serves me right for being English and passing my test in the United Kingdom. The DVLA were at obvious fault for issuing me with a British driving licence. Silly people; what were they thinking?

The Fourth of July in America. To be honest I wasn't quite sure what to expect, but I knew I wanted some sort of ebullient party atmosphere tempered by good taste. One reason for selecting Boston was that the population were more reserved than the rest of the country's inhabitants, and wouldn't decorate themselves with face paint and Stars and Stripes-style clothing to celebrate the anniversary of America's independence. Well, that's what I was hoping, anyway.

As we ate our lunch on Boston Common, there were no obvious signs that it was a national holiday, let alone Independence Day. A handful of people were wearing clothes which signified love for their nation, but not a great deal more than you would see on any day of the year. There were only a few silly hats, a paucity of flag-wielding families and not a single person dressed as Uncle Sam. This was what we had wanted, but actually Antony and I soon decided we were rather disappointed by the lack of patriotic attire, and considered visiting a shop and stocking up on American-flag bow ties, boxer shorts and top hats so we could instigate some kind of surge of Americanism. Luckily, we came to our senses before any purchases were made.

Making our way back to the hotel, we decided to visit a liquor store to stock up for our preliminary drinking before the evening's big party. It's strange that in a bar, I had to present an American state driving licence in order to be served just a small beer, yet in a liquor store, with only my appearance as proof of age, I was sold enough alcohol to kill me.

Independence Day reminded me that it was also my friend's daughter's birthday, so I rang them to bid Natasha a happy fourteenth birthday and was ready to celebrate America's 231st.

On our return to the city, we joined a swarm of people who were heading in the direction of the Charles River. By this time, the sun was beginning to set and, for the first time in the seventeen days since we had left the UK, rain began to fall. Hundreds of people were already lining a huge stretch of the dampening bank, competing for space in which to lay their picnic blankets and position their foldaway chairs in preparation for the firework display, which was still a good two hours away. Even here, there was little indication as to the significance of the day. Surrounding us were concession stands selling a range of different foods and, because of the weather, a supply of cagoules.

After a quick visit to a bar and then a portaloo in the dark back at the Charles River (the latter a near impossible task), we strolled down the embankment to find a place to see the fireworks. My trainers were suspiciously wet: either because they were old and had holes in them, or because I had urinated on them earlier. After almost thirty minutes of walking, neither the rain nor the crowd showed any signs of alleviating. We decided to make our way to the Harvard Bridge which, according to a Boston newspaper's top Fourth of July tips, was not normally congested and had a great view of the fireworks. From the amount of people fighting for position on the bridge, I deduced that everyone in Boston read the same newspaper.

It took us ten minutes to walk up the 200-foot zig-zagged walkway to the closed-off road. When on the bridge itself, it was nigh-on impossible to move and so we gave up trying to find a good pyrotechnical vantage point and remained just yards from the side in a space next to a couple who were entwined in each other's arms (probably to save room).

As the first firework shot into the air, the crowd silenced, leaving only the whispered 'Ooh's and 'Aah's to echo around the bay as the night sky was illuminated in astounding chromatic splendour. Five minutes in, the silence was broken by screaming just several feet from Antony and me.

'Phone an ambulance!' yelled one man to the mass of people who had no choice but to huddle around a girl who had fallen to the floor. 'Call 911!' Everyone reeled in shock and for a minute or so not a single person's interest was focused on the pyrotechnics. Personally, I was surprised that anyone had managed to find enough space in which to faint.

No sooner had someone dialled the emergency services, reported our position, which was hard enough for a human to reach, let alone an ambulance, than the girl came to and sat on the kerb to recover. With crisis averted we enjoyed what remained of the firework display. For the following twenty minutes Boston banged and flashed, detonated and discharged. With the breath-taking mêlée of explosions culminating in a dazzling array of rockets, the city rumbled and convulsed its inhabitants into a thunderous applause of unanimous appreciation.

*

Because 4 July fell on a Wednesday, we didn't have the usual weekdays break between festivals, and so the following day we had an afternoon flight to Jacksonville, Florida. Hotel check-out time was 11 a.m. and travelling to the city centre took a good thirty-five to forty minutes in the direction of the airport, so we saw little point in leaving our luggage at the hotel. Instead, we thought we would study the subway map and select a suitable place near the airport to kill some time. With his name on the door of our hotel room as an omen, and the fact it was just five stops from the airport, Revere Beach was a perfect choice.

In 1896 Boston was home to the first public beach in the country. At the turn of the century over a quarter of a million people would relax along Revere's five-mile shore on summer afternoons. The Great Ocean Pier jutted a quarter of a mile into the Atlantic and housed a ballroom and large skating rink, and there were half-hourly steamer services to Boston. The resort was most famed, however, for its amusements. Along with a Ferris wheel, Bluebeard's Palace and the Fun House, the beach was home to the town's biggest attraction: the Cyclone – one of the largest rollercoasters of the time where cars reached speeds of up to 60 mph and climbed to heights of over 100 feet.

Today, Revere Beach is a shadow of its former self. Just a handful of people take to its sands, nearly all of the town's attractions, including the pier, were demolished in a blizzard in 1978 and have been replaced with modern housing units; and the only fast-food vendor that can be found on the seafront is located, rather woefully, on the ground floor of a Government building.

The fast-food retailer, this being Massachusetts, is naturally a Dunkin' Donuts, and having put off visiting one for so long, an equal measure of curiosity and hunger sent us into the 'world's largest coffee and baked goods chain'. Basically, the franchise is a cross between a glorified bakery and a poor man's Starbucks. As well as serving an array of breakfast meals and flavoured coffee, the chain, as the name suggests and to presumably keep policemen happy, sells over fifty different varieties of doughnuts and other dough-based products. We purchased a bagel and coffee each and made our way in the direction of the beach, stopping at an area of covered benches in the centre of a small patch of grass. Two men sat on the bench opposite us and another was sitting to our right.

'Hey, is that thing online?' the man to our right asked me.

'I beg your pardon?' I replied, having no clue what he was referring to.

He pointed at my laptop bag. 'Is that thing online?'

'Oh, no. It's just a standard laptop,' I said, hoping he would believe the lie and not mug me for it. He stood up and joined us on our bench as Antony and I glanced at each other for reassurance.

'You know how to work one of these things?' asked the man.

'What is it?' I asked, glancing at it quickly.

'It's one of those GPS systems. I bought it this morning and can't seem to get the damn thing off camera.'

'Have you tried hitting it, or looking at the manual?' Antony suggested helpfully.

The man shrugged off Antony's advice and slipped the gadgetry into a black bag on the ground, suggesting to us that he probably didn't have the manual, and he probably hadn't bought it that morning either.

As he rose from the bench to talk to the two men opposite us, there was just enough time for me to lean across to Antony and suggest we ate somewhere else. But it was too late.

'Is that a Revere cop?' the GPS man asked the two other men as he looked down the town's seafront road. As he rejoined us on the bench, a police car left the road, mounted the public footpath to our covered seating area, and answered his question perfectly. Yes, it most definitely was a Revere cop.

'Hiya, Brian,' said the three men in unison as the policeman slammed his car door shut and approached them. The policeman exchanged pleasantries with the men and then strolled on through the area for a few moments before looking over his shoulder. As the man with the GPS system began to mount his bicycle, Antony and I learnt that the cop's affable remarks and relaxed departure were just a ploy to see if any of them decided to make a move when his back was turned. The mounting of the bicycle was enough to rouse his suspicions.

'Hold it there a minute,' shouted the cop as he ran back towards GPS man. In a little under two minutes, he had asked the man for some identification, another officer had arrived with sirens blaring, and all of the action had left Antony and me wishing we had popcorn with which to enjoy the show.

We had a front-row seat vantage point. The policeman spent the next few minutes questioning each of the transients about what they had in their possession. When a third policeman arrived, the first cop's attentions shifted dramatically to us.

'What's in the bag?' he asked, in the rude and abrupt way American policemen generally have.

'Um . . . clothes,' Antony replied.

'What!?'

'Clothes.'

'Where you from?' he asked.

We replied, trying to look honest and trustworthy, and after only thirty seconds, it seemed as if our accents and nationality had proved our innocence. The policeman made his way back to the three men, then noticed the bag containing the GPS system. With the innocence of two of the men proved, the first man was read his rights, bundled into the back of a squad car and driven away, leaving us with the first policeman. 'What do you do?' he asked Antony.

'I'm at university,' he replied.

'And you?'

'I've just left university with a journalism degree,' I said.

'Right, you then, come here.'

I felt proud that the cop held a journalism degree in higher regard than simply being at university. I was led to the opposite corner of the seating area and interrogated. I explained why we were in Revere and in the company of such unsavoury characters. Then we came to the main question.

'Was that his bag?' he asked in a let's-cut-to-the-chase-type way.

'To be honest, I can't say that it was his,' I replied. 'It

was just on the floor. But it is where he put the GPS . . .'

Never have I seen three letters bring such a smile to someone's face, nor can I think of a situation where it would happen again. (Well, perhaps the abbreviation 'HIV' with the words 'You haven't contracted' spoken beforehand.)

'That's all I needed to hear,' he told me.

He invited Antony over next to corroborate my story, and, after taking our details and reassuring us we wouldn't be required for the future court case, offered us a free ride in his squad car as a gesture of appreciation. When we discovered that the trip would only cover the Boston metropolitan area, and that Jacksonville, Florida was definitely out of the question, we thanked him for the offer and quickly returned to the subway station before we became key witnesses in any further criminal acts.

Glad to be away from Revere Beach's untrustworthy tramps and choleric cops, we checked our bags in at Logan International Airport for our afternoon flight to Jacksonville. We were about to head into America's Deep South to experience some God-fearing hospitality.

Luckily, I had the perfect book with which to get myself acquainted.

4

The Olymp-Hick Games

I haven't read a great deal of the Bible, but if *The Humor of Jesus* is anything to go by, I don't think the Lord had much of a future in stand-up. Not once does it claim he ever visited a Nazarene pub on Open Mic night to try his hand at the art; neither does it even hint that he made any rude or witty comments about any of his disciples' mothers. One sub-chapter, titled 'Humor stays with the "little ones"', tells of a time in March AD 30 when Jesus was being besieged by a large crowd of followers. Zacchaeus, a chief tax-collector who was vertically challenged, decided to climb a tree in order to get a glimpse of the great man. At spotting this, Jesus approached him and, straight off the cuff without hesitation, shouted, 'Zacchaeus, come down quickly!'

Now, I don't know about you, but I'm unsure as to how Zacchaeus didn't break his neck when, in fits of laughter, he had to somehow manage the climb back down. As I write this now, even I can think of some lines which would have made Jesus seem as if he had a comedic bone in his body.

'Zacchaeus, money doesn't grow on trees, you know,' would have done fine; or another adequate tree-related pun would have been: 'I was wondering which branch you worked at.' Even a plain and simple: 'Fall, you tax-collecting bastard!' would have probably raised a few smiles in the crowd.

But instead of listing the number of times Jesus told an English, Irishman and Scotsman joke (or, to be more precise, an Israelite, Palestinian and Mesopotamian joke), the book prattles on about how humour isn't making people laugh, but doing serious things without becoming conceited, in a lame excuse to cover up the fact that Mr Christ never cracked a single one-liner with precision timing. I doubt the Last Supper was much of a laugh-a-minute occasion either. Perhaps you had to be there.

As the two of us left the airport, I placed the book at the bottom of my bag as we picked up our hire car and made our way out of Jacksonville, through northern Florida and into Georgia, where it seemed as if Jesus had moved into every other building, and where Charles Darwin is a swear word.

Visiting America's southern states (or the 'Bible Belt' as it's sometimes called), is like stepping into another country. The humidity during the summer months is at an almost constant 100 %, the temperature rarely drops below 85 °F and religion is all-pervading. In a town with a population of just a thousand or so, it is not un-common to see seven or eight churches as you pass through. I didn't even know there were so many different denominations. I had heard of Baptists and Evangelicals, but the Assemblies of God, New Vision Fellowship, Pentecostal and the Church of God in Christ had me thinking that when it came to choosing a name, they simply picked religious words out of a hat.

East Dublin, situated in almost the centre of Georgia and, not surprisingly, to the east of the slightly larger settlement of Dublin, is a typical example of a Bible Belt town. With a combined population of just under twenty thousand, the two Dublins are home to over a hundred places of worship and the only Kentucky Fried Chicken in which I've seen the Ten Commandments adorn the wall beside the menu (presumably to show any murdering, adulterous thief who works on Sundays, uses the Lord's name in vain and had only popped in for a Crispy Twister, just how much forgiveness and birching is required of him). It is little wonder then that, owing to the town's over-zealous attitude to religion, under the 'Things To Do' category on Georgia's official Government website about East Dublin, the only thing to feature is the Altamaha River.

Once a year, however, the town plays host to something that typifies the region's jovial attitude to life and the admiration they have for an epithet that others assume is an insult: the Summer Redneck Games.

In 1996, when the Olympic Games were being held 150 miles up the I-16 in Atlanta, local radio station Y-96, and particularly its afternoon DJ Mac Davies, heard that many people thought the Games were 'being run by a bunch of rednecks who didn't know what they were doing'. As the criticism mounted, Davies and the station decided that if that's what the people expected, that is exactly what they would give them. They put together a true redneck schedule of events that took place in tandem with the Atlanta Olympics. A crowd of almost five thousand people arrived when the organizers were expecting a tenth of that number, and they knew they were on to a winner. Eleven years on, the radio station still sponsors the annual event, and people are drawn to the games from as far as seven or eight miles away.

To find out more, Antony and I entered the Dublin Information Center, approached a lady who sat on her own watching an American chat show and asked her if there was any literature on the Redneck Games. After listening to her for a few minutes, I wasn't sure if she had any to give us or not. Owing to her thick Southern accent, she could have had a cold and spoken Swahili through a hockey mask, informing me that she had all the records from the previous eleven events, and I would still have been none the wiser.

As we checked into our motel, the girl on reception greeted us with the similar 'And you came all this way for this?' reaction we had received in both Elko and Billings. But you could have bet me a million pounds to guess what she was going to say next and your money would have been safe.

'Are you going to Redneck Idol tonight?' she added.

'Redneck Idol?'

'Yeah, I think it's taking place at the racetrack tonight. The winner will perform at the games tomorrow.' As if that didn't sound strange enough, she added the killer line. 'All of that takes place after the mower racing, of course.'

Of course.

The 441 Speedway is located six miles south of Dublin, off US Highway 441, and for just five dollars we could witness an afternoon of top-notch lawnmower racing as an aperitif to tomorrow's games. And if the action lived up to its rather melodramatic name, we were in for a treat: the 1st Annual Dublin Chrysler Dodge Jeep Cadillac Pontiac Buick Deep South Lawnmower Racing Association Race of Champions (to give it its official title), didn't even take place on the speedway, instead using a small patch of dirt in the centre. The MC, a rather large fellow with beard, baseball cap and an XXL fluorescent green T-shirt, was not only a member of the Lawnmower Racing Association, but his obvious knowledge and love of the machines bordered on an unhealthy obsession.

Surrounding the lawnmower course, making full use of the rather dated and dilapidated speedway, were several military vehicles as well as a mini monster truck and a similar vehicle which, we were told, could climb a vertical wall. Even the vehicular attractions didn't do much to raise the morale of the crowd, who had to cope with the heat, humidity and the irritation of flies. At three p.m. on a Friday afternoon, it was fewer than a hundred strong. The MC gave us a long spiel about the 'sport', the association's long-standing credentials and its yearly events, and then explained the rules and regulations. This segment of the speech had me thinking. To make races equal, the power of the mower had to be limited according to the age of the competitor and class in which he had entered, but for some reason, presumably safety, the blades had to be removed. Surely without the blades the machine was no longer a mower but just a slow and appallingly unaerodynamic go-kart. How could it be called a lawnmower when it wasn't capable of mowing a lawn?

From what I could work out, despite the rules, the mowers didn't seem to be equal in power or speed, and in the majority of races, whichever driver took the lead on the first turn of the ovoid circuit would remain there until they took the chequered flag. The races that followed included a girl representing 'Team Jesus', a mower that tipped over, highly dangerously, and the first successful overtaking manoeuvre, when one man reached a speed of over 40 mph, which, on a circuit with straights of less than 100 feet, was pretty impressive ... for a lawnmower. Fortunately for us, the roar of the machines and the country music which echoed through the speedway's public-address system during each race was enough to drown out the commentary of the MC who, by this time, was enjoying the racing so much it seemed as if his relationship with lawnmowers went beyond just an extensive knowledge of the subject and into realms rather more perverse and sexually gratifying.

As the practice races gave way to the adult classes, where lawnmowers could reach speeds which rivalled our hire car's performance, it became obvious that the day's racing wouldn't be finished for quite some time. We made our way to a refreshment stand through the long blades of grass that surrounded the track. We had started to play a brand-new game – trying to detect when one country and western song ended and another began. With each one featuring similar melodies, singing style and lyrics about driving pick-up trucks and attending barn dances, it's not as easy as you think.

As we returned to our seats, there was some good news and bad news waiting for us. Sadly, for reasons I remain unsure of to this day, Redneck Idol had been cancelled and would not be featured in the evening's festivities. Luckily, the organizers, with a lot of persuasion from the MC I'm sure, decided on a back-up plan. The lawnmower races were now to include a greater number of laps per race and, later on, we would be shown a demonstration of the Dixie Chopper – the world's fastest lawnmower!

Woo!

After four more races, the crowd finally had a reason to get excited, as the mower duels were interrupted by the arrival of the General Lee (of *The Dukes of Hazzard* fame). People flocked around the famous orange 1969 Dodge Charger for a quick photo opportunity, to the chagrin of the MC, who seemed surprised that one of the most prominent and celebrated vehicles in television history could even come close to matching the attraction of a de-bladed lawnmower.

When he managed to get the crowd's attention back on the centre track, the racing continued and the first of the adult division produced a photo-finish . . . well, a shout-at-your-wife-finish, really.

'Sherri!' he bellowed. 'Who won that one?'

After deliberating for a brief few seconds, Sherri raised her two hands and held up six fingers. The MC turned to the two drivers.

'Number six won that race,' he informed them. The

driver of mower '6' began to celebrate, as did his rival, who was at the helm of '06'.

'Sherri!'

After the confusion had been sorted out, the racing took a brief respite – allowing a pick-up truck pulling a sheet of metal to flatten the course before lawnmower service was resumed. Two monster trucks were brought into action to entertain the crowd. As the wall-climbing vehicle began to struggle with any sort of climb, the so-called All-Terrain Monster was in full swing spinning and twisting its way through a routine of mechanical ballet. As the driver skidded and slid around the concrete circuit, he was invited nearer the crowd in order to perform a manoeuvre known as a reverse hurricane (a spin to you and me). As he powered the truck into the central reservation, he applied the brakes and pulled hard on the wheel, sending dirt into the air, raising cheers from the small crowd, and, because it had all taken place on the freshly flattened lawnmower course, outcries of anger from the lawnmowerers.

Amid shouts of 'Hey, what are you doing?', 'Get out of here, buddy!', and other less polite remonstrations, I could barely hear the apology from the owner of both trucks over Antony's and my laughter. As the pick-up returned for a second flattening job, we decided to head back to the motel, freshen up, and return when the temperature and humidity were more bearable, and hopefully when the lawnmower racing had been concluded.

After a quick shower, a swim in our pool and a light snack, we returned to the track and, above the ubiquitous sound of insect cries in the grasslands which surrounded us, we could hear the MC commentating on a teenager's lawnmower race.

'And the best thing about this sport,' he said, 'is that as youngsters, it keeps them away from drink and drugs and they are doing something productive with their lives.' Given the choice, I'd rather my son grew up to emulate Pete Doherty than a grass-cutting Nigel Mansell.

When the race finally reached its climax, the sun had set and, since the stadium floodlights didn't reach the centre of the circuit, three and a half hours of excruciatingly boring racing was finally over and the organizers made good on their promise by introducing the world's fastest lawnmower to the crowd. Looking like a cross between a go-kart and a mobility scooter, the Dixie Chopper has a 990 cc engine which produces a whopping 33 bhp. With a mind-blowing top speed of 15 mph, it has the ability to cut the grass of a football pitch in less than ten minutes, and turn 8.7 acres of grass into lawn every hour. Mind you, with a price tag of ten thousand dollars you would expect it to take the kids to school as well as thrill you in the bedroom (which, for the MC, it probably does).

The stage, which had stood empty for the entire afternoon owing to the cancellation of Redneck Idol, began to attract a crowd of revved-up revellers. Those who had brought along their own chairs sat at the foot of the spotlights. The evening's entertainment was to be a band by the name of Deepstep, a quintet from Dublin, named after the minuscule town of the same name 40 miles to the north. Although the chances of them not playing any country and western music was slim to none, we gave them the benefit of the doubt and decided to stand near the expectant crowd in the hope that someone would speak to us, or at the very least ask us how their stolen GPS system worked. After fifteen minutes of non-stop, knee-slapping country music, we decided to leave, but not before we noticed a young man wearing a ripped vest and sporting a rebellious baseball cap with the words 'Jesus is a nobody' written on it. When on closer inspection we discovered the cap actually read 'Jesus is my homeboy', my urge to speak to him dwindled. It seemed an appropriate time to return to our motel and prepare ourselves for an even stranger Southern experience the following day.

On the day where over 150 musical acts at twelve separate locations around the world, from Rio de Janeiro and Hamburg to as far afield as Shanghai and the British Antarctic Territory, were raising awareness for climate change at the request of Al Gore, Dublin's sweltering morning temperature made me wonder whether the series of global extravaganzas was a case of too little too late. With the mercury forcing its way into the nineties at only eleven a.m., coupled with the extreme humidity, it was only the event's online schedule which featured curiosities such as the 'Mud Pit Belly-Flop' and the 'Armpit Serenade' that spurred us into the car for the fifteen-minute drive to Buckeye Park in East Dublin.

If the queue of traffic waiting to turn off the highway and on to Buckeye Road was anything to go by, the Redneck Games was very popular indeed. As I looked behind at the increasingly lengthy line of traffic in which we were waiting, I realized we were the only two people in a conventional car. The remainder of the procession were arriving in 4x4s, SUVs, and, the most popular vehicle by far, pick-up trucks – with four crammed in the front and enough room in the cargo area for a family of six.

For five dollars we entered the hub of the Redneck Games, where the events, refreshment stands and entertainment would take place in an area no larger than a football pitch. At the very end of the park stood a boat ramp which met the Altamaha River. There were already a hundred or so people cooling themselves off. At the far bank, amid a flotilla of casual vessels sporting flags of the Confederacy, stood a tree whose branches were perfectly positioned to allow jumpers to leap from its height and fall into the river below. This attracted a great number of prospective jumpers who queued patiently for their turn. From the number of people waiting in line, I began to realize just why the river was the only 'thing to do' in East Dublin. Not even the earlier arrival of an ambulance to the water's edge had discouraged anyone from attempting the plummet.

At midday, the crowd were officially welcomed by some members of the Y-96 FM staff who still sponsor the event. They introduced a character they referred to as Freight Train, a gentleman with long grey hair, thin beard and a Confederate-flag-decorated hat, whose age was almost impossible to determine owing to his youthful attire and lack of teeth. With a propane torch made up of six cans of Budweiser in hand, it was Freight Train's job to light the ceremonial Barbeque Grill, the redneck equivalent of the Olympic flame. With the grill lit accompanied by the words: 'Let the gas begin', the games were officially under way. Thankfully there was little pomp and circumstance and no national anthem. Freight Train took some time out to mingle with the crowd and pose for photos, distorting his face by placing his bottom lip over his nose (an expression which could easily have won the man a gurning world championship).

We were informed by the announcer that the first event, the Armpit Serenade, wouldn't begin for another half an hour, so Antony and I decided to wander through the various stalls on the opposite side of the boat ramp to see what was available for lunch.

The choice of food on offer was extensive and reasonably priced, if not rather samey. Burgers were on sale at nearly every stand along with chicken, fries, hot dogs, and the usual array of carnivorous cuisine. To wash it all down, soft drinks, ice cones and water were sold in abundance and nearly always advertised with an incorrect apostrophe – something I loathe. Out of principle I avoided the 'burger's', 'hot dog's' and ... wait for it ... 'fry's', and was drawn to the only vendor who hadn't used a single apostrophe incorrectly.

'You wanna try summin'?' she asked, noticing my interest in the food available.

'Um, maybe,' I replied, pointing at a large sausage attached to the end of a wooden stick. 'What's that?'

'That's alligator on a stick,' she replied. 'It's real nice. You wan' some?'

'Er. Not right now. I'll work up an appetite first.'

Across from the alligator woman was a stand which, instead of selling food and merchandise, was advertising the Republican Party, a bulwark of the South. Confronted by a man clutching books titled *Why Lincoln*

Was Wrong and *The South Will Rise Again* as well as flyers for a local candidate, I had no choice but to talk to him. He had left his stand adorned in flags of the Confederacy in order to speak with me. Luckily, I had the perfect excuse as to why I didn't wish to listen to his right-wing conservative arguments: I was from the UK and was ineligible to vote.

In previous years, the Redneck Games have appeared on several American television programmes including MTV's *Real World* and Maury Povich's popular talk show. As we joined the crowd for the Armpit Serenade – an event which requires participants to produce a fart noise by using their hand and a sweaty underarm – it became obvious that this year's Southern extravaganza was no exception and would be making a return to the small screen. Before the contest took place, so-called 'celebrities' would demonstrate how the event was run, and try their hand before the real competitors took over. With microphone positioned directly under his armpit, Kyle, a young, shy-looking man who worked for a regional television company based in Atlanta, removed his shirt and attempted to produce the sound of flatulence. On a day of such humidity and heat, a sweaty underarm wasn't difficult to produce, but after witnessing Kyle's disastrous and not very crowd-pleasing attempt, it became clear that there was an obvious art to the Armpit Serenade. It was one that a fourteen-year-old was proficient in, as he took the crown when the real contest began, and won a trophy in the shape of a crushed beer can.

The Seed-Spitting contest followed and because so many people had entered, competitors' names were drawn from a hat. Once more, 'celebrities' began proceedings and Kyle embarrassed himself yet again when, following an almighty exhale, his projectile slipped from his mouth, bounced off his chin and landed just inches from his right shoe.

Having now worked up an appetite, I headed for some refreshments from the apostrophe-free stall. I sat on the bank of the river to watch the redneck lemmings fall from the tree, and tucked into what I hoped wasn't the alligator's penis. The arrival of yet another paramedic rescuing an injured jumper and carting him away in the back of the ambulance sweetened the afternoon, but did little to alter the taste of the meat, which can best be described as overly salted veal.

Bored with simply witnessing the events and paramedics at work, Antony and I made our way back towards the refreshment stands to wash the alligator out of my mouth and to see if we could sign up for any future events. I spotted the most official-looking person within a quarter of a mile (a lady with a pen not dressed in dungarees) and decided she must be the appropriate person to ask.

'Hi. Just wondering if we could sign up for an event?'

'Well, sure. Y'all too late for the Bobbin' for Pigs' Feet but you can still sign up for the Butt-Crack Challenge, the Redneck Horseshoe and the famous Mud-Pit Bellyflop.'

Two of the events were self-explanatory. We decided not to enter the Butt-Crack competition and enquired about what was involved in Redneck Horseshoes.

'I really don't know,' she replied with a large grin on her face.

'I thought it had something to do with toilet seats,' I replied, hoping to jog her memory.

'It could be,' she replied, 'but I really haven't got a clue.'

'OK then. Can you tell me what time the Mud-Pit Bellyflop is?'

'Sorry. I don't know that either.'

'Excuse me, but what is your actual job in this so-called information booth?' She laughed and posted our entry forms into the appropriate collection bins, as if to suggest that my last question was some kind of joke and not one which required a serious answer.

As the only information we gained from speaking to the lady was that we were too late to enter Bobbin' for Pigs' Feet, we decided to see what the event was all about. I thought that it couldn't possibly be what the name suggested, and believed it to be similar to games such as Murder in the Dark or Pin the Tail on the Donkey, in which no one is ever really murdered and a tail isn't ripped off a real donkey in order for it to be tacked back on to the animal by a dizzy child in a blindfold. As we reached the front of the stage, two see-through plastic tanks filled with water were placed on the ground, each containing eight real pigs' feet, skinned and looking as if they had been pickled. The rules appeared to be similar to apple-bobbing; Kyle was already in full swing, showing the crowd how not to succeed. His opponent, one of the ladies from the radio station, emptied the tank of feet in forty seconds, as Kyle, struggling to grab his second, looked as if he was more likely to drown than to finish in the ninety-second time limit.

During the drawing of the names for the real competitors, whenever someone's name was called and wasn't present, a large, shirtless fellow would always, without fail, call out 'I'll do it', before taking a sip from his beer can and cheering on whoever was selected to take part after the organizers ignored him. After four rounds of one-on-one pig-feet-grabbing duels, accompanied by at least seven or eight 'I'll do it's, the winner was a man who plucked the eight feet in a Redneck Games record time of only twenty-six seconds, beating a middle-aged woman from London. As the third beer trophy of the afternoon was awarded, I went to hunt for the lady from London. I wanted to hear an English accent and ask her what brought her to the Games. But, more importantly, the 'I'll do it' guy had just begun to speak to Antony.

I didn't garner much information from the lady from London, other than that she was with her daughter, but at least I was having better luck than Antony, who took a full five minutes to get away from Mr I'll Do It, or Drew Beard, as he turned out to be called. We escaped into the maze that was the area of refreshment stands, but our anonymity lasted for less than ten minutes, as Drew soon caught up with us.

'So where are you guys from?' he asked.

'England. Not London,' we replied in unison.

'You boys are a long way from home,' said Drew.

'Where are you from?' I asked.

'You see that hill over there?' he replied, pointing through the trees at a hill just over a mile away.

'Yes.'

'Just the other side of that.'

'Oh,' I said despondently. I'd been hoping that he lived further away than he did. Maybe he's travelled to other places, I thought.

'Have you ever been abroad, Drew?' I asked. Drew's answer was blunt.

'Where's that?'

'To another country.'

'Oh . . . um . . . I went to Michigan once.'

After talking of what we did back home and discovering what Drew did for a living (he worked as a delivery driver for a dump), he looked behind us with disappointment and anger – as if he was remembering the time he caught his best friend in bed with his mother.

'I hate that,' he snapped. I looked around. There didn't seem to be much apart from the boat ramp and some alligators on sticks.

'What?' Antony enquired.

'That,' Drew replied, pointing at two women, one black and one white, who were idly walking towards us side by side. 'It shouldn't be allowed. Makes me so angry.'

'Why does it make you angry?' we asked.

Drew grunted, stuttered and gestured with his arms, struggling for the correct words to sum up his feelings. 'It just shouldn't be allowed. We weren't meant to live together.'

Normally, at a point in conversation such as this, I would find any excuse to walk away so as to not be associated with the person. However, in Drew's case, I made an exception, mainly because he was so mind-numbingly stupid and had the IQ of a boiled sweet.

'You know there are two different kinds of niggers.

You can get white ones, you know. I just hate the lazy niggers,' Drew said loudly.

'You know, in England, that word is pretty bad,' said Antony cautiously.

'It's a bad word here too, but I don't give a shit.'

At this point, some of Drew's friends appeared and he introduced us as his buddies from London. He seemed to call them all 'cousin' in the same way that the English use 'mate', but from the look of them all, they could all quite easily have been related to Drew. As their racial hatred had already been exposed, it didn't take long for their second favourite topic to dominate the conversation.

'I'm a Baptist. That means I can't drink,' Drew said. He noticed me looking at the can of Budweiser in his hand. 'Oh, no,' he added. 'I can drink. I just can't get too drunk.'

'I see.'

'Do you go to church at home?' he asked.

'No. I'm not a very religious person,' I replied. Drew looked disappointed.

'You've gotta believe Jesus died and rose on the third day – how can you not believe it?'

'Sorry, Drew. I just don't. How religious is this town? Do many people go to church?' I asked.

'Most of 'em – probably about ninety to ninety-five per cent of 'em.'

At this point, I felt safe in the knowledge that Drew liked us enough to not hurt us. I decided to see how vicious his views actually were.

'What do you think about same sex couples?' I asked. 'Many states like Massachusetts have already legalized gay marriage. What are your thoughts on that issue?'

'Oh, that ain't right, man. Just ain't right!' he snapped, before stopping and staring straight through Antony. 'You two aren't . . . ?'

'Oh, no,' I said quickly.

'That's OK then,' he said before pointing at Antony. 'It's just that with a haircut like that, you never know.'

'Is that sort of thing not looked upon favourably?' asked Antony.

'Well, at my high school prom, some fag came dressed in a skirt.'

'Yeah?'

'Yeah,' Drew said defiantly. 'He went home in an ambulance.'

On that rather solemn note, Drew signed up for the Mud-Pit Bellyflop and agreed to meet us there when it all began. He and his friends departed, leaving Antony and me by the side of a stand which, ironically, promoted the Redneck Games and a love of the Confederacy as 'Heritage, Not Hatred'.

As a JCB arrived to prepare the mud pit for the belly-flopping, a man dressed in a long Confederate-flag coat took to the stage and sang some classic country tunes to a crowd who were more interested in how the pit preparations were coming on. Thirty minutes later, the microphone was handed back to the Y-96 DJ, and a crowd about six deep surrounded the pit, awaiting names to be drawn out of the hat. First though, as always, the 'celebrities' would take to the pit. An elderly lady known as Grandma Redneck – who wouldn't look out of place on a front porch in a rocking chair with shot-gun in hand – was selected to lead the proceedings and dunk herself into the 4-foot-deep pit, which was similar in size to a garden pond and contained muddy water which was an unhealthy shade of bright orange.

As Grandma Redneck stood at the bog's edge, adopting a dive position for photo opportunities, a small child ran out of the crowd and ran into her behind, attempting to force her into the mire. Thanks to her impressive girth, Grandma Redneck didn't even lose her footing and when she finally took to her downward plunge, her size and weight played a major role in covering a large majority of the crowd in some of the escaping mud.

The rules, from what I could work out, were pretty simple: each competitor was to fall into the pit in a belly-flop position. Judges would then decide on which 'flop' was the best. If the contest was judged on how much water left the bog, Grandma Redneck had set the benchmark pretty high. According to the Y-96 DJ, the contest would take place in the form of heats, with the winners of each progressing to a flop final. With every name announced, a shirtless newcomer would approach the pit, push members of the crowd back to make room for a perfect run-up, dive into the mud, and return to the surface completely covered in a skin of orange muck, looking like a monster from *Doctor Who*. With each belly-flop, the audience (and especially Drew) shrieked and applauded as more and more mud splashed into the crowd.

Midway through the second heat, when a member of the audience was pushed into the pit, all hell broke loose. The crowd took this as their cue to enter the bog too. In under a minute, dozens of people were crammed into the pit. Many more hovered at the edge, looking for a space into which they could squeeze, bringing the official contest to a premature end.

'Shall we?' I suggested to Antony.

After removing our shirts and flip-flops, we entered the pit slowly and methodically so as to not trample anyone. We did not emulate some other 'swimmers' who ran and jumped in, with no regard for anyone who would be underneath them in the pit when they came crashing down. The first thing I noticed was the warmth of the water. The second was that the bottom of the pit was incredibly difficult to wade through, as the muddy bed produced a drag effect on your legs similar to walking through a children's ball pool. As if rubbing shoulders with muddy rednecks wasn't enjoyable enough, I met Drew in the centre who decided to slap me on the back and show me a personal alligator-wrestling technique of his which he had earlier attempted to describe verbally. Being sufficiently covered in Georgia's finest, I suggested that Antony and I wash ourselves off in the river before returning to the motel for a proper clean, and a spot of dinner in Kentucky Framed Commandments.

Even though only an hour had passed when we returned to the Redneck Games, the scene had changed dramatically. People were still playing in the mud pit which had lost so much water it now looked more like a muddy paddling pool; the setting sun had drawn people out of the river and to the foot of the stage, and an entire day of drinking had had its effect on a now energized and raucous congregation. Drew, who had earlier told us that his religion compelled him to drink responsibly, was staggering around with a girl in tow apparently oblivious to what was going on. He only settled when a Y-96 FM staff member announced that a wet T-shirt contest was about to start.

To whet the crowd's appetite, the four contestants were exhibited on the front of the stage, and to raise money for charity an auction began for the right to hose the ladies down. This was eventually won by a German who paid a hundred dollars for the honour, who also won the right to sit as a judge for Mr and Mrs Redneck, which would precede the hosing.

From what I could make out, Mr and Mrs Redneck was just a talent show, and the entrants didn't seem to have a single skill between them. One competitor showed that he could shout rather loudly and another, a man named Cletus (yes, that was his actual name), could crush a beer can by placing it into his dungarees. The winner, however, was a woman whose 'talent' was that she had given birth to five children. As the time for the wet T-shirt contest grew ever closer, you could detect that the crowd were ready owing to their oh-so-subtle signals: they were shouting 'WE WANT TITTIES' over and over again. On hearing this, a rather drunk girl ran to the front of the stage and lifted both her top and the spirit of the crowd. As event organizers forcibly removed the girl to the continual 'titty' chant from the rowdy gang, the host took to the microphone and tried to calm the situation.

'Hey, everyone, this is a family event,' she said calmly. 'Let's be classy.'

Classy? At the Redneck Games? The crowd weren't going to buy that, surely. They had just witnessed a talent contest in which the ultimate in stereotypical rednecks was placed runner-up to someone whose only skill was the art of procreating.

'WE WANT TITS. WE WANT TITS!' the crowd cheered. The host tried to laugh the chants off but they went on for so long that she stormed to the front of the stage.

'Hey!' she bellowed back, before adding to the lewd atmosphere herself. 'There are children in the audience, so there'll be no more bullshit!' Whatever respect she had commanded flew straight out of window as she swore. The crowd responded by chanting 'bullshit' in unison, the wet T-shirt contest was cancelled, and it was up to the winner of the previous year's Redneck Idol to play to the hostile audience.

After only five minutes the artist was interrupted by the games' closing firework display. The attitude of the crowd, coupled with the sporadic fighting that had broken out in sections of the park, had probably persuaded the organizers that they should end the games as quickly as possible. Antony and I scrambled to a nearby bank to escape the possibility of being involved in any skirmish, and found ourselves torn between which explosions to gaze at – the colourful ones in the air, or the ground's more brutal appeal. As police and security guards were called into the darkness for the almost impossible task of finding a young man who had produced a knife, we decided it was in our best interests to leave.

The slamming of the car door ensured our safety as I took a last look at my fellow deserters. Suddenly, I felt out of touch with the human race. It was obvious that with the exception of shape and skin colour, they and I had almost nothing in common. I knew that presumably not everyone who had attended the games shared Drew's views, and yet realistically nothing I had seen or experienced suggested anything to the contrary. In democratic societies, freedom of speech is embedded into constitutions and everyone has the right to express their opinion, even if you don't like what they have to say. I had assumed 'redneck' to be a slang term, indeed more of an insult, but it seemed that to be a redneck is something held in high regard in the South and a label which most of the working class wear with pride. For the best part of the day, the Redneck Games had been a source of family fun and downright tomfoolery, but when old-fashioned ideologies rise to the surface I wonder whether their love of the Confederacy and its way of life *is* a case of heritage and not hatred, as was suggested.

The only thing that was certain, as I looked back at people staggering into their cars, stopping for the occasional vomit, was that there would be a high proportion of the congregation nursing a severe hangover in church the following morning.

5

Cracks at the Tracks

I hate Los Angeles. Absolutely loathe the place, and I have done ever since I first visited the dump in 1997. Back then, the City of Angels was an unrelenting urban sprawl, populated by over eighteen million people (most of whom didn't speak English) residing in an area stretching more than 120 miles from the Pacific Ocean to the south-western tip of the Mojave Desert. Owing to the city's rather limited public transportation network, LA was home to no less than twenty-seven intertwining freeways which still couldn't cope with the demands of the population's sixty-five million daily commutes. Even Hollywood, known for its prestige and allure, is no more than a street of souvenir shops where rubbish covers many of the stars on the district's famous Walk of Fame. Ten years on, and fate had cruelly returned me to the city, but this time I decided to wipe the slate clean, hoping things would have changed and that the glitz and glamour had once again replaced the blitz and clamour.

However, this visit began worse than the first.

In my eternal quest to save a few dollars, I had booked my hire car with a company named Deluxe Rent a Car. Now, I know as well as you that the name was most probably ironic and not representative of their fleet, but at the time I was happy that I was making a huge saving of three dollars a day. Antony and I trudged away from the crowded baggage carousel and made our way to the rental car pick-up point located just yards from the airport's exit. There we awaited Deluxe Rent a Car's shuttle bus.

And waited. After twenty minutes Antony and I slumped on to our bags to recover from the early morning flight from Jacksonville to Los Angeles, which had taken eight hours, owing to a horrendous 500-mile detour via Washington DC. The flow of rental car shuttle buses was becoming almost hypnotic and every one had passed at least once. Avis arrived and was quickly followed by Hertz and Advantage, then Dollar; Thrifty preceded Budget, who made way for Avis and Hertz to arrive for their second laps. There was no sign of Deluxe, nor did any of the hotel chains have the company's logo on their vans symbolizing any sort of partnership. A further ten minutes passed and once Avis and Hertz had passed us for the third time, I made my way back into the airport terminal and approached the information desk.

'Excuse me, but I'm waiting for a rental car's shuttle bus. Do you know if they have one?' I asked.

'What's it called?' she replied.

'Deluxe Rent a Car,' I said, rather embarrassed.

'I've never heard of it,' she said bluntly. 'Oh, hang on

a minute . . .' She consulted some notes and a list on her desk, running her finger down a list of names. 'Nope.'

'Um, thanks anyway.'

As I made my way back to Antony, I passed a pay-phone with a telephone directory hanging underneath and decided to ring the company for instructions on how to reach them. There appeared to be a Deluxe Clothing, Deluxe Hair Salon, Deluxe Jewelry, but then, where Deluxe Rent a Car should have featured, was Deluxe Rooter Sewer & Drain Service. Maybe it was the same company. As a last resort, I rang my girlfriend who logged on to my email account back in the UK and gave me the number for the rental firm.

Having dialled the number from the payphone with the useless phone book attached, my call was sent directly to a recorded message which gave clear and concise instructions for reaching the rental centre.

'Hello, and thank you for calling Deluxe Rent a Car,' it said. 'To reach our rental centre please exit the terminal building and wait by the sign marked "Hotels and Courtesy Shuttles" for the white shuttle van that's marked "Jonnypark". It arrives every fifteen minutes and will deliver you safely to the facility. This payphone will self-destruct in ten seconds.' (Actually, I made that last bit up.)

Of course! It was so simple. I'm surprised we didn't think of it earlier. It was obvious, staring us right in the face. To find 'Deluxe Rent a Car' we had to keep our eyes out for the van marked 'Jonnypark'. It made perfect sense. They are, after all, nearly identical names, aren't they? Antony and I were kicking ourselves at our own stupidity for thirty minutes, until the van finally picked us up.

Upon arrival at the company's 'headquarters', the sizeable queue gave me some time to look around. Outside, among the throng of cars parked in no particular order, stood a giant electricity box, similar to the ones found at the top of high-voltage transmission pylons. The office inside was a tasteless mix of purple and grey and wouldn't have looked out of place in a 1970s office block. In fact, a small child standing just in front of me summed the place up rather nicely after he tugged on his father's trousers and whispered, 'This place is horrible, Daddy.'

Finally, after an interesting conversation about why I had to pay eleven dollars just because I had a foreign driving licence – 'We can control three pedals in the UK, you know,' I told her – I was handed the keys to our new hire car and we made our way out into the forecourt to locate it. Much to my dismay, it was a Chrysler PT Cruiser. My three-hour wait for a shuttle, then in the queue, had rewarded me with a car that was a cross between a 1930s limousine and a hearse. To make matters worse, the colour was – well, *they* called it gold. I thought 'shitty brown' was a more accurate description.

Leaving the rental centre to join the San Diego Freeway and the inevitable traffic jams, I noticed two concerning facts about the car. It had little fuel and, according to the digital display, had an oil level of 0 per cent. Fixing the problems, however, would prove to be a little more troublesome. After stopping in several petrol stations I finally found one that would accept a credit card. I made a mental note that upon returning the car I would simply drive around the block as many times as it took to empty the tank, to leave them with the same amount of fuel as they had left me. As for the rather disturbing oil level, I simply turned the digital display off. Problem solved.

Although our first day in Los Angeles hadn't got off to a flying start, we were sure that as long as the car didn't seize up until the second we returned it to the rental centre, things were bound to improve; and to help them along, we headed for Santa Monica. Santa Monica has everything you would expect from a beachside city: golden sands, palm trees, a beautiful ocean and an abundance of tramps who seem content to bask in the summer sun. After a quick stroll along the famous pier, Antony and I made our way through the Third Street Promenade, past the expensive designer outlets and sports shops, which kept informing us that in just four days' time, David Beckham would join the likes of Pele and the great Franz Beckenbauer by joining the LA Galaxy and ending his illustrious career playing football in a country where they don't even call the sport by its proper name. Mind you, for seventy thousand pounds a day, I wouldn't complain.

David Beckham wasn't around to have a quick chat to, but fortunately for us, ahead of me in a queue and having a bit of trouble with his credit card, ex-Arsenal and England left-back Lee Dixon was. After confirming his identity, Antony and I collared him to see why the Premiership stalwart was in Los Angeles.

'Hello, Mr Dixon,' Antony shouted, to get his attention.

'Hiya, lads,' he replied, as if we were team mates of his.

'Must be great for you in LA,' I interjected. 'I guess you never get noticed,' I added, instantly realizing that our very interruption defeated my point entirely. I decided to move things swiftly along. 'You out here for *Football Focus* or the BBC for Beckham's unveiling?'

'No, but I've got a meeting with FOX. How long are you guys out here for?'

'Just a week.'

'You've come to LA for just a week?'

Not wanting to go into the odds and sods of the entire trip, I decided to play it safe. 'Yeah, kind of. Do you actually like it here? Because we aren't the biggest fans of this city.'

'Where do you like?' he asked.

'Boston's lovely,' I replied.

'Yeah, well. LA is great. My wife lived out here for fourteen years and you really need to know where to go.'

With that, Lee left the shop and made his way into another clothes shop. As we set off in the opposite direction so as to not look like a couple of minor celebrity stalkers, it suddenly dawned on us that not only had we not asked him for his views on Thierry Henry leaving Arsenal just a week before, but, most importantly, we hadn't asked him where we needed to go to make the most out of this horrible city. As we looked back down the street, Lee Dixon, the guy who's never noticed, was being asked for an autograph by a couple of guys who had recognized him.

So Santa Monica hadn't really helped. By the next day, something was definitely wrong with the atmosphere between Antony and me. I wasn't sure if it was the drone of Los Angeles life or the fact that we had now spent almost a month together. Neither of us was talking that much, but we both sensed that it definitely wasn't a character clash: he didn't have a problem with me and I had no quarrel with him. I think the hatred that seemed to pervade the air of Los Angeles was contagious and the thought that we still had three days to waste until our next event sent a shared shiver of dread down our spines.

Stuff it, I thought to myself. Neither Antony nor I wanted to spend another day in this dump, so I was willing to throw caution to the wind and run the risk of seizing the car's engine in the middle of a desert and hundreds of miles from anywhere. What we needed was a 500-mile round trip to Las Vegas. That should cheer us up.

Although Las Vegas is a city in the middle of the desert, established through gambling and expanding on greed, it is a truly fascinating and quite staggering spectacle. Where else in the world could I see both the Eiffel Tower and the Empire State Building as a 40-foot Rita Rudner stares back at me through my hotel window? Owing to the almost intolerable heat, where during the summer overnight temperatures are still in the mid nineties, we decided the best idea was to remain in our room with some cooling beers and take to the city streets when the sun had disappeared.

A walk down the famous strip is a strange experience and, if you can resist the temptation of a flutter in one of the city's 1,700 licensed premises, the stroll past 15,000 miles of neon lighting and free entertainment is enough to pass an entire evening. Each and every hotel dedicates itself to a theme and with the pyramid at Luxor and an almost perfect replica of the St Mark's Square Campanile amid the gondolas and waterways of the Venetian, Vegas seems like a city into which the whole world has been squeezed. Treasure Island Hotel and Casino puts on a free seventeenth-century pirate show known as the *Sirens of TI* for passers-by four times a night, and the luxurious Bellagio is famed for its 32,000-square-metre artificial lake and truly spectacular musical fountain display. As Antony and I perched ourselves on the casino's wall, 'My Heart Will Go On' bellowed out of the speakers and the lake's hundred or so fountains, accompanied by 4,500 lights, danced to the melody. We waited a further fifteen minutes until the Sarah Brightman and Andrea Bocelli song '*Con Te Partirò*' had stunned the crowd into a state of enraptured awe. As the song reached a higher key, the carefully choreographed display made full use of its 1,200 nozzles, dazzling the crowd and passers-by alike with a show which befitted the beauty and elegance of the piece.

I think Las Vegas and especially the fountains of Bellagio did the trick. We returned to our hotel feeling thoroughly uplifted. When we consulted the Bellagio's playlist, we realized it was a good job we had only stayed and watched the fountains perform two songs. Our good mood could have been quickly quashed if the casino's random selection of their thirty available tunes had chosen Lee Greenwood's 'God Bless the USA'. Fortunately it didn't and Antony and I were back to our usual selves. And we needed to be. In a little over two days' time, we weren't only going to spend the day together, but we were expected to drop our trousers and pants more than thirty times with a bunch of complete strangers.

In 1979, K. T. Smith was drinking in the Mugs Away Saloon in Laguna Niguel, southwest of downtown Los Angeles in the highly affluent area of Orange County. Smith reputedly told his friends that he would buy anyone a drink if they approached the railway track opposite the bar, lowered their pants and 'mooned' at the next passing train. Many did and, over twenty-five years later, they continue to do so one Saturday a year in July. Sadly K. T. is no longer there to reward them. Today, the 'Mooning of Amtrak' at the Mugs Away Saloon is an event that attracts hundreds of people each year. Southern California's Metrolink regional rail system began weekend service in 2006, and the number of daily trains which pass the bar on the selected Saturday between dawn and midnight totals thirty-six. Although attending such an event meant we would have to spend an entire day in or around a bar, Antony and I were willing to make such a sacrifice. We checked into our motel, then immediately made our way to the Mugs Away Saloon to scope the place out the day before the mooning was scheduled to begin.

Located on a long, dead-end road just off the San Diego Freeway, the Mugs Away Saloon seems to be more of a small business on an industrial estate than a bar. With a single pool table and a tiny outside drinking and smoking area, the pub isn't the largest I've ever ventured into either. However, as we approached the bar lady, pre-empting her request for ID by already reaching for our passports, a picture of a dozen pairs of bare buttocks signified we were definitely in the right place. Although cocktails were on offer for the weekend's extravaganza – with names such as a Wet Pussy, Dripping Dick or a Royal Fuck, proving that the art of drink-naming innuendo has been lost – Antony and I opted for a pint of beer each as we made our way outside just in time for a band to take to the stage and begin the saloon's 'Pre-Mooning Party'.

In anticipation of the big day, the Mugs Away Saloon had more than a dozen camper vans and RVs already parked alongside the road, and nearly every parking space belonging to the bar and nearby businesses had been filled. Above the door, northbound and south-bound train times were emblazoned across two huge posters. If Antony and I were to take this thing seriously (as seriously as you can take showing your bare arse to commuters), we were going to have to arrive back at the saloon before the first scheduled train at seven thirty-five a.m. That was bad enough, but Antony had more pressing matters on his mind. As we arrived back at our motel for a good night's sleep, he shared his concern with me.

'Rich?' he asked with a serious look in his eye. 'Do you think I should shave my ass?'

Even for me, seven a.m. is a ridiculously early time to begin drinking and yet outside the Mugs Away Saloon people were already sipping from cans of Budweiser and a lot of bikers had congregated.

'You reckon we should go inside and get a drink?' asked Antony.

'I reckon we should get a leather jacket,' I replied.

It was outside the bar that we met Mark Braconi, a young-looking 38-year-old who works with server operating systems, IP addresses and other computer-geek-related things I know nothing about. Mark was in the same boat as us, as although he lived just five miles from the bar, this was his first Mooning of Amtrak.

'Most of the people here are W. T. you know,' he commented as he took a swig from his vodka and orange.

'Yeah,' I replied slowly, not knowing what on earth W. T. stood for. Wearing trainers? White teeth?

Mark saw the perplexed look on my face: 'White trash.'

At this point, the barmaid who IDed us yesterday approached us.

'You were here last night,' she said. 'Have you been to bed yet?'

'Yeah. Had five and a half hours last night,' I replied.

'Want a Bloody Mary?' she asked.

'It's just gone seven in the morning!'

She looked at me with utter disdain. 'I have one word for you.'

'Slack?' I suggested.

'Pussy,' she replied.

'Ah, thought it may be something like that,' I said, before turning my attention to the bikers. 'Are they friendly?'

'Them? They're the Capistrano Eagles, our local biker group. They're fine.' She pointed to a burly fellow with a can of Budweiser. 'Just don't piss him off.'

At seven thirty, Antony and I dragged an unwilling Mark to the chain-link fence to wait for the first of the day's thirty-six trains. Joining us across the road from the bar were maybe six or seven people, leaving more than double that number in and outside of the saloon. At twenty to eight, the 7:35 came into view and the few that were present at the fence dropped their trousers and shorts and pressed their buttocks up against the chain-link fence. The first thing I noticed was that the cold metal fence was rather comfortable on my bare skin and I felt totally at ease. As the train slowed down for the benefit of the people onboard (the trains are booked up months in advance), all the passengers raised their right arms to wave as it sauntered by, whistling in appreciation of the nakedness on show. The whole mooning experience was hardly embarrassing at all, and reminded me of my days as a secondary school pupil, when you were fully entitled to misbehave and feel as if no consequences would befall you, as long as the entire class was joining in with you.

The next train wasn't due for almost an hour, so Antony and I made our way back to the bar and continued to talk to Mark, telling him the best way to travel to Ireland from the UK for his forthcoming European vacation with his wife. Although he already knew about the ferry crossing from Holyhead to Dublin, he wasn't wise to the existence of Ryanair and their ridiculously low fares.

'And you're sure that's on a plane?' he asked incredulously.

At eight, the Highway Patrol pulled up outside the bar. Two policemen exited the vehicle and a sudden undercurrent of comments such as 'They have no jurisdiction' and 'Rent-a-cop' echoed quietly through the ranks.

'What do you reckon they're here for?' Antony asked Mark.

'I reckon someone must have complained about your arse, mate,' I replied.

At eight twenty, we made our way back over to the fence for the first of three trains which were scheduled to pass in the following twenty minutes. It was here we would moon not only our first Metrolink train, but the first public conveyance travelling southbound too. After the 8:23 whizzed by without a whistle or slowing of speed at eight thirty, twenty-one people now joined us at the fence for the following train, one of whom was a woman in her forties who was dressed in preparation for the heat in sunglasses and a small white dress.

'Are you from England?' she asked.

'Yeah, good guess,' I replied, having realized by now how difficult it is for an American to distinguish between an English accent and the ghastly Australian twang where every sentence ends on a high as if something amazing has just happened.

'You live here then, do you?'

I scoffed at the suggestion. 'No. I couldn't live here,' I replied.

'England home, is it?' she asked rather compassionately.

'Yes. I suppose it is.'

As I leant against the fence to appreciate her kind words and the thought of home it had provoked, the crowd that had amassed to watch the mooning of the 9:09 southbound broke into rapturous cheers. Just a couple of feet from where I was standing, the woman who had just spoken to me had pulled her short skirt up and lowered the straps from her shoulders, revealing two medically enhanced breasts with what looked like Playboy bunny piercings through her nipples and a vagina complete with stud. Cameras were quickly whipped out by members of the excited crowd as the woman placed her hands either side of her groin and showed off the piercing, of which she seemed immensely proud. In a little under a minute, she had gone from quite affectionate and touching to just plain touching herself. Ironically, the only item of clothing which was left in place was the crucifix round her neck.

Whilst most people were still awaiting the arrival of the train, she continued to prance around, much to the delight of Kris, whom she didn't describe as her partner or husband, but as her 'soul mate'. He seemed quite content to stand back and admire her as other men ogled at her and posed for pictures alongside her breasts. The 9:09 Metrolink train zoomed by, ten minutes behind schedule but, as far as I was concerned, not a minute too soon. She turned, showed her bottom to the crowd, then returned fully dressed to the fence next to me, and continued her conversation as if nothing had happened. 'England's out there, huh?' she asked. I didn't quite know what to say.

'Um, yeah. A bit. Think you'd fit in nicely though.'

As the mooners dispersed, an elderly gentleman sporting a big white beard and wearing a Mickey Mouse T-shirt approached the woman. Any thoughts that he reminded me of Santa Claus were quickly dispelled when, instead of making her sit on his knee, he pointed at her breasts and said: 'Can I have a look at your tits?' You didn't need to ask her twice, and as she swiftly acquiesced to his request, cameras were focused on her again, transforming the mass of people into a horde of amateur paparazzi as Santa surveyed the woman's lower piercing like some sort of over-zealous gynaecologist.

During the commotion, Mark spotted a television crew and thought it would be a great idea if he informed them of the distance we had covered just to attend the day's event.

'You'll get on for sure,' he insisted.

'But I don't really want to, Mark.'

'Yes you do. Hey, buddy! These guys came all the way from England.'

Before we knew it, a father-and-son camera team had us sign disclaimers, and we were talking to what may have been another member of their family about our time in America and our reason for attending such an event.

'Um, just for a laugh,' was the best reason we could muster.

As the 9:27 Metrolink northbound passed, Mark introduced me to a woman called Laurie, a lady who thankfully kept her replica Jeff Gordon NASCAR top firmly on. She was much taken with the English word 'bum', but took obvious exception to my low opinion of her beloved NASCAR – a sport in which cars drive round and round an ovoid track for hours on end, only ever needing to turn left, presumably making the members of the audience feel rather dizzy. As we chatted by the fence, a newspaper reporter approached and asked me for some quotes he could use for the local paper. Struggling to find anything interesting to say to him, I was luckily saved by the bell – the bell of the 9:47, passing twelve minutes late.

By eleven, cars had blocked others in and the entire area surrounding the bar looked more like a refugee camp – albeit a Butlins-style one with paddling pools, barbeques and giant caravans. Inside the bar, a band had already begun performing. The pool table had been covered with a sheet of plywood and a girl was dancing on top of it dressed in only a pink bra and panties and a bottle opener. Reaching the bar now seemed a near impossibility.

Outside, five men had arrived in ideal attire for mooning: kilts. Presuming that the men all hailed from Scotland or had ancestors from a Celtic nation, I was surprised to hear that they were Sicilian, and that kilts had been standard dress (no pun intended) for the inhabitants of the Italian island since the Seaforth Highlanders fought there in the late eighteenth and early nineteenth centuries.

The 10:34 (passing at ten thirty-eight) slowed down so much that it almost came to a complete standstill, with people managing to take pictures from the back of the train's rear carriage. Boobs were still on show. Antony and I remained at the fence, prepared to moon both the 10:54 northbound and southbound 11:01. When a train shot by at ten fifty-seven journeying south, we weren't sure which train had just passed. To add to the confusion, another hurtled by twenty minutes later, travelling in the opposite direction.

Because there wasn't another train scheduled for fifty-nine minutes, it gave us at least an hour and a half before, realistically, it would pass. Antony went to buy a burger, but I'd seen far too many baps already that day and retired to the car to indulge in some air-conditioned relaxation. As Antony joined me in the car, we realized we were parked in between Mark and his wife, who had just arrived. Mark announced he was leaving before 'things got out of hand', so we exchanged mobile numbers and agreed to all meet up in less compromising circumstances before we left LA. Such was the demand for a parking space that as soon as Mark's wife vacated her space a man in a pick-up truck quickly pulled in.

'Fucking hell! There are more people here than last year,' the driver bellowed as he slammed the door shut. 'Why aren't you guys out there?'

'We've been here since seven and fancied a breather,' I replied.

'Oh, man; so many people. We're giving out free liquor at a stand this afternoon for anyone getting their tits out. This is their Mecca.'

I struggled to keep up with his rapid speech and simply nodded my head whenever he stopped for air. It was clear he was excited about the prospect of what might happen in the afternoon, and as he bid us a good afternoon, he looked into the air with arms outstretched, as if a friend of his had just died and he was asking God why.

'Woo! Titties!' he shouted, and with that, made his way to the front of the building to join his ilk.

After our air-conditioned break in the car from hell, we returned to the bar where the number of bikes parked outside now totalled well over a hundred. The atmosphere had completely changed. What had begun as a frivolous day of fancy-free mooning had turned into a sordid reunion of exhibitionists and moustaches. The last time I had seen so many bikes in one place was when Bateman and I were in a town called Hagerstown, Pennsylvania – a town whose outlet store acted as a checkpoint for the 5th Annual 9/11 Commemorative Ride, only fours years after the attacks on New York, and the day before I was to sleep on a refrigerator (long story, about three hundred pages, ISBN 9780552154062 . . . well, I have to earn a living).

The scene that greeted us opposite the fence, just yards from the bar's entrance, was nothing like the atmosphere of the early morning mooning. The number of people in leather jackets had exploded, bandanas were prevalent and the number of biker girls out-numbered the other females present by eighteen tattooed breasts to two. There was certainly no violence, but the crowd were boisterous and loud, and middle-aged women were being photographed topless and encouraged to either mount their bikes or their partners.

As Antony and I strolled through the bar's car park, many of the bikers were trying, in their own imitable way, to make a bit of money, or simply to see more naked women. Such men included Glen, who was sitting relax-ing by a paddling pool filled with dozens of one dollar notes and a single five dollar bill. As he supped at his can of beer, he noticed our interest in his 'creation'.

'It's for women,' he said. 'But there aren't enough drunk girls. They have to be naked, you know.'

'Could I have a go?' asked Antony. Glen simply turned in disgust and encouraged us to find drunk girls who could flash their breasts at the George Washingtons, Lincoln, and, most importantly, Glen himself. Opposite the paddling pool, the man who parked next to us had just opened his stall, which he had named 'Shooters for Hooters'. Clearly he was still offering drinks for tits. Behind the table, he and three other men stood with beers in hand, awaiting desperately thirsty women to approach them.

By one fifty-eight – the time both the 1:27 and 1:39 passed the bar – the idea of mooning all thirty-six trains that day was fast becoming something I didn't really want to do. It was hot, the mood had changed completely, and although a mooning festival wasn't the most dignified of activities, I never expected the Mugs Away Saloon to host a Hell's Angels reunion. Outside entertainment was provided by local band Ex-Paladin, a two-piece heavy metal band who, according to their myspace page, sound like 'the type of music you would hear if you were in the dark ages, and you heard a desolate wounded warrior rage about futile battles and failed courtships, alongside a rebellious maiden who is beating the hell out of her drums, ranting about her hamster that died . . .'

Noisy. That's how I'd put it.

Back at the fence, awaiting the 2:18, the spirit of innocent fun was still hanging in there, exemplified by a dad who had his young child on his shoulders, lowering his little pants in order to join in the action. Next to me, an elderly gentleman, who was engaged in earnest conversation about college education and had paid over a quarter of a million dollars to help his daughter through a three-year course, noticed my height and eagerness for the train, and tapped me on the shoulder.

'Do you mind warning me when the train's coming?' he asked.

'Yeah, sure,' I replied.

'Just say something like . . .' He struggled to find a perfect codeword or phrase.

'The train is coming?' I suggested helpfully.

'Um . . . yeah. Perfect.'

What was becoming more odd about the mooning wasn't the fact that everyone was drinking, but what they were drinking out of. Everyone was storing their beverages in a similar vessel, a container that I had seen on many American films and television programmes and yet hadn't ever seen outside of the US. That day in Orange County, there were hundreds and hundreds of red plastic cups. If you are American and reading this, you'll wonder 'What's the big deal with red cups? We see them all the time,' and you'd be right to think that. But if you're also thinking that it's strange for someone like me to write a paragraph or two on the subject, then you are sadly mistaken. Everyone had a red cup. *Everyone*. To me that was just plain odd. I have been to many countries other than America and never seen a single red cup, and yet here they are everywhere: in Hollywood movies (traditionally when some sort of high school party is in full swing); stacked high in shops and supermarkets; a cup even provides the centrepiece for a poster I saw advertising a new ABC family television show about college life called *Greek*.

A red plastic cup *is* America, a symbol which typifies the nation, as evocative as the bald eagle, the Liberty Bell, the Statue of Liberty and an uncontrollable problem with obesity. The stereotypical Frenchman would be a bike-riding, baguette-carrying, onion-necklace-wearing artist in a black and white striped jumper and tilted black beret. A German would be dressed in lederhosen, dancing strangely and drinking from a huge half-litre beer glass. An American would be enjoying a burger and drinking from some sort of red plastic beaker. Don't be fooled into believing that the thirteen red and white stripes on the American flag signify the founding states of America. Oh no. The white is probably the South's doing and the red expresses love for the national plastic cup.

OK, perhaps I'm wrong, and I've ranted on about plastic cups for long enough, and maybe the stripes don't symbolize a beverage holder after all. Mind you, I reckon if you study an American flag closely, those may not be fifty stars after all.

By late afternoon, interest in mooning had dwindled, leaving only a few people actually baring their buttocks whilst concentrating on other things. Antony and I decided that the squalid, raucous atmosphere that had enveloped the event wasn't a scene we wanted to be a part of. As we made our escape, negotiating the car through the parked bikes so as to not clip the first, beginning a domino effect and angering a hundred owners instead of just the one, my last glimpse of the Mooning of Amtrak were several hydraulically aided cars bouncing and a navy T-shirt which informed me that the acronym for the 'The War Against Terrorism' is TWAT.

With only two days remaining in Los Angeles, Antony and I were determined to find something positive about the city. The following day, we finally found it.

Twenty miles south of downtown Los Angeles lies the city of Long Beach, a shining jewel in the tainted and decaying crown of LA. Its quiet, palm-tree-lined streets and quaint shopping districts draw your attention away from the myriad corporate skyscrapers and the dock-yard which dominates most of the city's coastline. Its cosmopolitan feel exudes an air of prosperity on a level with Monte Carlo. There's even a Grand Prix held there each year.

Across the bay stands the RMS *Queen Mary* – once the pride of the Cunard White Star Line – an elegant reminder of Britain's Empire and her history as a ship-building nation. Today, more than seventy years after her launch, as the world around her looks to the future, the *Queen Mary* stands as a reminder of the past, a hotel and museum embedded in tonnes of concrete, looking out rather forlornly at the Long Beach skyline.

In the evenings, the city's peaceful streets are a joy to stroll. After many turbulent years of gang-related crime, Long Beach has imposed an evening curfew on un-accompanied youths. This, coupled with the fact that the local police force question anybody who blinks awkwardly, creates a splendid ambience in which an evening drink can be enjoyed. It was in one of these friendly bars, spurred on by the broadcast of a NASCAR race on the bar's television, that Antony and I decided to write down a list of things we liked and hated about America. The list grew as we discussed it with the two barmen. So engaged we were by the task that the ink was still flowing when we returned to the motel. As I switched the bedroom light off to bring our penultimate day in Los Angeles to an end, I placed the notebook on the bedside table, closing its pages on seven in the like category, with the number of hates totalling sixty-four.

On our last full day in Los Angeles, we passed the morning in an outlet mall, taking advantage of the favourable dollar/sterling exchange rate. In the afternoon, we rang Mark from our motel room, and agreed to meet him and his wife Aleks in a shopping centre just a few miles from the Mugs Away Saloon. Somewhere in the Irvine Spectrum Center, a huge outdoor mall inspired by the architectural magnificence of the Alhambra in Granada, Spain (complete with twenty-one-screen cinema complex, extravagant fountains and a Ferris wheel), lies the Yard House – where we were scheduled to meet Mark and Aleks.

The Yard House boasts of having the largest selection of draught beers in the world – and with 147 to choose from, it may in fact be true. We were shown to our table and presented with the menu: the overwhelming choice felt more like reading a Tolkien novel than simply deciding what to drink. Preceding the unveiling of our list to Mark and Aleks, the waiter approached our table and illustrated point number one perfectly by asking Mark for some ID. Mark, don't forget, is a 38-year-old man, and although he has the look of someone younger, believing him to be under the age of twenty-one was really pushing the imagination to its absolute limit.

'That's what I don't get,' both Antony and I said, interrupting each other. 'Why on earth are they IDing you? It's obvious you're older than twenty-one.'

'I kind of like it,' Aleks replied. 'Makes me feel young.'

I took an instant liking to Aleks. Not only was she attractive, funny and intelligent, but was also well travelled and was definitely switched on when it came to American cultures and her opinions on them. She was a defiant patriot and proud American but only flew the flag on Independence Day and was a stalwart supporter of the Democrats but hated Hillary Clinton. Most importantly, however, she seemed intrigued by our list and wanted to hear it.

We tried to mix the likes with the hates for the sake of balance, but since one column outnumbered the other by almost ten to one, it didn't seem possible. We started on a cheery note.

'We like the car pool lane,' I said, before moving swiftly on to a hate. 'You don't use adverbs.'

'Pardon?' replied Aleks, who was probably expecting something to do with driving on the wrong side of the road or some sort of observation about obesity.

'You might,' I replied. 'But most people never use adverbs. They use adjectives instead. They forget all about the L and Y on the end of a word. "You drive too quick" instead of "quickly", for example. And the worst one, "You did bad", instead of "You did badly". That one really annoys me.'

Aleks simply nodded in agreement.

'And your coins are rubbish,' I added anxiously. That should win them back.

'In what way?' questioned Mark.

'Well, the five-cent coin is bigger than the ten for starters. How stupid is that?'

'Oh, yeah. I've never thought of it like that before,' he replied.

For the following half-hour, Antony and I detailed all the things that really annoyed us in America. These included such major flaws as America's international dialling code, which is somehow 001, even though we invented the phone, and minor niggles (that still managed to bother us) such as the way vinegar isn't readily accessible in restaurants; major television networks fill primetime slots with pitiful sitcoms based on a family and a moral dilemma they must overcome; and toilets being called bathrooms even though I've yet to see even a bidet in one.

I expected some sort of backlash from Aleks after discovering her patriotic streak, but much to my surprise she agreed with every single criticism. You could tell Mark had some points to make but after admitting he once bought a pick-up truck seconds after Aleks and I agreed that Americans drive unnecessarily large vehicles, he thought better of it.

The evening continued in much the same vein, as we used our liking for the turn-right-on-a-red-light rule and beer glasses kept in fridges to temper our criticisms of aspects of American culture. These included the constant advertisement breaks on television; no relegation policy in any American sport; fully grown adults wearing baseball caps; the dangerous two-prong electrical sockets; the adding of sales tax at the counter; and the phrase 'I was, like' often used by teenage girls.

When Aleks decided to split the bill with me, after I had insisted on paying, it proved either that she and Mark enjoyed our company a great deal, or the drink had gone to her head and she was getting frisky with her credit card. Either way, after sharing the cost of the evening, she disappeared for fifteen minutes and returned to the table with a Yard House pint glass and hooded top for both Antony and me.

Outside the bar, we bid farewell to Aleks and Mark and exchanged addresses in the faint hope that we would one day spend another evening together, perhaps in a British pub listening to a list of their own.

It had been almost a week since we landed in Los Angeles, and we had wanted to leave after only a day. However, the evening spent in the company of Aleks and Mark and our time gently strolling around the streets of Long Beach had almost made up for LA's shortcomings. We left the Irvine Spectrum Center with a stirring of respect for Los Angeles, only to climb into the Chrysler, which reminded us of the cycle of hatred once more.

There was no time to give the city another chance, however. Antony and I had to leave the home of movies and had already planned to attend our very own premiere. The only problem was that with just a week before the opening night, we were 1,000 miles away, and the movie didn't even exist.

6

And the Winner is . . .

Early the next morning I was back at Deluxe Rent a Car.
I don't mind admitting that I had cleverly rationed the
fuel to the extent that the car was running on fumes. I
handed the keys back to the woman behind the counter
and we moved our luggage from the boot of the car and
into the airport shuttle bus we had managed to miss for
two hours when we first arrived. It was only on
slamming the boot shut I noticed that not only did the
car have neither oil nor gas, but the licence plates had
expired over a month before.

LAX is the fifth busiest airport in the world by
passenger traffic, and handles more origin and final
destination passengers than any other in the world.
Such is the demand for the port that when we
were dropped off by the shuttle bus, people were
checking in using the desks positioned outside of the
terminal building. Further queues greeted us inside
the terminal and two hours later, we were sitting in

the departure lounge, awaiting our flight to Portland.

Following our time in Los Angeles, our arrival in Portland couldn't have been more propitious. Compared to the barren landscapes and urban sprawl of LA, Portland was a literal breath of fresh air. As our plane touched down, a quick peek out of the jet's windows was pleasing to the eye. Desert plains and clogged interstates had been replaced by alpine horizons and gently flowing rivers winding their way around the arboreal landscape. Portland is definitely a pleasant place to be – a city home to half a million people and a manageable downtown area, with the distant Mount Hood dominating the view.

After a night in a nearby Econo Lodge, we returned to the airport to pick up a hire car in which to make the 80-mile journey south to the city of Corvallis, where the premiere was now a day closer but the film hadn't taken a single step closer to completion. Right now, it wasn't even an idea in someone's head.

After the debacle of Deluxe Rent a Car and the unacceptable state in which I received the PT Cruiser, a reputable company (complete with obvious shuttle bus) was selected for our week-long Oregon car hire. Dollar offered us a free upgrade, and we departed Portland International Airport in a 2006 Ford Mustang – a car complete with both fuel and oil. With the whole day before us and no rush to check in to our motel, we decided to drive forty miles to the coast and follow the Pacific coastline down to the inland route to Corvallis. As we departed Portland, the interstate gave way to winding US highways (allowing the Mustang to show us what it could do). The sky had turned an overcast and daunting grey, temperatures had plummeted into the mid seventies, and it had started to rain. Life couldn't get any better.

The Oregon coast is rugged and certainly not the paradise that the words 'Pacific' and 'summer' conjure up in the mind's eye. Cliff edges were windswept and beaches were long, empty plains of dark yellow sand, and for the first time since arriving, reminded me of home. As the road snaked its way in a constant shadowing of the shore through such native-sounding towns as Tillamook and Neskowin, the coastal Route 101 threw up more ordinary names such as Lincoln City and Newport. It was at Newport that we began travelling inland until we had reached our destination – Corvallis, two days before the beginning of the city's annual festival of art, science, technology and kinetic energy.

Corvallis's rather eccentric da Vinci Days is the longest running festival of its kind and, although the three-day event bears his name, celebrations are concentrated less on the artist himself, and more on his legacy and ability to conceptualize ideas and inventions centuries ahead of his time. During his sixty-seven-year life, da Vinci sketched early designs for many inventions including a helicopter, odometer, catapult, tank, machine gun, and still had time to thrash out a couple of paintings here and there. It's the creative and conceptual part of the fifteenth-century polymath's life that the people of Corvallis choose to embrace and, as the brochure explains, 'Where else would you find art that makes you think, mini-race cars built by school kids, juggling physics lessons, a race of human-powered, artistically designed kinetic vehicles, award-winning music, a film festival, a keynote speaker, street performers, and interactive art and science activities and events . . . all in one weekend festival?'

See, I thought you couldn't think of one. (I thought of Cannes, but that only covered the film festival bit really.)

The city of Corvallis has a population of just over fifty thousand and was briefly the capital of the Oregon territory in 1855 before the state was welcomed into the union four years later and Salem was selected. The city is also home to Oregon State University, a college which during term time adds a further twenty thousand to the population. Nothing could speak more profoundly of Corvallis's character and geographical surroundings than the three top-tier programmes studied at the university: forestry, engineering and environmental studies; and OSU's motto 'Open minds, open doors'.

Since leaving Boston, Antony and I had endured a tiresome couple of weeks of exhausting heat and religion in Georgia and the frustration and rumpus of traffic-ridden LA. Corvallis seemed the perfect antidote. Not only were we surrounded by rivers, mountains and forests in a stimulating alpine environment but Corvallis was recently voted one of the top ten bicycle-friendly cities in America and the nation's twentieth safest city. Ironically enough, Benton County (the majority of whose population lives in Corvallis) has the lowest church attendance rate per capita in the entire country.

The following day, the eve of da Vinci Days, Antony and I took a short walk through the leafy streets of downtown Corvallis to the tourist information centre where our weekend tickets were being held. The 'tickets' came in the form of a coloured wristband, which would allow us access to all events, activities, exhibitions and general revelry taking place during the weekend. With a day in hand before Corvallis's annual spectacle began, I consulted the brochure stand to see what we could do in the local area to pass the afternoon. It boiled down to two things – a drive through the spectacular volcanic Cascade Mountain Range or a self-guided tour of Oregon's most popular covered bridges.

It was an easy decision to make.

The Hayden Covered Bridge – located just off Highway 34 – was built in 1918 and is one of the oldest in the state. The bridge, 91 feet long, spans the Alsea River and was of absolutely no interest to us as we travelled east out of Corvallis in search of the Cascades.

The Cascade Range stretches 700 miles from Northern California through America's Pacific Northwest and into Canada. The section in Oregon contains its fair share of volcanoes, and we were to pass the northern trio: the Three Sisters, Mount Jefferson and Mount Hood. This is where my map, which had served me well for three previous trips to the US, was proved to be useless. We navigated our way through the bizarrely named towns of Sweet Home and Upper Soda, and things were still plain sailing when the four-lane US highway changed to a more modest country road. It was only when we turned on to the Oregon state 22 that we found we had a problem. From here, the roads were single lane and simply did not exist as far as the map was concerned. And the signs didn't help us much either, being either painted on the ground (and impossible to see) or written on crockery.

Yes, crockery.

If road sign pots and pans weren't enough to prove just how deep in-the-middle-of-nowhere we were, an accurate indicator of our godforsaken location was provided by the Mustang's radio. In a built-up area in America, a scan through the FM band would normally result in the discovery of thirty or so stations between the 87.8 MHz and 108 MHz frequency. Here, where soup bowls and plates informed you of your position, only one station came through Russell's speakers (Russell is what we had named the Mustang). Unfortunately, the radio network's playlist was exclusively Christian rock – which wasn't too bad actually, as long as you could mentally block out most of the lyrics. After an hour of non-stop Bible ballads, we finally reached the thriving metropolis of Detroit. Not the city in Michigan, you understand, but with a population of 260, Detroit was easily the largest town within a 30-mile radius of our current position. Having not seen a single one of the town's people we continued on to the NF-46 (well, at least I think that's what was etched into the colander).

After a further hour of such classics as 'It's All in His Hands' and 'You're Ever So Inviting', Russell had delivered us safely to Mount Hood – Oregon's tallest peak and the Cascade Mountain Range's most-likely-to-erupt volcano. Unfortunately, we had driven into the town of Mount Hood and had somehow missed the turning to Trillium Lake – where the best views of the stratovolcano are to be had. How we drove straight past an 11,000-foot mountain without noticing I'll never know.

On the shores of Trillium Lake, surrounded by a family of ducks feasting on the remains of our Doritos, Antony and I stood in awe of the magnificent spectacle of Mount Hood. Its 11,249-foot peak disappeared into the drifting clouds and snow seemed to trickle down its slopes as if poured on by God's own hand. Either that or I had left the radio on for too long.

The millpond conditions and the bright daylight created a striking mirror image in the lake and we returned to the car with a vision of unrivalled environmental beauty forever etched in our minds. We also made the discovery that the mountain is over five hundred thousand years old, is made up of twelve separate glaciers, last erupted at the end of the eighteenth century, and as much as ducks enjoy Doritos crumbs, they aren't the biggest fans of Maltesers.

We made our way towards the interstate for a quick and easy return to Corvallis, where road signs were metallic and radio stations covered a range of topics. The Mount Hood Highway might as well have been called 'Silly Name Drive'. In just ten minutes, we had passed the town of Government Camp at the foot of Tom, Dick and Harry Mountain and the slightly larger settlement of Rhododendron and its neighbour Zigzag. In the thirty miles which followed, we were welcomed to the towns of Wildwood, Salmon, Sandy and, at the end of the highway, the town of Boring – where we enjoyed such sights as the Boring Fire Department, Boring Square Garden Center, Boring Middle School and Wally Road where the Boring Farmers' Market was held every Sunday morning during the summer.

*

Although the campus of one of the largest universities in Oregon sits on the outskirts of the town, Corvallis doesn't really have the kind of nightlife one would expect, and little bars with a live band are as crazy and exciting as it gets. Still, following a Thursday night special at the Peacock Tavern with drinks at just $1.50 (and a favourable exchange rate which priced the pints at less than 75p), we were fed and made significantly merry for less than twenty bucks, leaving us with hangovers for the opening day of the festival. Because da Vinci Days didn't officially start until the evening, our early afternoon rise from bed meant we hadn't missed a single minute and gave us plenty of time to try and remember why a girl had slapped Antony the previous night and to make our way back to the bar to locate the pile of sick he'd produced outside.

Running concurrently and in conjunction with da Vinci Days was the 8th Annual da Vinci Film Festival, a celebration of independent film including short films, feature films and documentaries submitted by local and national filmmakers, which the organizers had whittled down to a dozen or so that would be shown at two of the college's auditoriums. Although a mini film festival was of only minor interest to Antony and me, the debut of a film competition certainly was and we were gearing up for victory.

The rules were simple. The da Vinci Fast Film Project, according to the programme of events, involved the writing, shooting and editing of a ten-minute film in just forty-eight hours. All a team needed to do was to arrive at the LaSells Stewart Center in the college campus, be given a theme for their piece and a prop that had to appear at some point within the film, and then make the movie. We quickly decided that if we could scam a camera from the organizers, our lack of experience in filmmaking and non-existent editing software would prove no impediment to the project. We would write credits on pieces of paper, and sing over the top of the filming whenever a tune or incidental music was required. The entire half-assed effort, complete with horrendous acting and British accents, would gain us so many sympathy votes that surely we would be victorious.

That was the plan anyway.

At four forty-five – a clear fifteen minutes before the competition began – we arrived in the LaSells Stewart Center and approached the sign-up desk under our new guises as Rich Hitchcock and Antony Spielberg. Behind the desk sat a young woman and a small man in his mid twenties with short, curly hair.

'Are you directors?' asked the woman.

'Um. Not really,' Antony replied.

'We'd like to be though,' I said. 'Is it possible to enter the Fast Film Project?'

'Yeah, sure.'

'Can we borrow a camera though?'

She shook her head. 'You can't borrow one. You have to use your own.'

Plan B it was then: stand around waiting for a team to arrive which we could latch on to, appear in a scene in the background, and claim victory for ourselves.

As we waited, we discovered that the short man sitting alongside the woman wasn't a member of the organizing committee, but was in fact a competitor in the Fast Film Project. His constant references to himself and his film course at OSU made us take an instant dislike to him. He was the kind of smarmy guy who instead of listening to anyone else would switch the conversation around to something which reflected well on himself. Even worse, he looked like the sort of person who would wear a scarf. Terrible. Because of this, Antony and I didn't ask to join his one-man 'team' and instead of asking his name, we simply gave him a more fitting one: the Turd.

We had a new purpose in Corvallis now. Our main priority was beating the Turd. Winning the competition would just be a bonus. But as more and more teams arrived, all looking very professional and, more importantly, complete, our prospects were looking bleak. It was likely that we would have to abandon our plans of taking on the Turd and instead try to join forces with him and, through some sort of elaborate inside job, destroy his victory from within. As we wallowed in thoughts of treason and treachery, a young man with blond hair and glasses tapped me on the shoulder. 'I hear you're looking for a team to join.'

Without even having to wow him with my grade A at GCSE Drama or the fact that Antony can do a masterful impression of Borat, we were welcomed on to our new team. Our crew consisted of Andy Foster, the guy who invited us to join the team in the first place; Mary Jeanne Reynales, a middle-aged woman with long dark hair and a Bluetooth earpiece; and her husband Dave Grucza. They had already drawn 'Fall from grace' as the film's theme, and had been given a booklet of da Vinci's inventions as our prop. As we shook hands with our new partners, Mary Jeanne suggested we should follow her and Dave to the Lower Campus area where the da Vinci Days Festival had just begun and where we would meet the rest of the team to hatch a plan.

Following Mary Jeanne and Dave was easy enough, but managing to actually find a way through to a parking space near the campus was a different matter altogether. It wasn't that the streets were busy or that parking was prohibited, but every time we began to make good progress, a battery-powered car would shoot across our path and a 'road closed' sign would force us to detour. The reason for the constant diversions was the ENTEK International Grand Prix Electrathon, the first race of the festival and, according to the organizers, the longest-running Electrathon America-sanctioned event in the country. I'll take their word on that one.

Eventually we found a place to park just a couple of blocks from the campus. With a garden table and some fold-away chairs, we made our way to a park just outside of the main da Vinci Days exhibition venue. We sat down beside a painted wagon they had used in a production of *The Wizard of Oz* that was now serving as an information stand, and discussed the brief outline of the movie. Luckily Dave had a plan.

'The idea is that it's all based on a focus group,' he said. 'And da Vinci is planning on marketing his helicopter as some kind of commercial airline.' He continued talking for quite some time. After a few minutes I switched off. I didn't know what on earth he was talking about.

'So all we need is a punchline,' he ended.

'Right,' I said vaguely. 'Well, I just want to beat the Turd,' I added helpfully.

'You two go and get some food,' said Mary Jeanne. 'You must be hungry.'

After purchasing some chicken fried rice from one of the many stands selling everything from curry to couscous, we wandered around some of the exhibition stands. Nearly all of them were promoting things like more efficient energy use. 'Paint with Soil' was a particular favourite of mine. Opposite the soil stand was an energy-efficiency desk, at which members of the public were invited to list ways in which energy could be saved. Before returning to our team, I happily joined in and scrawled the words, 'Leaving the television on standby is the Devil's work.'

Settling back into our garden chairs, we were introduced to new recruits Bill Powell, a friendly faced man with short grey hair and matching moustache, and his effervescent wife Michele, and learnt more about our team's backgrounds and the skills they were bringing to the table. It was quite like the dossier scene at the beginning of *Mission: Impossible*. Not the terrible, gung-ho films starring Tom Cruise, you understand, but the classic and cleverly written 1960s television series to which the films don't do justice. It appeared that we were in good company: Mary Jeanne was a member of the Corvallis Community Theatre, and although she was the spitting image of the actress Kathy Bates, she decided against appearing in the film and was instead bringing her experience as a theatre director to it. Her husband, Dave, was a whizz with editing software, and could easily solve the problem of creating a life-size model of da Vinci's helicopter by superimposing a miniature model of one a friend of theirs had already made. And Andy was an experienced cameraman and part-time video production type-person. He then stood up and, adopting a commanding stance (it seemed to me as if he was now in charge), began to explain the idea, which this time I actually understood.

'Right, we have the plot now, guys,' he said proudly. 'Basically it's a news report about a scientist who has created a helicopter from da Vinci's designs. The report will be of the first launch—'

'—at Grace University,' Mary Jeanne interjected (she was proud of that one) before Andy continued. 'The report will be of the first launch and as you are British we thought you, Rich, could play the reporter—'

'Nigel Huffington,' Mary Jeanne pointed out, before Andy finally finished his spiel with, 'Antony, you'll be the voiceover announcer.'

Owing to our short walk, I hadn't been there to interrupt their thinking process, and as a reward was handed the lead role. I was so surprised I quickly turned around to check if my name had been written on the back of my garden chair, before I made one stipulation.

'I'll be a BBC reporter, right?' I asked with the utmost solemnity. 'Because I'm not gonna pretend I work for ITV.'

Bill was the first to act on my sudden mood change. 'Why? Don't you like ITV?' he asked.

'Don't get him started on ITV, Bill,' warned Antony.

It was too late. He had.

'Bill, it's a channel that doesn't broadcast a single programme I enjoy. Their sports coverage is appalling; all they show are soaps and terrible "documentaries" about fat people or celebrities. Basically, its target audience are the people who read things like *Take a Break*, *Heat* or *OK* magazine. Now you can even get ITV 2, 3 and 4! Why have those when you can't even get ITV 1 right? The only reason it appears as quite a popular channel in the UK is because it's left on in retirement homes twenty-four hours a day and the old biddies can't be bothered to change the channel for something better—'

'BBC it is then,' bellowed Mary Jeanne, defusing the situation as I paused for breath, halting my rant before it turned into a one-man crusade against the network. I calmed down, sat back in my chair and learnt more about the film.

During the report, the helicopter would eventually crash, and the punchline would be that the failure would be due to a cleaner at the lab turning the design of the craft upside down. Because we didn't find their idea of a punchline particularly amusing, Antony and I sat back in our chairs thinking of jokes which could appear before the ending of the short film.

'We have to have that annoying satellite delay and touching of the ear,' I said.

'Good thinking,' Mary Jeanne replied.

'When it crashes, can I shout the exact same lines as that Hindenburg commentator did? You know, the "Oh, the humanity" line.'

'I like it.'

I was on a roll and they hadn't even heard the best one yet.

'Can't I have a double-barrelled surname? If I was called Nigel Huffington-Fall, I could end my report by saying, "This is Nigel Huffington-Fall from Grace University." You see, a very cheeky way of getting the words "fall from grace" into the piece.'

Clever, hey?

The group were so impressed that they turned their attentions to Antony and awaited a comedic gem. Antony raised his finger and his lips parted. 'You know, Rich, we only needed to buy one wristband – we could have passed it through the fence.'

By the time the meeting ended, two hours had passed and we had only forty-six hours until the deadline. In order to make full use of the time we had available, Mary Jeanne advised us to enjoy the evening's performance by Pink Martini, a local band who had made it big, as she went home to write the script.

We only watched them for an hour or so, not because Pink Martini weren't good (quite the opposite, in fact), but because of the unearthly start time of eight the following morning. We didn't want to make the mistake of arriving late for our acting debuts.

At eight twenty, Antony and I arrived at the very same park where the plot was first discussed, and realized we weren't even the last to arrive. A couple of organizers were already marking out an area of the park for the Canine Frisbee competition later on that morning. Mary Jeanne and Dave were standing beside a table of filming equipment and approached us with the script. At over ten pages, it seemed quite substantial, until I realized that the words were typed in a large enough font for the pages to be held above the camera as a sort of rudimentary autocue.

After Bill and Michele appeared, Mary Jeanne handed me an Armani suit with shirt and tie, and asked me to put it on, before informing me it had cost three thousand dollars.

'I hope you have a belt,' she said. 'It belonged to my brother-in-law and he was a larger man than you.'

As Bill and Michele adopted the role of wardrobe supervisors by brushing random hairs from the jacket and even straightening my tie before adding a clip, it became apparent what 'larger than me' meant. The trousers would be put to better use as an expensive designer wind sock. The jacket, although perfectly comfortable, was very loose around the chest, and had enough slack to hold our crew and most of the equipment. Luckily Mary Jeanne had a solution. She presented me with two giant plastic clamps which were attached to the back of the jacket, making me look as if I was the victim of a brutal stabbing by an army of Lego men.

As I went through my opening line in my head, Andy arrived clutching a tray of drinks from Starbucks, supplying everyone else with an early-morning cup of coffee, and Antony and me with our first cups of tea in over a month.

After a quick tie-straightening by Bill, who had now donned an authentic brown leather bomber jacket with white scarf around his neck in preparation for his role as test pilot Brent Collander, the camera was pointed in my direction, Mary Jeanne thrust a microphone into my hand, and we were ready to begin filming.

So as not to confuse me and Antony too early in the filming process, the first scene we were to shoot (I obviously began to pick up the terminology) was the opening scene of the film. However (and try and keep

147

up with this), this would end with a link to a scene I would claim the 'BBC' had filmed earlier, yet in reality, we were to record it later and splice it into place when we came to editing. (Media studies students will be familiar with the concept.)

We filmed several attempts – sorry, 'takes'. Some weren't to Mary Jeanne's liking; others I completely ballsed up because the piece was so long. We worked on the opening lines for quite some time until (it seemed to me) Andy and Mary Jeanne had a hundred different versions from which the best (or 'least worst', in my case) could be extracted and put into the final edit, thankfully relieving me of ever having to say the words 'gyroscopic' and 'Professor Cornelius Whalborne' for the remainder of my life.

The following scene was very straightforward. I just had to say the simple line, 'And you rejoin me here at the launch site where the anticipation is palpable', then turn away from the camera. As we filmed the five-second line a number of times in search for one for the final edit, it became apparent why big Hollywood blockbusters take many months to shoot. The reason for my turn at the end only became apparent when Mary Jeanne marched across the park with a small crowd of confused-looking people in tow. Directly following my turn, another scene would be edited in that showed that the crowd that had arrived to witness this historic launch would total only a dozen or so (one of whom appears on his disability scooter, takes one look at what all the fuss is about, and simply continues on his way). With the helicopter only existing through the wonders of computer-technology, a double-rung ladder was positioned where the craft would be placed so the crowd and I had a common target on which to focus. Sound effects were to be added later, so the helicopter's 'launch' and subsequent 'crash' was demonstrated by Andy's right arm, which, when raised in the air, was to encourage noises of approval throughout the crowd as if the experiment was turning out to be a huge success. At the moment his hand dropped back to his thigh, the crowd was to become dejected and turn away in disgust, leaving me to look at the camera apologetically defeated amid a plume of smoke created by a fire extinguisher set off by Mary Jeanne.

With this scene, using almost ten minutes of video tape and a dozen close-up shots of the frustrated and by now impatient crowd, my work was effectively complete. Bill, the test pilot, was then filmed approaching the craft, with a separate shot showing his death. I then shouted the Hindenburg lines down the microphone (several times, of course) so it could be edited in when the helicopter fell to the ground and finished with a typical sign-off line and the clever 'Fall from grace' line attached.

In all, almost an hour of film had been shot, of which only two minutes would make the final edit. I removed the suit, changed into my usual clothes and was shocked to discover that it was already early afternoon.

Mary Jeanne suggested that the entire crew should meet up later in the evening to grab something to eat and meet the final members of our cast, including a few extras and Peter Platt, a proper actor with on-stage experience, who would be playing the crucial role of the professor.

*

The Fox and Firkin pub in downtown Corvallis (and before you look it up, a 'firkin' is an old English unit of liquid volume equal to 40.9 litres, and not an indiscreet way of getting a swear word into the name of a drinking establishment) is a pleasant place to spend one's evening, and it wasn't simply down to the company we kept. Fish and chips, curries, pies and ploughman's all appeared on the 'English pub' menu, and so it was with fond thoughts of home that I opted for bangers and mash. By an overwhelmingly strange coincidence, we were also reacquainted with Jean Dick, an OSU student who we had met in a bar in Corvallis when we had first arrived. She was joined by three fellow students, Julia Clark, Alex Svela and the fantastically named Kendall Zwang. Luckily, none of them was the girl who had slapped Antony.

Over an hour later Peter Platt rushed in and shook us by the hand. I'd had a mental image of what our professor would look and sound like, and Peter was not what I'd expected. Our 'professor' was in his late twenties, had olive skin, and although he had a full set of hair and a beard, both were jet black and neatly trimmed. To my mind, a professor didn't care about his appearance, had glasses and grey hair as wild and eccentric as him. Mind you, if Peter had seen me earlier on wearing a pair of trousers four hundred sizes too big for me and two giant clamps hanging from my jacket, he'd probably have thought I didn't look much like a BBC reporter, so who was I to complain? And anyway, Peter had already appeared in countless amateur dramatic productions and was a graduate of Harvard University. The closest I have come to acting stardom was appearing as an Oompa Loompa in a primary school production of *Charlie and the Chocolate Factory*. Oh, and my granddad appeared as an extra in the 1977 war movie *A Bridge Too Far*.

By now our cast and crew totalled twelve people and we only had the last few scenes left to shoot. For these we required Peter, his entourage of scientific assistants and a plausible set for a professor to work in. Whether we were allowed to be there (let alone film) or not, the dozen of us made our way to a federal laboratory where Bill worked on the outskirts of town.

The Environmental Protection Agency building wasn't much to look at from the outside: it seemed more like a comprehensive school than a government build-ing. Like thieves involved in an inside job, we parked around the back of the building and waited to be let in by Bill as the rear door could only be opened from the inside. Once inside, Bill led us through narrow corridors, past locked doors and finally into a room which looked like a lecture theatre-cum-classroom. As I undressed to don the Armani suit once again, Jean, Alex and Julia sorted through the miniature models of da Vinci's designs we had brought along and put on white lab coats in an attempt to make the classroom look more like the den of a da Vinci-obsessed professor. Peter put on his own lab coat, a pair of plastic safety glasses, perched himself on a stool beside an overhead projector and awaited Mary Jeanne's instructions.

It was only then that Antony and I realized just how good Peter was, and what a sublime choice to play the role of the professor he had been. Clutching the da Vinci design booklet – the prop that had to appear somewhere within the film – Peter went through his repertoire of accents, characteristics and general idiosyncrasies. At times, Professor Whalborne was a French aristocrat, at others he was from the Deep South. Then he became an eccentric doctor who was angered at people's lack of understanding. Such was the brilliance of each take that the outbreaks of laughter from me and the rest of the crew were ruining the scene and beginning to irritate Mary Jeanne, who wasn't enjoying the range of characters on display and wanted something more sensible than a Dutch or Jamaican drug baron professor.

After a dozen hilarious takes, Peter presented the pro-fessor as a restless, slightly schizophrenic character who was meant to make me, the BBC reporter, feel uneasy about interviewing him. This was conveyed in my reaction to his statement on the materials used, when I ask the professor what the crowd should expect from the launch, smiling encouragingly so as to not show my unease.

'Success!' Peter blared. 'Absolute, uncontroversial success!'

With that, my work was done, and as Andy and Dave filmed the lab assistants for some extra material and the final scene involving Kendall as the cleaner who turns the projection upside-down, I changed back into my casual clothes and set off down the corridor in search of some illegal biological experiments or governmental cover-ups. Twenty minutes of serious sleuthing later, all I had discovered was that we were in the Western Ecology Division of the EPA's office of Research and Development; that the facility's primary mission was to study the response of terrestrial, coastal and regional-scale ecological systems to pollutants and other human stresses; and that the face staring back at me on the wall of reception between George W. Bush and his vice president, Dick Cheney, was that of the EPA administrator Stephen L. Johnson. (I didn't even find that one out myself, Bill told me.)

With filming completely finished (or is that called a 'wrap'?), Antony and I were invited to Mary Jeanne and Dave's house along with Bill, Michele and Andy. As some voiceover work was required of Antony and me, we were only too happy to accept and caught a lift with Bill and Michele to the north of the city.

As soon as you enter their house, the framed movie posters, motion picture soundtracks and musical scripts littering every room mean you don't need Loyd Grossman to point out Dave and Mary Jeanne's obvious love of show business. They enjoy the thrill of a live audience and a theatre so much, that in May they had been married in one, live and unrehearsed in front of an audience who had turned up to watch a matinee performance of *Ragtime*. Before the show, Dave had shouted down the proposal from the balcony and Mary Jeanne, trying to look shocked, paused and duly accepted. After the closing of the curtain, the musical conductor began the 'Wedding March'; Dave appeared in a tuxedo, Mary Jeanne's cousin performed the ceremony and the audience were left wondering whether what they had witnessed was real. Only a handful of people were let in on the secret and Mary Jeanne got the no-thrills, no-gifts, no-nonsense, spontaneous wedding party she had always wanted.

While Andy and Dave locked themselves in the

computer room to edit the film, the rest of us chatted at length about a host of subjects ranging from why all American radio station names seem to be made up of four letters to what Dave did for a living. This gave Mary Jeanne an idea to pass the time.

'We'll play twenty questions!' she said. 'Twenty questions to try and identify his job.'

I was never any good at this game, and Antony proved to be up to my standard. By the time we'd used up all our questions we were none the wiser. Although he was very competent in digital editing, it was simply a pastime and Dave didn't even work with computers. The main clues we had established was that he was a tradesman, worked indoors, used tools, modified and repaired things, made a mess in his line of work, but he wasn't a plumber, carpenter, builder, plasterer, decorator or electrician.

Give up?

So did we.*

As if Dave's job wasn't difficult enough to get, Michele ran a yarn shop in Corvallis. We could have played fifty questions and I would never have guessed that one. Mary Jeanne's job never came under scrutiny. Her job as a nurse wasn't the most difficult to guess, and I think she remembered giving me her business card earlier in the day. Meanwhile, in the editing suite (or the study), Andy and Dave were beavering away in full nerd mode. They called all of us in and showed us some

---

* He was a cobbler. Incidentally, his business was called 'Dave's Family Shoe Service' (a name which he must have spent many sleepless nights thinking up).

of the scenes they had already pieced together. I didn't want to see a great deal, and purposely looked away, saving myself for the premiere.

After Antony and I had recorded quick voiceovers for segments of the film, Bill and Michele decided it was time they were leaving, a prompt for us to make a move too – partly because it was late, but mostly because they were giving us a lift back to the motel.

As we were led through another hallway of their more-than-modest abode, a certain picture caught my eye. It was of Tony Blair, Gordon Brown . . . and Andy.

'What's that all about, Andy?' I asked.

'Oh, yeah. I used to work for the Labour Party,' he said breezily.

It transpired Andy had worked as an intern for Blair and co. in 2003 and as a contractor during the 2005 general election. If only I had known before we agreed to join his team.

We left Andy in Mary Jeanne's house to work through the night on the editing. As we passed the night lights of Corvallis we realized that our final day in the town would end with us either as bona-fide winners, or feeling exactly like the Hollywood actors and directors who can merely claim to be 'Academy Award nominees'.

The previous day's filming had meant that with the exception of the 'Paint with Soil' stand and the hour we had spent listening to Pink Martini, we hadn't really seen a great deal of the da Vinci Days, so early on the Sunday morning we headed down to the Crystal Lake Sports Park for one of the many kinetic races that take place over the three-day weekend. A kinetic race is an event in which the vehicle is powered without an engine or other means of propulsion other than human movement.

The Kinetic Challenge Mud Bog is the third leg of the weekend's race, and is like every dream I've never had. The previous day, the entrants had pedalled their way up a steep sand dune and then showed how quickly their vehicles could travel on the road. Today, they were pitting their creations against 100 feet of knee-high mud, before entering the nearby river for the fourth and final section of the race. Owing to the four differing terrains and challenges, there is no ideal design and so the vehicles come in all different shapes and sizes. One, a black school bus bearing the words 'Deliverance Truck', waited patiently for its turn behind an old black Ford named 'Henry Ford Goes Surfing', 'Chariots of Tire' and a giant caterpillar.

Things became even more surreal when a giant tomato with huge wheels took to the mud with the crew on board yelling 'Hiya Del Tomate' over and over again, as an elderly lady appropriately dressed as a tomato raised support from the crowd. When the vehicle became stuck, the crowd cheered and yelled encouragement until, bizarrely enough, several Vikings appeared from nowhere to help move it through the viscous course. A big yellow school bus followed. As a vehicle named 'Patriot Act' entered the fray, I thought what a perfect festival the da Vinci Days was, because of both its location and the people of Corvallis, and whether such an event would work anywhere else. I imagined Rod and Bob would have lost interest, owing to the lack of guns; there was nothing Spanish or Basque about the event; and if Drew had heard there was a festival dedicated to the genius of an artist called Leonardo, he'd be on the lookout for the other three ninja turtles. Being a university town, Corvallis is the ideal home for such a festival because it is liberal and interested in science. It was also the town which might just turn Antony and me into winners, and so we headed to the LaSells Stewart Center to breathe in the atmosphere of the film festival before the evening's premiere.

Before setting foot on the red carpet which led to the double entrance doors of the LaSells Building, Antony and I took a look at the Reser Stadium opposite. We couldn't believe that such an impressive construction was home to just a university football team (the American kind where the players hardly use their feet but still insist on calling it 'football'). As 'phase two' of the 'Raising Reser' project renovation work was being completed at the southern end of the structure, we crept inside for a closer look and discovered that the inside was just as impressive as the view from the outside. With a seating capacity of over 46,000, the stadium could house almost the entire population of Corvallis and would rival any of those found in the English Premier League. It was so awe-inspiring that we didn't arrive at the LaSells Stewart Center for a further thirty minutes.

The previous day, between leaving the park and meeting up at the pub, we had managed to watch a selection of different films ranging from a terrible Mafia-style movie called *On Top of Spaghetti* and a feature film called *The Mini*. As we approached the information desk in an almost abandoned foyer, we asked what films would be showing soon.

'There's an excellent comedy called *Last Stop For Paul* which starts in the Construction and Engineering auditorium in a few minutes,' she said.

'What's in the other auditorium?' I asked. She consulted her list.

'It's called *Fairy Tracks*. It's a documentary about whether there truly is a nature fairy and how we can define nature.'

I paused for a moment. 'What time does *Last Stop For Paul* start?'

After the movie, which was – if I had to describe it in one word – 'watchable', it was already three in the afternoon, and the forty-eight-hour deadline was less than two hours away. I was mildly concerned, so I rang Mary Jeanne's mobile and she told us that Dave was still in the process of finishing the DVD but would be at the auditorium within the hour. Reassured, and with time to spare, we lay in the sun outside before watching a short documentary about Kamikaze, a bicycle messenger in New York City, whose nickname certainly fit his character.

With only an hour until the premiere and none of our crew to be seen, I was now moderately concerned. I phoned Mary Jeanne for a second time to ask if she was anywhere near the auditorium. Luckily, she and the rest of the crew were in the Hilton hotel across the road from the LaSells Stewart Center. They must have arrived when we were busy watching a middle-aged man weave in and out of traffic whilst 'surfing' the back of vans and buses.

As the bar at the hotel was still closed, Mary Jeanne, Dave, Andy and the rest of the crew were all sitting around a large table drinking glasses of water. Unfortunately Peter couldn't make it owing to a rehearsal for *Much Ado About Nothing*. We were, however, introduced to John Herrmann, the creator of the miniature model of the helicopter we'd used, who demonstrated his genius further by offering us some whiskey out of a hip flask he had managed to smuggle into the hotel with him.

'Apparently there are ten teams entered,' Mary Jeanne informed us.

'Yeah, and I think the organizers are having problems with some of the DVDs,' I replied, relaying some gossip I'd overheard after I'd left the auditorium.

'Really?' Dave said, looking in Andy's direction. 'We'd better check that one isn't ours.'

At ten to five, we made our way into the auditorium and discovered that only seven entries had made it to this final showing, and that our DVD was one of the ones that the organizers were having trouble with. I was really worried now, but had no choice but to sit down and watch as the same woman who had been behind the desk all weekend appeared at the foot of the stage and introduced us to the showing of the da Vinci Days Fast Film Festival.

The rules were simple. Each of the films would be shown, and the winner would be decided at the very end by the good old-fashioned voting system of applause. With over two hundred people in attendance, it seemed that Mary Jeanne's plan of bringing along as many people as she knew in order to increase the volume of our combined clapping seemed a fruitless endeavour. Without knowing in which order the movies would be shown or if the technical problems had stymied our entry, we subsided into silence as the auditorium's lights dimmed and waited to see what would be the first movie that appeared on the screen.

From what I can remember, the film was about two men who met at a bus stop. Each day one of the men would unintentionally stop the other boarding the bus. For a week (which is also what it seemed like when you watched it), the same thing happened until, at the very end of the film, it turned out that the man who had never managed to get on the bus was the driver, and had been failing deliberately in order to make his passenger's life hell. I think.

The second film was completely bizarre and was something about a vortex. The cast didn't help the audience's understanding with their constant screeching and shouting, and the script was impossible to follow. Antony summed it up perfectly when he leant over to me during the lacklustre and quite brief applause and whispered: 'What the fuck was that all about?'

Film three was something to do with a fitness-obsessed man and his lazy friend. One would constantly sit on the sofa (sorry, 'couch') eating junk food whilst his friend was in the garage making use of the multi-gym or jogging down the street. I believe it ended with the health freak being knocked down by a car or a tragedy of equal magnitude. To be honest, I found it impossible to work out their theme, but I didn't try very hard, because if the entrant wasn't ours or the Turd's it wasn't really of that much interest to me. Then the group of people sat around the Turd began to grow restless and tap each other on the shoulders. I knew his film was next.

I'd overheard a brief chat he and Andy had had in the foyer before we were asked to enter the auditorium, and knew the Turd's theme was gossip. He didn't like this at all, and had admitted that he had simply added a minute's worth of footage over a documentary he was making for college . . . the cheating bastard.

I needn't have worried. His movie wasn't the greatest. It was basically a selection of clips with people regaling the audience with inane anecdotes, broken up by blank screens with a sentence like: 'That was nice, please tell us another' written over it. One sketch followed another until the film finally fizzled out and I glared in disapproval at any of our entourage who dared to applaud his unscrupulous and deceitful efforts. Others in the audience, however, most of whom were sitting around the Turd, didn't heed my facial warnings and began to clap. It soon became obvious that because of the voting system, any old piece of shit could win the award (remember *Titanic* won eleven Oscars!).

The fifth film was so short that if you had taken your eyes off the screen to adjust your shoe lace or have a word with anyone who applauded the Turd, you would have missed it. It must have been on for less than a minute, with the credits doubling the duration of the film. I think it was set in a shop and had no speech – relying on subtitles to carry the story. Unfortunately, I leant across to Antony to speak ill of the Turd's entry and by the time I glanced back at the screen, the film had finished.

A Rubik's Cube was the main feature of the following film and was the first one, other than the Turd's, to hold my attention from start to finish. It was basically a mild horror film in which no matter what the owner of the Rubik's Cube did, the handheld puzzle would return to him until it had been completed. To be perfectly honest, I thoroughly enjoyed it. Dave was not so impressed and argued that there was too much in the movie for the team to have shot and edited it in just forty-eight hours.

As the room fell silent for a few moments, it seemed that our DVD's technical problems had finally stopped it from entering. Just then, the BBC logo appeared on the silver screen and Antony's voice filled the auditorium. 'And now we go live to Nigel Huffington-Fall on location.'

Antony and I eased back into our chairs, I appeared on the screen with not a single clamp in sight, and we began wishing we had some popcorn with which to enjoy the show. My opening line linked in with the lab scene brilliantly, and the superimposed model of the helicopter looked . . . well . . . superimposed. My close-up reaction to the professor, which I had been very proud of, sure that I had managed to pull off an expression of uncertainty and unease, in reality looked more as if I was midway through a giggle. Dave and Andy had accidentally edited an outtake into the final piece. My turn on the 'palpable' line made perfect sense now I could see it work with the size of the crowd, and the sound effects and launch worked brilliantly with the fire extinguisher and my look of disapproval. If there was a performance worthy of some sort of recognition, however, it was Peter's. The scenes shot in our absence, of the professor giving his final test instructions to the pilot, and his hilarious reaction when the entire launch ended in disaster, were comic gems and certainly made the film. If I'd had to point out some negatives, it would have been that the Hindenburg line had been removed (it was probably in the deleted scenes on the DVD extras), and that the final punchline did anything but punch. At least we managed to get a groan of pun-like dissatisfaction from the audience following my 'Fall from Grace' sign-off. At less than four minutes, however, at least we hadn't wasted a lot of everyone's time, like some of the entrants.

All seven movies had been shown and now it was time for the completely unfair system of voting by clapping for the victor, a method which could see the Turd take the crown because of his cortege of class 'colleagues' (I was sure it would be inaccurate to call them mates). In fairness, I thought the Rubik's Cube film was at least equal to our movie. Fortunately, I've watched enough Eurovision Song Contests to know that going last is a huge advantage, and although the stars of the Rubik's Cube were in attendance, we had the Eastern Bloc on our side.

After applause was offered for all seven films, the organizer paused for a moment and announced that the winners of the da Vinci Fast Film Festival would be . . . decided by a clap-off. She couldn't seem to separate two of the teams . . . us and the Turd's! Now it was time to be serious. Everyone in our team and those who had come in support of us were ordered to keep their hands at arms' length when the Turd's film received its applause, and then break the rules of 'clapping only' by bellowing in a boisterous and obnoxious fashion when it was our turn. It did the trick.

'And the winners are the *Fall from Grace* team,' she

said. 'Can I invite the team up to the front?' Mary Jeanne darted from her seat and we all followed her to the front of the stage.

With the auditorium now quickly emptying, there was no need for an acceptance speech or any sort of berating of the cheating Turd. There was also no award for us to receive, but we were told we would be sent certificates in the post. There was no cash prize, but our film would be on the official da Vinci Days Film Festival website.

It was all rather anticlimactic.

Still, although it had taken two attempts, the Turd had been flushed, and that's all Antony and I cared about. Victory was ours, and I at least had the pleasure of being mobbed by a fan as I departed the auditorium. A girl in her late teens approached us and noticed my accent wasn't put on for the purpose of the film.

'Oh, my God! I love your accent,' she screamed as if I was a member of a hunky boy band who had just handed her his boxer shorts. 'It's real, isn't it? Oh my God!'

After following Andy to the nearby university campus to inform Peter of our victory, disrupting his rehearsal and irritating his colleagues, we made our way to McMenamins, a bar just a few blocks away, for our post-victory party. With all tables already booked, and with the size of our group demanding quite a large table, we decided to perch ourselves at every available seat at the bar and ordered our food and drink.

By now, the sun had started to set, and with an early morning flight to catch from Portland, Antony and I quickly cleared our plates and said our farewells, shaking hands and hugging each and every member of the group. Although we'd taken an active role in the Custer's Last Stand Reenactment, the bulls' non arrival in Elko and our names never being drawn at the Redneck Games had meant we hadn't had a chance to take a competitive role in a festival (barring bare buttocks in California). Finally we had competed and were leaving Corvallis as two of life's winners. We both said we were going to miss our crew, Oregon, its people, its mild climate, and the Mustang.

Our next flight was to return us to the Deep South after only a two-week hiatus. Once there, our task was to build a boat in just four days. The thought of something involving construction filled us with dread. I once went camping in France and struggled to pitch the tent. Luckily, I had a trick up my sleeve . . . well, not up my sleeve as such, but aboard a flight from London.

7

Back on Dry Land

Arriving in Little Rock was a shock to the system. We were once again in a major city, the temperature was uncomfortable and Little Rock was situated in the middle of land-locked Arkansas, meaning our surroundings were bare and flat.

In just five days' time, the 21st Annual Cardboard Boat Races were to take place in the little town of Heber Springs, 60 miles to the north of Little Rock, and Antony and I were going to enter. The only problems were: we had no boat, no materials with which to build one, and our plans were completely up in the air. Literally at 30,000 feet. Perhaps I should explain.

In order to preserve both my hopes for a second victory and my relationship with my girlfriend, I had flown her out to meet us in Little Rock. On Bec's insistence, she was going to travel with us for two weeks before returning home. As an added bonus, she was bringing six packets of pickled-onion-flavour Monster

Munch with her. Luckily her dad, Dave, is an engineer, and although he is more familiar with designing tools and parts for mechanical machinery, the idea of drawing up a blueprint for a cardboard boat was well within his capabilities – a task that had seen him happily sitting at a table with a blank sheet of paper in front of him and a pencil behind his ear. I'd put him to work before I ventured out to the States and now, refusing to entrust the documents to the mercy of the United States' postal network and instead using the most expensive hand-delivered method, I would have the fruits of his labours.

Antony and I touched down at Little Rock National Airport in the early evening, and because Bec's flight had been delayed and wasn't due for several hours, we picked up our hire car and drove in search of a motel. Because of Bec's imminent arrival and citing reasons such as privacy, noise, 'it's been a month' and other cryptic messages which left me none the wiser, Antony insisted we check into separate rooms. Checking my emails and tracking Bec's plane on my laptop to make sure I left for the airport on time, I glanced occasionally up at the television, changing the channel until something caught my eye. CNN had coverage of a political debate involving all of the Democratic candidates for the 2008 presidential election. Members of the public had been asked to use YouTube to record questions they would like to ask the panel, a selection of which were then put to the likes of Barack Obama, Hillary Clinton and some people I'd never heard of. A shopping channel was offering me an indestructible razor, built from carbon and stainless steel which would end the need to ever buy another razor again. If I rang straight away I could get a second one absolutely free. And on CNN Headline News, there was live coverage of horrendous flooding which, according to the host, was devastating parts of 'Glow-ster-shire' and 'Wer-sester-shire'. I lay back on my bed and breathed a sigh of relief. From the familiar-looking live pictures and aerial shots of the flooded plains, I was beginning to think that something had happened in England.

Bec's plane finally touched down at ten thirty and I set off in search of my blueprints. I was eager to bring her back to the motel so we could all find something to eat. By eleven o'clock, most of the restaurants and bars surrounding the motel had closed, and we were left with just a nearby Taco Bell. It had just closed its doors to the public but was still serving people through the 'drive thru' hatch. It was a great opportunity to show Bec the type of service one expects from American eateries, and although it's difficult ordering food via a speaker installed into a menu board, because the person you're talking to always sounds as if he/she has been kidnapped and gagged, the genuine kindness and courtesy demonstrated by people in the service industry stateside is second to none.

I have a few problems with Taco Bell. Firstly the pictures don't really represent the products well, and secondly the speaking menu board didn't understand me saying, 'Hang on a minute.' Thirdly, the names of the dishes mean a degree in Spanish or modern languages is crucial when ordering. Take a quesadilla for example. Living the sheltered life that I have, I had never seen that word before and when I came to ordering one, I pronounced it exactly as it was written: 'cwes-a-dilla', thus managing to make it sound less like a Mexican dish of melted cheese and meat and more like an Australian prehistoric reptile.

The menu board did react, saying something about 'Kay-sa-deeyas', but sounding as if he had added to his ball gag by placing a welder's mask over the top. I tried to add a drink to my order before having a go at the simple numbering system they had. At that, transmission was terminated and all I could do was drive to the window to see what our incoherent conversation had produced in the kitchen. I drove several yards forward until the assistant aggressively pulled the window open. 'Here's ya food,' he shouted, thrusting three tin-foil-wrapped packages into my hand.

'Um, thank you,' I replied.

'You really English or were you fucking with me, dawg?' he asked.

'I beg your pardon?' I replied, as politely as I could. 'Yes, I am English, yes.' I decided to be a disgruntled customer.

'Oh!' he exclaimed. 'I thought you were . . . um . . .' He struggled to find the words as I prepared to reply in a perfect English accent.

'Fucking with you, dog?'

'Yeah. Summin' like that.'

So Bec's introduction to the delights of American cuisine was something or other from Taco Bell eaten at the motel with a can of lager bought from a 24-hour garage.

The next day, we had two things on our mind: to get a decent meal without being involved in an altercation with someone who thought I was trying to do something unmentionable with their pet, and to find some cardboard with which to start work on our boat. The latter was hopefully to be supplied to us by a Yamaha and Honda bike dealership which Bec assured me her dad had already contacted and was conveniently located just two miles from our motel. What she failed to inform me until we pulled into the dealership's forecourt was that the shop had never replied to his email. However, Bec has a good knowledge of bikes owing to her father's amateur career in motocross, and this, coupled with the fact that I once crashed into a hedge on a moped, meant I was happy to let her do the talking. If need be she could talk about bikes in a confident charm offensive. Striking up a conversation about a Yamaha YZ 125, Jeremy, the assistant, seemed impressed and invited Bec into the back. She'll do anything for cardboard.

We left the business with several flattened boxes of sturdy, corrugated cardboard; enough for the sides of the boat but nowhere near robust enough for use on the base of the vessel. As we began our 60-mile drive north to Heber Springs, we left the interstate on the outskirts of Little Rock and pulled into a café for some breakfast. The host was affable and kind, if a little ill-informed about the world.

'Oh, I love your accents,' she said after we had asked for a table for three. 'Where are you from?'

'Have a guess,' I replied.

A puzzled look covered her face before she replied. 'Where's that?'

After explaining where in the world the United Kingdom was, we were shown to our table. The waitress presented us with the menu and the clever system they had adopted, naming each breakfast meal after a southern state of America, inserting a pun if the circumstances were propitious. Well, I say clever; there was 'Yolklahoma' for the meal with two eggs instead of one. Then the menu seemed to lose its linguistic flair – the other breakfast choices were Missouri, Kentucky and Arkansas.

As we left the interstate and joined the northern highway towards Heber Springs, main roads and large settlements gave way to quiet scenic byways, small towns and the obligatory churches. So ubiquitous were the places of worship that to pass the time, we would look at the map, find the name and population of the next town, and guess how many churches we would pass. The game continued until we reached our destination of Heber Springs. Population: 6,500. Churches: 13.

Usually when we check into a motel, we do so based on one thing: price. Other criteria such as the accommodation's amenities, comfort and location come as a mere afterthought. Heber Springs, however, was to prove a mighty challenge as not only were there only five to choose from, but we required one with an owner who was sympathetic to our cause and didn't mind us using his motel as a temporary dry dock and cardboard shipyard.

The Budget Inn, conveniently located just a few blocks from the centre of town, half a mile from where the races were to be held, and owned by an Indian family, was perfect. It was quiet, close to a supermarket and hardware shop, and because the owner for the first time in ages had someone with whom he could talk about cricket, he was more than happy to allow the construction of such a vessel in his car park. He thought his family might attend the event for the very first time, and even offered to load our boat on to the back of his pickup truck on the day of the races. Brilliant.

With both a construction yard and accommodation secure, all we needed before undertaking such a monumental development project was alcohol. Famous British engineer Isambard Kingdom Brunel was never seen without a cigar in his mouth, and so, to create HMS *Bateman* (fittingly named in his absence) – a ship that would rival Brunel's SS *Great Britain* and *Great Eastern* – we needed our own trademark accessory. Beer. A quick trip to the supermarket was required before the long, hot days of construction could begin.

Just across the road from the motel lay the welcoming car park of Harps Food Store, a large grocery store which was probably last refitted in the 1980s. As Antony marched up each and every aisle in search of beer and wine, Bec and I scanned some of the shelves for items we could use as cheap tools for the boat. Antony re-emerged empty-handed.

'I can't find it,' he said.

We all walked to the far aisle where the alcohol is normally sold and were greeted with nothing alcoholic and a young girl in her Harps Food Store uniform whom we asked where the beer section was.

Nothing at all could have prepared me for her response.

'Oh, we don't sell it,' she replied. 'This is a dry county.'

Bec and Antony looked puzzled by the girl's words, but I knew exactly what she meant. If you are in the same boat (see what I did there?) as Antony and Bec, I shall explain.

In 1933, the Eighteenth Amendment, more commonly known as 'Prohibition', became the only one in America's history to be repealed, leaving states to decide whether they wanted to re-legalize the sale of alcohol. Today, counties in America are either 'dry', meaning the sale of alcohol is forbidden, or 'wet', where alcohol is sold. Because certain cities and municipalities in the country have the right to make their own laws, some cities within dry counties have declared the sale of alcohol to be legal. These are called partially dry or 'moist' counties. This is all in complete contrast to what we are used to in the UK, where the terms 'wet' or 'dry' wouldn't be appropriate. To describe the scenes one witnesses in most towns on a Friday night the words 'drenched' or 'piss-stained' are much more fitting.

Seventy-four years after the repeal of prohibition, 10 per cent of the country remains completely dry, including almost half of Mississippi's counties. It is also illegal even to transport alcohol across any of the dry counties in that state. Although recent research has shown that dry counties have a higher proportion of alcohol-related traffic accidents, due to the distance residents will drive after drinking to return to their 'dry' county home, forty-two of Arkansas's seventy-three counties prohibit the sale of alcohol.

It was only then that I realized that whoever came up with the crazy concept of a cardboard boat regatta did so when he was sober!

Now, I'm not an alcoholic or heavy drinker, and in the thirty-six days Antony and I had spent in the States together, we must have been inebriated only two or three times. However, with a hard graft ahead and cama-raderie required for the construction of the boat, some refreshment was definitely needed, and I headed back to the motel to check on the internet for which of our neigh-bouring counties sold the stuff.

Heber Springs sits almost centrally in Arkansas's Cleburne County and the district is surrounded by five adjacent municipal areas. Travelling to Stone County would mean a drive around Greers Ferry Lake to the north, a futile endeavour anyway due to the county being dry. Although the Searcy Country Club was one of the few venues in White County to the southeast of Cleburne that was allowed to sell alcohol, I wasn't pre-pared to join a golf club just to enjoy a tipple. Cleburne's south-western neighbour, Faulkner County, was just as dry, and Van Buren, whose border stood less than ten miles to the west, was dry too and had been for almost two hundred years. Our final hope fell on the shoulders of Independence County, a name which sounded as if it embodied the spirit of the right to free choice. Surely it would have repealed the only amendment in the American constitution that removed freedom rather than ensuring it?

Nope. It was dry.

Our only choice was to embark on a 100-mile round trip to Pulaski County, home to Little Rock (and also Jacksonville, which is in a rather unlikely position of being one of the few 'dry' towns within a 'wet' county). With little time to spare, we all leapt into the car and made our way south on a pioneering expedition of exploration and unwavering valour, worthy to rival those of Marco Polo and Sir Francis Drake. Kind of.

Driving in Arkansas was a real frustration. The roads were wide and empty and yet the speed limit was a pitifully slow 55 mph. There were few schools to pass, only a small number of towns through which the road meandered, and the only houses on the side of the highway were large farms which were set back a considerable distance from the tarmac. I didn't put my foot down but the ease of driving subconsciously helped me speed up. In the rear-view mirror I saw the bright glare of flashing blue lights and the beam of a police car's headlights. Goodness knows how long he'd been following me; I only looked into the mirror to wipe away a smear I had seen.

I can vividly remember where I pulled the car over to the side of the road. I stopped barely 50 yards short of the White County line, about 20 miles south of Heber Springs. As the cop took his time climbing out of his vehicle, I wondered if a stealthy freewheeling of the car across the county line would make as much difference as it does in the movies, resulting in no jurisdiction for the officer and a clever escape of a fine for me.

It was too late. While I had been musing on *Smokey and the Bandit* and *Dukes of Hazzard*-style judicial loopholes, the officer had had enough time to approach my window.

It's not the first time I've been stopped by the police in America. In fact, I can't remember any time I've driven stateside when the law enforcers haven't ticked me off about something. My dad and I were stopped in Seattle for not pulling over to the side of the road when an emergency vehicle was making his way through the traffic, even though the paramedics already had a clear 50 yards of space through which to charge. And the last time Bateman and I were in America, he was stopped by the police in Wyoming for speeding. A week later we were held at gunpoint by three undercover police officers just because of a Cornish flag on the parcel shelf of our car. Anyway, I digress. Where was I? Oh, yes, the police officer.

As he tapped on the window, I remembered the two main rules for escaping fines in foreign countries: act very British and very ignorant. I stabbed at the button that operated the electric windows, only to realize the keys weren't in the ignition, and so I fumbled around some more until the keys were slotted in and the window began to sink, perfectly demonstrating imbecility without acting.

He asked for my driving licence, car-hire details and – for some reason – Bec's passport. Then, whilst trying to make sense of a United Kingdom driver's licence, he began the questioning.

'Do you know what the speed limit is on these roads, sir?' he asked.

'Um, well in England . . .' I said, careful to get the word 'England' into my opening sentence to make sure the officer knew that was where I was from, '. . . these sorts of road are sixty mph, and I must admit, I don't know what it is out here. I've only been here a few days,' I lied.

'Well,' he said, breathing out a sigh of disappointment. 'Most roads in Arkansas are fifty-five mph. When we approached you, you were doing sixty-five and then you sped up to seventy-one.'

'Oh,' I replied, thinking the policeman must have thought I was trying to evade capture. 'Sorry about that.'

'You in a hurry to get somewhere this evening?' he asked.

'Yes, officer. I'm setting off in search of a week's supply of alcohol which I intend to bring back and store in your dry county whilst we build a cardboard boat.' Obviously I didn't say that. That would be madness. I merely replied briefly and ambiguously: 'Nowhere special.'

After more questioning to which I lied – no, withheld the exact truth – he returned to his squad car for a moment or so, then came back with mine and Bec's ID, my hire-car details, and a blue piece of paper in his hand.

'I'm giving you a warning, Mr Smith, because I wouldn't want you to have to return on vacation here again to appear in court,' he said sternly.

'Oh that's OK, officer, give me the fine,' I didn't say. 'I would just fly home and not pay it anyway.' In actual fact I said, 'Thanks,' and after a brief ticking off and reminder of American driving laws, I was on my way to the Promised Land. It was only after a few miles that I realized I had given the policeman the hire-car details for the Mustang in Oregon.

After forty police-free minutes, we finally reached the interstate, just a few miles from the Pulaski County line. Such is the number of dry counties in the state that I saw the colossal Ace Liquor Store before the welcoming sign to the county. Liquor stores and alcohol-endorsing gas stations cluttered the first hundred yards of Pulaski County; simply crossing the county line was like disembarking from a ferry in the port of Calais on a booze cruise.

Because Ace Liquor Store was on the other side of the highway, we visited Harvey's Liquor instead where we made the employees' day simply by speaking in an English accent. In return they made ours by selling us three crates of Coors, some wine and several more bottles of beer. With our expedition at an end, safely returning to Heber Springs with no interference from the law, we smuggled the alcohol into Antony's room, filling every single available space in his fridge with the contraband.

Day one of construction was interrupted by the realiz-ation that I had been wearing the same T-shirt for six straight days and required a launderette before the search for tools and more cardboard could begin. The Sugarloaf Laundry Mat was run by a genuinely amiable and polite gentleman who didn't at all mind washing Antony's sick-stained clothes which he had kept with him since his drunken episode at the Peacock Tavern in Corvallis. The owner also took a keen interest in our boat-building endeavours, and revealed that he had once entered the competition.

'Have you got any tips?' Bec asked.

'Elephant glue,' he said. 'Elephant glue will stick any-thing down and it doesn't take a lot of time to dry.'

With a full day before we could collect the clothes, we decided we should return to the motorbike shop and see if Jeremy had any more cardboard for us. Jeremy remembered Bec and had even taken the trouble of logging on to the official website of the races and had put the correct type of boxes to one side for our collection. He was a jolly nice man. Although we were very appreciative for his interest and dedication to our cause, the boxes were still not enough to complete an entire boat, nor were they sturdy enough for the base of the vessel.

We continued on the interstate towards Little Rock, wondering where a mass of cardboard could be found that would be of adequate thickness, until, by an utter fluke, we came across the most fortuitous of billboards, one that proved that someone or something was definitely on our side and had summoned the cardboard genie. Hovering seventy feet above the interstate was a sign advertising a cardboard box factory! Owing to the utter shock of seeing such a conveniently placed bill-board, I only managed to see that the business in question was proud to stock 'over 500 different sizes', and so had to leave the interstate in order to drive back the way we came and record the name and address.

I don't know about you, but I've never seen a bill-board (or any advert in any publication or medium for that matter) promoting cardboard boxes. Yet the only time in my life I have been desperate for such a thing, one appears. Perhaps there is a God after all, and my often-negative references to religion within this book should be stricken from the record.

Or maybe not. You can cross them out if you like.

Whether it was the doing of a sympathetic deity or just a stroke of luck, I passed the billboard for a second time, and instead of marvelling at its existence, we all managed to remember the name of the company, the Riverside Box Supply, and each of us memorized a segment of the telephone number. With no phone to contact the company, and no map on which to mark their position, we decided that the best course of action would be to find a suitable tourist information centre and use them instead.

Our next stroke of luck was finding the most beautiful tourist information centre, set in a magnificent historic antebellum home in downtown Little Rock. Below a glistening chandelier sat a small table with a computer. In less than ten minutes, I had the directions to Riverside Box Supply and the nearest hardware store to us, and was finally ready to hunt for our very own cardboard version of El Dorado.

Riverside Box Supply is located in what some would describe as the economy housing district of Little Rock, set in a barren landscape on a minor service road leading to the airport. By the look of the business's foyer and reception area – where a tacky aerial photograph of the business was surrounded by effigies of Jesus, and framed psalms and passages from the Bible – it seemed that if it was indeed God who was behind the placing of the billboard, he was now attempting to complete the job and convert us. The husband and wife managerial team welcomed us, called 'Tony' in from the back and made small talk, encouraging us to 'just say anything' so they could listen to our accents as if our speech were as melodic as that of angels.

Tony arrived minutes later, relieving us of our vocal duties, and led us into the back of the store. Piled to the very top of the room, just short of the 30-foot ceiling, stood hundreds of pallets of flat-packed cardboard and boxes of varying size and thickness. Although we were just after some materials for a sturdy base and support joists for our tiny vessel, there was enough cardboard in the Riverside Box Supply to assemble an armada.

For our base, I opted for one of the thickest sizes they had, a triple-corrugated piece of cardboard, which took two of us to carry, and several pieces of the double-corrugated variety which could be used as the sides and joists of our boat. As I drove the car around to the side delivery doors, it soon became apparent that owing to a discrepancy between the size of the saloon-style boot and the sheets, loading the vehicle was going to be a bit of a struggle. With Tony helpfully suggesting that it would be easier if we put the car in the box instead of the other way round, we were left with no choice but to bend the base sheet in half and, with help from two other assistants, force it sideways into the back of the car. With the vehicle crammed to breaking point with cardboard, Antony wriggled his way into the back seat of the car where he remained uncomfortable but uncomplaining for the two hours it took us to visit the hardware store and return to the motel. At least the cardboard god who had led us to the box supply store continued to watch over us as we carved a safe passage back to Heber Springs, protecting us from the policeman who had stopped us the previous day and the remainder of the Cleburne County sheriff's office.

Finally, on the Wednesday evening, with fewer than three days until the big race, construction on HMS *Bateman* was under way, and we made the startling discovery that, although located in a dry county, the handles on the Budget Inn's cupboard made brilliant bottle openers.

As with most construction jobs, there was a budget to keep within, and the *Bateman* was no exception. The cheapest spray paint was bought; a clothesline was purchased in place of the more expensive rope; low-cost 'Gorilla Glue' was substituted for the 'Elephant glue'; and with proper oars carrying a price tag of well over thirty dollars, I opted for the more economical solution of using three four-dollar dust pans (the brushes were an added bonus).

Bec's dad knew only too well of mine and Antony's DIY skills and had designed the size and shape of the boat accordingly. If we followed his plans correctly, HMS *Bateman* would be 7 feet in length, 3 feet 10 inches wide, and would narrow at the front of the boat to produce a 2-foot bow. We would sit in a central hull measuring 5 feet 6 inches by 3 feet which would be held in position by 26 rolled cardboard joists, adding strength to the sides of the boat. That was the plan, anyway.

Construction began in the early-evening, 90-degree Arkansas heat as I cut my way through the thick base with one of my four steak knives (which I had bought to escape the price of a hacksaw), and Antony and Bec measured and cut precise amounts of cardboard for use on the body of the boat. As darkness fell on Heber Springs, with the car's headlamps as our only source of light, the first day of building came to a close when the varnishing had been completed and there was nothing we could do but retire to bed to allow the cardboard to dry. We finished our beers, collected the tools and swept away the debris with the oars.

*

Early next morning we checked on the varnish and decided we should make a start on further construction. After only an hour, we were forced to take several breaks because of the intolerable heat and the lack of shade in the motel's courtyard. It was a unanimous decision that efficient work on the boat could only be achieved in the evenings when temperatures had dropped and the sun wasn't as intense.

To be on the safe side and to make sure we weren't unintentionally breaking any of the stringent rules laid down by the race organizers, I decided to visit the town's Chamber of Commerce to see if there was any literature on the regulations. Not only did I leave with an eighteen-page booklet on cardboard boat basics called 'What Floats Your Boat', but I was also handed an entry form and learnt, quite surprisingly, that there was a twenty-four-hour Wal-Mart Super-center on the opposite side of town.

The rules of the race stated, not surprisingly, that the structure must be made entirely of cardboard with the exception of the propulsion system, oars and the steering device. Check. There was one rule, however, that we had overlooked, which was that every member of the team must wear a life jacket – something we definitely had not packed. With Wal-Mart charging an extortionate amount for something we would use only once, and armbands apparently not a sufficiently life-saving device, we headed to a nearby marina to see if we could rent some.

The nearest beach to Heber Springs is a nine-hour drive away in Louisiana. The town, however, is situated on the banks of Greers Ferry Lake, an artificial reservoir named after the town situated on the opposite shore. It was formed by the creation of the Greers Ferry Dam in 1962 and was dedicated by John F. Kennedy the following year, his last major public appearance before his ill-fated trip to Dallas a month later.

Thanks to the newly formed lake, both towns profited from a tourism boom which saw the area become one of the country's most popular destinations. Today, the popularity of the region may have diminished but the Heber Springs Marina is one of many dotted along the shores of the lake where out-of-towners moor their boats for weekend breaks on the water.

As we wandered up the jetty to the building at the end, the overhead sun shone on the surface, seemingly cleaning the water so that large fish could be seen between the hull of the boats and the bed of the lake. After waiting patiently for a woman and her family to rent one of the many boats available, I approached the counter and asked if they hired out the life-vests we had seen in the store. We were in luck. For fifteen dollars and my 'fascinating' driving licence as collateral, we could borrow three life jackets and were even offered two oars for free, meaning only one of us would have to endure the embarrassment of using a dustpan during the race. With two days before the event, we agreed to pick them up the following day.

In the early evening, work recommenced on HMS *Bateman*, although the heat was still a major problem. The base was taped together and the varnish had dried nicely but the glue we had used on the numerous other sheets we'd packed into the base refused to dry in the overwhelming temperature. Our best bet would be duct tape and, given it was going to be of integral importance to the structure of the vessel, I visited the local hardware store and bought 125 yards of the stuff. At the checkout, my confidence in our project took a bit of a knock when the assistant revealed that he too was entering a boat into the race.

'Yeah, I'll be there,' he said, before adding the confidence booster: 'I've been working on it for about six months now and she's still not finished!'

Upon my return, Antony and Bec managed to duct tape the base together and started work on our central seating section. By nightfall the inner hull was complete and had been varnished, ready for gluing to the base, but insect bites to both of them were compounding the misery of the heat and impending deadline. When tools were downed at the end of the working day, the inner hull stood firm and we hoped it would stick to the base of the boat by sunrise.

Friday would be the last day on which we could work on the boat, and if it was too hot for us to work during the daylight hours, we would be left with only the evening hours and early morning to get HMS *Bateman* ready for Saturday's nine a.m. registration. The glue would need adequate time to adhere and if it was applied too late the boat would leak almost instantaneously, thereby wasting our hours of work and condemning the *Bateman* to a watery grave. Construction was going to go down to the wire; we had only seven hours remaining, and just twenty-four cans left in the fridge.

Friday began with a trip to Wal-Mart for some anti-bug repellent and itch cream with which we could all treat the injuries we had sustained the previous day, and a visit to the marina where we collected our life jackets and oars. By the afternoon, we had dragged our boat to the rooms on the opposite side of the motel's forecourt so we could shelter from the sun's glare.

As we set up a production-line system to create the twenty-six rolled joists, Becky on rolling duty, Antony sticking, and me as the duct-tape cutter, we began to notice that the motel was quickly filling up with week-end customers. For the entire week, we had effectively been the only people staying at the motel, but now, early Friday evening, half of the rooms had vehicles parked outside – one of which pulled into the space beside our current working position with a cardboard kayak attached to the roof.

The Neumaster family were from Missouri and had entered their ten-year-old son, Hunter, into the youth division of the cardboard boat races. Hunter took an immediate interest in our construction but couldn't disguise the disdain in his voice.

'That gonna float?' he asked.

'Probably not,' I replied pointing at the roof rack of his car. 'That yours?'

'That's *Skeetle*, my boat.'

'That's right,' his dad interrupted. 'What's a boat, honey?' he shouted to his daughter.

'A hole in the water,' she responded as if rehearsed.

Hunter and his dad were only too happy to offer equally helpful hints on construction and suggested materials to aid buoyancy. As the children's grandparents were due to arrive in the very space we were working, it gave us the perfect excuse to drag HMS *Bateman* back across the forecourt to escape the constant interference from Hunter. Stupid name anyway.

We continued working on the boat as more and more people checked into the motel. Before too long, the 'No Vacancy' sign was lit and our efforts came under further scrutiny from our new neighbours. By now the sides were glued to the base of the boat and our rooms had been nearly emptied of heavy objects to weigh down the flaps and help it stick. Two wooden desk chairs along with two armchairs were both put to good use, and to compensate for the potential deficiencies in the bonding of cardboard to glue, I was sent to Wal-Mart for yet another roll of duct tape.

Worried that the strength of the boat had been called into question, we worked tirelessly into the night as the duct tape began to peel. We did our best to ignore the man who had checked into the room next to ours. Smoking a cigar, he watched us for several minutes before returning to his room and reappearing with a camera. There he stood, just feet from us, amongst discarded tools and cardboard scraps, not saying a word. Then he began sidestepping his way through the work area taking pictures, still in utter silence, with no expression on his face. As Antony, Bec and I hinted in his direction with our eyebrows, wondering what he was doing or from which mental illness he suffered, he finally removed the cigar from his mouth and broke his silence.

'Is that a boat?'

Cheeky bastard.

By midnight, there was nothing more we could do. The glue required hours to take effect, we had no more durable cardboard at our disposal, so all we could do was wait. Having been wrapped in almost 200 yards of the stuff, HMS *Duct Tape* was a far more appropriate name. Owing to the Arkansas temperature, an early-morning paint job would dry in no time and with any luck, once HMS *Bateman* was emblazoned in the Cornish colours of black and white, it would transform from a shit state into ship shape.

'That looks great,' Bec called across the motel car park to the grass bank at the back where I was busy spraying the finishing touches to the boat. A thick white cross covered all four visible sides on a black background, creating the flag of St Piran anywhere you looked, with the words 'HMS *Bateman*' emblazoned across the stern. The boat was sturdy enough and the drying of the glue had turned the previous evening's structural frailties into a vessel which was at least . . . how can I put this kindly . . . whole – a single entity.

We decided against an official naming ceremony, just in case the boat wasn't strong enough to withstand a collision with a bottle (empty or otherwise). The owner of the motel parked outside our room and pointed at the cargo space. 'We go?'

Complete with board shorts for when (not if) the boat went under, and a captain's hat (which I had purchased from a Dollar Tree store earlier in the trip), we tied the boat with the clothesline to the frame of the pick-up, and hopped into the cab. Dollar Trees are incredible shops. They are the American equivalent of pound shops, but with the current favourable exchange rate everything was less than fifty pence – including a pregnancy test which Antony and I saw in their Corvallis branch. For that kind of money tossing a coin would probably be just as accurate.

Sandy Beach has everything you'd expect from a seaside location. It has a car park, an area for volleyball, hordes of people in revealing swimwear and golden sand. The only thing it lacks (and I must admit it's a bit of a howler) is the sea. The Greers Ferry Lake, however, makes up for the lack of an ocean, and its clear waters and flat conditions create a pleasant and tranquil artificial seaboard.

As we located the organizers and registered our boat into the 'adult team' division, we noticed we were the only people not from the states of Missouri, Oklahoma, Arkansas and Mississippi to enter. Our international entry would truly make this year's event a 'World Championship'. We were then handed a schedule of events and found a suitable location on the sand, away from the crowds and in the shade. The course was pretty simple. A semi-circular swimming area had been cordoned off by continuous lines of plastic tubing and approximately 30 feet further into the lake a row of buoys provided a boundary beyond which people had moored yachts and speedboats using the cockpits and bridges of their luxury vessels as grandstand seats. The cardboard boats were to use the central division in between and would have to navigate an arching course roughly 200 feet long.

According to the schedule, awards weren't just presented for the fastest boat. A team could pick up a trophy for a wide array of achievements, all of which I instantly doubted we would be collecting at the day's end. 'The Pride of the Fleet' award would be handed to the team whose boat had an innovative and unique design, and who had taken the important matter of science and physics into account. A Cornish flag and a name that meant nothing to anyone (in addition to the fact that I had tried to incorporate Archimedes' principle without any luck) would definitely see us miss out on that particular medal. And our discordant dress sense and gloomy fears that our vessel was one of the worst in the competition wouldn't help us pick up the prize for 'Team Spirit'. Our best hope was to aim for the 'Titanic Award', won by the team who suffered the most dramatic sinking and who demonstrated the best efforts to prevent such a disaster. This, at first, seemed easily attainable: sinking was the one thing at which we were all sure HMS *Bateman* would excel. Unfortunately, to 'win' the award, the boat had to travel at least 50 feet, and that was at least 48 feet farther than we anticipated reaching.

From our vantage point, by the side of a spacious and tall power boat, we had a great view of the course and wondered why hardly anyone was sitting alongside us, with the watercraft's supports providing a pleasant backrest and adequate shade. By ten a.m., it became apparent.

A sharp, eardrum-shattering squeal filled the beach and a booming voice welcomed everyone to the 21st Annual World Championship Cardboard Boat Races. Sitting alongside Gary Redd, a past Chamber of Commerce president and local bank manager, was Laine Berry, better known as Mrs Arkansas 2007. The married beauty queen would be co-commentating with Gary and presumably was there to provide the crowd with detailed analysis of the races and the crafts involved. Her encyclopaedic knowledge in her specialized field of pageantry and make-up would no doubt be very helpful.

Just when we thought the space and shade compensated for the vociferous ramblings, Gary announced he was going to throw some merchandise from Sonic, a chain of drive-in diners and sponsors of the event. In little under a minute, a multitude of beachgoers had gathered in front of us, unintentionally kicking sand in our faces and aggressively competing against one another for frisbees, mobile phone pouches and inflatable beach balls; begging for further freebies with arms outstretched as if they were refugees at a UN food package drop.

Once they'd stopped throwing tacky gifts over our heads, we were free to admire the last few races of the youth division, and the marvellously satisfying sight of Hunter struggling against his competitors and travelling in the wrong direction.

As the races continued, the brilliant commentary skills of Mrs Arkansas were exposed. At the start of each race, she would struggle to read the names of the boat and crew from a sheet of paper and then, when one of the boats led its adversary by several feet, she would bring the microphone close to her lips and say: 'Wow! They have a commanding lead.' That was the extent of her analytical talent.

The youth races came to an end, and as they left the water, preparing themselves for their second run, the start of the adults' heats was announced. This was our call, and we left our perch beneath the commentators and dragged HMS *Bateman* to the far shoreline to meet our fellow competitors. Two rows of cardboard boats in front of us, collecting plaudits and looks of awe, was the boat that was not only a definite contender for the 'Team Spirit' award, but an absolute shoo-in for 'Pride of the Fleet'. The crew was dressed in matching bandanas and the 'Pirates & Paddles' boat was a piece of papier-mâché perfection. John Bartlett was the chief designer and captain of a stunning miniature replica of an eighteenth-century frigate decked out and decorated in the style of a pirate ship. His team were proud of their creation and had already decided not to enter it in the afternoon's finale: the demolition derby, open to any of the boats that survived the rigours of racing.

Next to the pirates stood the *Sprocket Rocket*, a floating cardboard platform powered by a bicycle mounted on top; an invention whose engineering genius put an end to our incredibly slim chances of picking up any kind of notable award. Because there were twenty-five teams in the adult classes, most heats were contested between two or three entrants and whilst viewing wasn't easy due to the bustle of 'the pits', at least I was within audible distance of Mrs Arkansas and could hear which boat had a commanding lead.

Pirates & Paddles may not have been the quickest team in the competition and wouldn't be winning the title, but the ship took to the course graciously amidst a chorus of horns from the boats and cries of encouragement from swimmers who had sprawled themselves on the floating boundaries to gain a closer look.

We were having a splendid time with our competitors, sharing jokes with the other teams, when a man with a clipboard called our name. Well, I thought it was ours.

'HMS *Batman*?' he asked.

'*Bateman*,' I corrected.

We were positioned in the waist-deep water alongside *Flower Power Unsinkable* and a brown boat with a yellow bolt of lightning drawn on the side called *White Lightning* (although they had misspelt their name and had 'White Lighting' written on the hull). The captain claimed it wasn't a mistake and that 'lighting' was a colloquialism in Mississippi. He was definitely lying. I've heard of 'Lightnin'' as a different pronunciation, but 'lighting'? What do they say when they really do need to use the word 'lighting'?

But now I had to concentrate. All attention was on the mayor, who stood with the starter's gun on a speedboat behind the grid. We clung to the 'gunwhales' of our vessel, reluctant to step inside and cause damage to the base or flood it before we had even set off. No one wanted to be responsible for sinking it.

A loud bang filled the air and water splashed in our faces as our opponents raced off. We all jumped in and for the briefest of seconds things appeared to be going well. We may have already been a good five or six lengths behind *White Lighting*, sorry, *Lightning*, but we were all aboard with Bec in the bows using her dustpan as a rudimentary rudder, attempting to direct the boat in the right direction. Ten or so seconds after we had clambered aboard, however, it became obvious that the only direction we were headed was down.

'We're leaking!' Antony shouted, trying to keep his panicky giggling to a minimum. He wasn't joking either. We were all kneeling in the boat and already the water was up by our thighs.

'Bail, Bec. Bail!' I yelled.

The water might or might not have been seeping through the badly glued gaps at the side, evading the seal of over 200 yards of duct tape, but it was certainly cascading over the stern which cleared the surface of the water by only a matter of inches. As Bec converted her dustpan-cum-oar into a bucket-cum-dustpan-cum-oar Antony and I paddled like madmen just to see how far we could get. Not very. Before we knew it, we were up to our necks in the Greers Ferry and were kneeling on the floor of our boat which, in turn, was now resting on the bed of the lake. Things weren't going swim-mingly (well, they kind of were, really). We had sunk. As we dragged the soggy mess out of the water, all I could hear was the jeering of the crowd and Mrs Arkansas claiming that as a result of our sinking, *White Lightning* had a commanding lead.

Well, to the best of my imagination, that is how our entry into the races would have gone – had we registered. Readers, I promise this is the last time I'll lead you on.

In the early hours of Saturday morning, as we laboriously reapplied peeled duct tape and ladled on further coats of inadequate glue, whilst battling the heat, humidity and insect bites, the decision had been made to abandon ship. If you had seen the exhaustion and sweat on our faces and what kind of a 'nautical vessel' all the effort and money had got us, you too would probably have admitted defeat.*

With only the evenings in which to work, a car boot which had meant all of our cardboard had had to be folded and therefore weakened, and the temperature preventing the glue from setting, we were always facing an uphill struggle. And although Bec insisted it would float and we should continue working through the night until its completion, the fact that the sides wouldn't stand firm meant Antony and I knew when we were beaten. If they couldn't withstand the light breeze in the car park, what would happen when they came into contact with thousands of gallons of water? After what I had paid to build the piece of crap, I wasn't prepared to put down a further fifty dollars registering it and a twenty-five-dollar deposit I would face losing if we failed to drag the stricken vessel from the depths of the lake.

Bec might have been correct, however. The following morning, before we headed to the races, we tested it for durability. We had already wasted the owner's time by not appearing from our rooms in time for a lift, and so we didn't wish to incur his wrath by trying the boat out in the pool. Instead, we opted for a far more strenuous trial: Bec drove the hire car into it . . . twice. At approximately 10 mph, the boat simply dragged across the ground, trapped under the grille, and I asked Bec to reverse the car and really have a go. This time, at about 25 mph and with a longer run-up, HMS *Bateman* stood no chance.

* You can see an artist's impression of what it should have looked like, and what it ended up resembling, at rich-smith.net. Abysmal doesn't even begin to describe it.

Surveying the wreckage, Bec was quite impressed. 'See, it survived the first one,' she said.

As we headed back to Little Rock the following day, the atmosphere in the car was one of deathly silence. Bec was still upset that we hadn't entered and I, too, was regretting the decision I had made the previous day. The hire car had shown that HMS *Bateman* was durable, and would have withstood whatever the nautical equivalent is of being hit at 10 mph by a Nissan Sentra. We would never know how that would have translated into nautical miles travelled.

We pulled into the same motel we had left five days before feeling defeated and downhearted. Avoiding Taco Bell, we ordered a pizza and decided that as we were lodging in a wet county for the first time in almost a week, we should drown our sorrows with a drink at a nearby bar or, at the very least, back at the motel.

We even failed at that. Arkansas doesn't sell alcohol on Sundays.

8

The Longest Yard

'Thanks for everything,' said Antony. I shook his hand and Bec wrapped her arms around him before kissing him on the cheek.

'Right then. We'll see you when we get back, mate,' I replied. 'Hope everything goes well.'

This Monday morning was especially depressing.

After we had arrived in Heber Springs, Antony had learnt that his grandmother had been diagnosed with a brain tumour and had been given just two weeks to live. For the next hour, Antony agonized over his course of action, whether to stay for the remainder of the trip or fly home before it was too late. He decided that after we returned to Little Rock following the boat races, he would return to Cornwall. As the doors closed behind him, Antony made his way towards the check-in desk while Bec and I returned to the car. We both hoped that he would arrive home safely and that his nan would be well enough to see him. As it dawned on me that if it wasn't for Bec's arrival I would be on my own, I thought of all the good times Antony and I had experienced together during our fifty-day adventure. For some reason my mind could only muster images of him being sick in Corvallis.

We changed all of our remaining flights from Antony's name to Bec's and her stay with me was to become a permanent one.

Our final day in Little Rock was to be our first as a duo, and we had a day to waste in the city before our flight to Louisville later in the evening. In a hope of avoiding malls (or more precisely the Build-a-Bear Factory outlets which lie within them, where I would have to buy clothes for Bec's companion bear, Gary), I suggested we visited the William J. Clinton Presidential Center, one of twelve such buildings in America which preserve papers, records and historical materials of presidential tenures. The library is the second largest of its kind and is housed within a futuristic glass structure which cantilevers over the Arkansas River and a disused train bridge, echoing Clinton's 1992 presidential campaign promise of 'building a bridge to the twenty-first century'.

Covering 20,000 square feet of exhibition space, including a 110-foot timeline centred on the eight-year Clinton administration and a life-size replica of the Oval Office, the library contains 2 million photographs, 80 million pages of documents and nearly 80,000 artefacts from Clinton's time as president. The Presidential Center is a truly magnificent sight and does a fantastic job of demonstrating what a popular and productive premiership Clinton had. With exhibits documenting his work for African-Americans and his handling of the Kosovo Crisis (a conflict which didn't see a single death among NATO peacekeeping forces), you leave with a distinct sense that although Arkansas is the origin of some crazy limitations on alcohol consumption, the state has managed to produce someone of significance and of great benefit to the modern world.

By the way he loaded our bags into the back of the shuttle bus, you could tell that the driver was either in pain or had experienced a chronic injury at some point in his life. He appeared to be blind in one eye and walked askew as if one of his fists weighed substantially more than the other. As we locked in our seatbelts, he jumped into the driving seat and lowered the volume on the stereo.

'Guess what happened to me?' he asked. 'I was shot!' he continued without giving us any time to answer.

'When?' I asked.

'Oh, many years ago now,' he replied, breaking into a childish giggle as if he had fond memories of the event. 'Yeah, it was at a motel I was working at twenty-three years ago, when I was twenty-two,' he added, with a second chuckle. I was less shocked by the shooting than by his age. He certainly didn't look as old as forty-five.

'So you from London?' he asked.

'No. Not really,' we replied.

'I used to live in London.'

'Oh yeah? Did you like it?'

'No. It was cold and it rained a lot,' he laughed.

I enjoyed the shuttle run a great deal. It might have painted a pretty bleak picture of street life in Louisville (and London's climate for that matter), but the driver's cheery yet humble attitude was as infectious as his child-like laugh, and I wanted the drive to continue all morning.

When he arrived outside the terminal, he looked up at the rear-view mirror, caught our gazes and paused for a moment, releasing another smirk and short burst of laughter. 'The shooter got seven years.'

Until now, the festivals I had attended all centred on one town, city or, in the reenactment's case, field. Our next festival (if one can call it that) was unique as it didn't take place in just one city but on a single road. It snakes its way through five states, living up to its name of the 'World's Longest Yard Sale'. Also known as the 'Highway 127 Corridor Sale' (named after the road on which the hundreds of yard sales lie), the annual event began in 1987 and was used as a way of luring travellers away from the nearby interstates and proving to them that the back roads still had something to offer. And this one certainly does, all 450 miles of it.

The 2007 event was the first in the Yard Sale's history to include an additional 180-mile segment which would take the shopper through Ohio, and extend their itinerary to an unprecedented 630 miles. Because the event only operates from the first Thursday in August to the following Sunday, we decided we would stick to the traditional 450-mile trail to give us a chance of com-pleting the route whilst still having enough time to experience the sales.

With it only being Tuesday, we had two days before we began our long bargain-hunting trek and so instead of making our way to the starting point in Covington, the most northerly part of Kentucky, we continued across the Ohio River and into neighbouring Cincinnati. It was here we experienced the Budget Host Town Center Motel.

When I'd booked the motel online two days before, there was only the one picture: a motel situated in a shaded, leafy area of the city. It had a pool, the rooms looked clean and it was just off the I-75, perfect for getting to Covington for the start of the Yard Sale, and with easy access to the downtown area. At fifty-six dollars per night, it was one of the cheapest in the area, but I had paid less than that before and been happy with the resulting accommodation. I reserved two nights without a moment's hesitation.

Upon arrival, Bec remained in the car as I made my way to the front office to check in. It was only four in the afternoon, but there was already a raucous noise coming from the bar adjacent to the front desk. As the clerk turned in his chair, raising his eyebrows in acknowledgment of my presence, I gave him my name and reservation details before noticing that as well as the usual signs informing residents of the checkout time and policy on pets, a third notice stating 'NO DRUGS' was stuck to the wall. That should have been my first clue.

Our room was on the ground floor, just two doors down from the chained-up and abandoned swimming pool, and I entered the room a full five minutes before Bec (as she took a 50-foot detour to avoid the hornets' nest that lay just where one might find a welcome mat). When she entered, Bec headed straight for the curtains, pulling them open and flooding the room with light. She was not impressed with what she saw.

Although it was a non-smoking room, a definite smell of stale smoke clogged the atmosphere and couldn't be expelled as the windows wouldn't open. Bec found chewing gum stuck to the walls; there was what appeared to be blood on both the back of the curtains and on the ceiling; the carpet looked like it hadn't been cleaned since Ronald Reagan was president, and all the table surfaces were sticky. I won't even comment on the state of the sink and shower. Suffice to say, Janet Leigh had a more pleasurable experience in her bathroom at the Bates Motel.

'It's not that bad, Bec,' I said trying to remain upbeat and positive. 'At least it's got wireless internet access.'

Bec didn't care. She sat on the bed, not willing to walk around the room or unpack any of her belongings in case they became 'contaminated'. She hated the place. And she wasn't the only one.

I know you didn't buy this book as a travel guide or an AA accommodation handbook, but allow me to just share some reviews of the Budget Host Town Center Motel I have found on various travel review and opinion sites. I won't bore you with the entire passage, but here is a summary.

At time of writing, Tripadvisor.com has seven reviews on the motel and they are titled thus: 'No Way Jose', 'Keep Driving', 'Absolutely Disgusting', 'Too bad to even stay', 'Don't waste your money . . .', 'Stay Away', and 'Why can't I give it a rating of 0/5?' (I have to take credit for that one.) Yahoo travel isn't an improvement and posts six reviews including: 'We thought it looked clean until . . .', 'Keep Driving! Do Not Stop Here!' and 'Gunshots outside the door'.

The accommodation's only tick in the positive column, the internet access, proved a godsend as it helped us out of the Budget Host and into a Super 8 motel, which was not only far superior but cheaper too.

The first day of the Yard Sale was upon us, and after two nights' sleep in a place that wasn't also home to some of the world's most infectious diseases, we were ready for the monumental task. I had planned to turn the entire four days into a *Bargain Hunt*-style competition of epic proportions between me, Antony and Bec in which we all had thirty dollars to spend before we arrived in Gadsden, Alabama, where we would use the remainder of the Sunday attempting to sell them to see who could make the most profit (or suffer the smallest loss). Antony's departure had left the game in doubt but it was still quite a good idea and since we both still harboured bitter feelings about our time in Arkansas, we agreed to compete. We both wanted to win at something to remove the nasty aftertaste of failure.

Although US Highway 127 was to be our home for the next four days, it wasn't easy to find it from the centre of Covington, despite having the official Yard Sale brochure – which also pointed out areas of historic and general interest along the route. However, after taking some wrong turns, we found Pike Street, which took us to the Dixie Highway and a conveniently placed road sign that at last confirmed we were travelling south on the 127 and had officially set off on the trail of the World's Longest Yard Sale.

Fifteen minutes in, on the outskirts of Covington, we passed the first of the yard sales – a set of stalls located in a gap between two buildings. No one stood behind any of the tables, and although children's toys, one-dollar sunglasses and some second-hand batteries were mighty tempting, we decided to move on before the owner of the goods appeared and persuaded us to part with our money.

Next we pulled into a housing estate and followed the signs to a garage sale which was trying to get in on the act. It may not have been located on the side of the highway, but as we had only driven past one so far, we thought we should visit an actual sale. Outside of a garage stood an assortment of lamps, lampshades and badly damaged furniture. Inside, three members of a family sat in silence until one of them overheard us talking.

'Australian, hey?' asked one of the two women.

'Um, no. We're English,' Bec replied.

The lady pointed at me. 'Well, he's definitely got something Steve Irwin about his voice.'

'Yes. Although I doubt there's a similarity in our voices now that he can't speak,' I remarked.

We finally left Covington and came across the first large-scale yard sale, one that had dozens of vendors, numerous refreshment stands and hundreds of shoppers. And how could we not stop at a sale in a town called Beaverlick?

Here we were determined to buy the first of the stock that we would resell three days later, and so we were now forced not only to haggle but try and surmise what would or wouldn't be of interest to Alabamans. That meant things like pick-up truck paraphernalia and anything linked with the Confederacy were in, whilst books or anything with words were definitely out.

I decided against buying an antique-style map of Great Britain so as not to confuse prospective buyers, and Bec dabbled with the idea of purchasing a Jesus figurine. Taking into account that her prospective customers in Alabama would probably already own six or seven miniature models of the Redeemer, and with no one operating the stall, we moved to a nearby booth where delights on sale included a North American road atlas from 1967 and a television recording of *Uncle Buck* on an old VHS tape.

The Beaverlick yard sale wasn't a complete waste of time, however, and both Bec and I managed to make a purchase. After haggling the owner down from five to three dollars I secured a product called Tic-Tac-Putt,* a moulded plastic putting practice game where balls were putted into spaces using the same rules as Tic-Tac-Toe (known as Noughts and Crosses by anyone with any sense). Bec was pleased with her purchase too: an un-official US Army cap for five dollars. The only problem with my purchase was that there was a golf ball missing – an orange one – an item that wouldn't be easy to replace before we reached Alabama.

With our first items purchased, we took a solemn oath to stop at every yard sale on the route. That way we could claim to be the only people who had truly experienced the event and had seen it in its entirety (and I could search golfing stands high and low for a replacement orange ball). There couldn't be that many sales,

---

* I've just scoured the internet for Tic-Tac-Putt to discover that Dick's Sporting Goods are selling it for $32.95. Bargain!

surely. We were well outside of Covington now and had only seen three. And it wasn't as if the 127 passed through a lot of large towns and cities. It was a Thursday too; some people could be at work and others wouldn't want to spend a further three days roasting in the southern sun trying to flog their junk to unsuspecting travellers. I mean, there couldn't be many yard sales at all. Could there?

How wrong I was.

Our new tactic was put into practice and in the three and a half hours that followed we managed to travel just 37 miles (an average speed of 10.5 mph), stopping at 46 separate sales. At that speed, assuming the yard sale stalls would be available to view between ten in the morning and five in the afternoon, we would have needed until the following Tuesday to see it all (and the Friday after that if we had chosen to travel down the new 630-mile route).

The next sale we came across was in a field at the side of the road, and although I was tempted to invest in some John Deere coasters, I decided against it and moved in the direction of a stall which specialized in guns, guns and more guns. It's remarkable that in the UK, even a farmer would have to wait for weeks for the paperwork and red tape to allow the purchase of such a weapon, but here in Kentucky, I could buy any firearm I wanted, no questions asked, from a guy in dungarees. In the corner of this medium-sized 'yard' sale stood a pair of hillbillies (it's the only way to describe them) who had positioned themselves behind a table with random junk sprawled across it and were playing banjo music as an incentive to approach them. If only, at that precise moment in time, a special camera had been invented that not only captures the image but records just a few seconds of audio to set the scene (like those annoying birthday cards that play a snatch of music when they're opened), my American photo album would be a much happier place.

We knew by now that it was impossible to stop at every single sale, so we decided we would only venture into a yard sale if it was one of the big ones (or if there was a chance I could find a replacement golf ball). We returned to the car and travelled all of 800 yards up the road.

This one was the daddy of all sales, situated in a huge field on the outskirts of Owenton, Kentucky – named after Abraham Owen who died at the Battle of Tippecanoe in 1811 (sorry, quoting from the brochure here). I approached a nearby stand selling golf bags and clubs, and quickly located a big blue tub full of hundreds of golf balls. Most of the visible ones were white or yellow, and as I delved deeper it became clear that not a single one was orange. Bec, on the other hand, had secretly made her second purchase after locating a rather special stand whilst I was up to my neck in balls. She approached me holding a necklace. 'Look at this, Rich.'

'What is it?' I replied.

'It's an alligator tooth.'

Bec had purchased the item for seven dollars from a table which had a wide array of similar collectibles. Horns of different animals sat alongside crocodile heads and bits of leather. Even human teeth were up for sale. What made the stand unique was that displayed along-side the numerous anatomical oddities was a sporting almanac of the Cincinnati Reds' World Series winning season of 1976.

By six o'clock we had checked into a Best Western in Frankfort, the state capital of Kentucky, only 77 miles south of Covington. With a population of less than thirty thousand, Frankfort is by no means a metropolis, but the small city is a charming blend of old and new. Modern financial institutions and Georgian antebellum buildings, evidence of a bygone era of historical significance, overlook the Kentucky River which flows calmly beneath bridges of varying age. Today, Frankfort only just sneaks into the top ten of Kentucky's largest cities. Its popularity was evident as Bec and I entered an Italian restaurant in an eerily desolate and somnolent town centre.

Over a dish of spaghetti meat balls, we realized that we would have to pick up the pace if we were going to make it to Alabama with enough time to sell our haul. My idea to stop at each and every sale because there 'wouldn't be many at the side of the road' had been proved comprehensively and thoroughly misguided. In one afternoon we had passed 231 of the bastards and managed to cover just 77 miles of the 450 required.

With three more states to pass through after Kentucky, we were determined to use Friday to make up lost ground, aiming to check into our next motel in Tennessee. By ten a.m., we had already passed several minor yard sales, staying true to our commitment. It wasn't until we had covered ten miles that we were finally enticed by a sale situated in the grounds of a church. There wasn't a great deal to buy, but for obvious reasons the sale would only be held there until the Saturday. This started alarm bells ringing; the farther south we travelled, the more religion would have an impact on the sales held on Sundays, and I began to wonder if Gadsden, deep in the Bible belt, would even hold such an event on the Sabbath. And, worse, there wasn't a single orange golf ball to be found.

The second yard sale of the day was the biggest we'd seen so far and, with over three hundred vendors in an air-conditioned warehouse and a large outdoor area, it would prove the largest we'd pass during the weekend's festivities. The bulk of the indoor merchants specialized in guns and firearms, which explained why so many people were strolling casually down the aisles clutching rifles and handguns. It was like being at a car boot sale during a military occupation. Amongst the plethora of sport-orientated stalls, I was frustrated when, after searching for over fifteen minutes, I came away from all of them orange ball-less. The closest I came to my dream was when I found an unopened pack of Wheaties which was clearly years old because of the picture of Tiger Woods on the box and the cereal's special giveaway in conjunction with the 2002 PGA Championship. Included in the pack were two free golf balls, but the risk of spending ten dollars on a breakfast cereal four years past its sell-by date, in the hope that one of the two balls would be orange, wasn't a gamble I was willing to take. I was, however, coerced into listening to the spiel of a nearby vendor who tried to make me buy a pair of thirty-dollar sandals (the kind old men wear over socks) which, according to the seller, made the wearer feel as if 'he was walking on marshmallows'.

We were only six miles away from the motel we had woken up in two hours before and decided that, if we wanted to avoid making the same mistake as the previous day, we wouldn't stop for another sale until the town of Danville, 40 miles further south. Just two miles later, I pulled off the road and parked up on the side of the road alongside another yard sale. Well, I had to. There was a sign claiming it sold 'Golf clubs, balls and shoes'.

No luck.

We set off again with renewed determination, and as we passed no fewer than ninety yard sales en route to Danville, by not stopping we were certainly clawing back a great deal of time which would have been otherwise wasted looking for golf balls and other random tat. The lengthy car journey also gave us time to devise another game to play in addition to our amateur *Bargain Hunt*. Whilst we searched through endless stalls for our personal plunder, we now had to look out for a specific item selected by our opponent. To keep things simple, things that weren't likely to exist, such as an Edwardian pneumatic drill or a 1984 A-Team annual signed by Joan of Arc, were barred. For Bec, I chose any dish, plate, or any type of crockery that depicted George Washington. Bec, on the other hand, came up with a challenge so cunning it could have once been an idea belonging to Baldrick's fox.

'So, what do I have to find?' I asked.

Bec smirked and her face lit up. 'An orange golf ball.'

Clever bitch.

Our first chance presented itself at the first yard sale in Danville, a city famous for an international news story in

210

which a female fraudster with a sense of humour had purchased an ice cream sundae in a local fast food restaurant and attempted to pay with a two-hundred-dollar bill depicting George W. Bush and the White House with lawn signs saying such things as 'WE LIKE BROCOLLI' and 'NO MORE SCANDELS'. The Dairy Queen cashier accepted the note and gave the woman $198 change.*

With nothing of great interest in Danville's largest yard sale (except for a brilliant NASCAR play rug and cars which I bought for fifteen dollars), we continued south towards the Tennessee border 90 miles away. Because every motel we passed had a 'NO VACANCY' sign, we were desperate to get to Tennessee with plenty of time to secure ourselves a bed for the night. We put orange golf balls and George Washington crockery on the temporary backburner, so we could increase our current average speed – which at 15 mph was an improvement on the previous day, but would still leave us miles short of the border – reach the new state and find a place to stay.

As we journeyed ever farther south, churches, bill-boards relating to Jesus, the Confederate flag and unattractive homemade quilts became more frequent. After passing 309 separate yard sales including people with simple tables on their porches, in just over 100 miles of travel – stopping at just a handful, which we left

---

* Apparently, the same happened in Roanoke Rapids, North Carolina in 2003 when a man used one of the bills to pay for $150 of groceries, and then Deborah Trautwine, a 51-year-old Pennsylvanian woman, was arrested after using a similar note in a clothes shop. (Just thought you might be interested.)

empty-handed – we entered Tennessee and arrived in the small city of Jamestown.

With fewer than two thousand residents, Jamestown wasn't one of the largest cities we had encountered, but it was definitely the most significant. Because it lay approximately 234 miles from Covington, and was therefore more or less the halfway point of the event, the Fentress County Chamber of Commerce in Jamestown was considered to be the headquarters of the Yard Sale. We couldn't simply pass through without showing our faces, and as the chamber clerks would know of all the accommodation within the entire county, we decided to kill two birds with one stone.

As we hopped up the rotten wooden steps of the sandstone building housing the chamber – deciding against using the even more precarious-looking ramp for wheelchair access – we passed a sign welcoming us to Ye Ole Jail.

Bec and I stepped in and perused a brochure stand. A voice from a side room said, 'Can I help you?'

The voice belonged to Gale Reed, a woman in her fifties who was positioned behind a computer screen. She was the office administrator of the chamber and she sat opposite Walter Page, the director of tourism and membership.

'Yes,' I replied. 'We've been on the Yard Sale route and were wondering if there's anywhere to stay. I think the closest place could be by the interstate but that's about sixty miles away.'

'I'll contact Julia,' she replied, picking up her telephone.

The room didn't look much like the headquarters of

Jamestown, let alone a 450-mile festival: it was small and quite cramped. One of the clerks of the chamber, however, a young man sitting at the side of the room with no desk, redressed the balance. He was dressed in an expensive suit and looked like a mannequin in Austin Reed. His name, Ruble Upchurch III, certainly did his formal and punctilious appearance justice.

'Oh you do!' said Gale excitedly as she lowered the receiver from her ear, covering the mouthpiece. 'Clare has a room at the Wildwood Bed and Breakfast. And she's English,' she whispered.

That sealed the deal; not only would we not have to travel sixty miles to the interstate and then the same distance to rejoin Highway 127, but a B&B run by an English lady meant continental breakfasts of cereal and disappointing things from a waffle iron were out and a good old fashioned fry-up was on the cards.

'Excellent,' I replied. 'We'll check in and have a drink. We need one after the last few days we've had.'

'That might be a problem,' said Ruble. 'It's a dry county.'

'For Christ's sake,' I snapped. 'Not again. What's with this country?'

Ruble looked startled then moved quickly towards a cupboard as if I had scared him and he was looking for an escape route. He returned with a bottle of table wine in his hand.

'Here, take this,' he said. 'They make it at a winery just out of town.'

We thanked the chamber clerks for the wine and for managing to do the almost impossible in finding accommodation so close to the 127 at a bed and breakfast which, according to the woman, people normally had to book over a month in advance during the busy season. They then invited us to take a walk upstairs and see why the building is billed as Ye Ole Jail.

On the top floor of the chamber, in a hot and stuffy room which felt and looked like a badly converted attic, stood a solid steel cage, separated in the middle to form two formidable and incommodious cells into which a small mattress and toilet had been squeezed. Untouched since their final day of use, the damp and repugnant cells conjured torturous visions more befitting the Tower of London. It was hard to believe that the jail saw its last inmate as recently as 1979.

We checked into our room at the Wildwood Lodge at five in the evening, just before one of the two austere and rather eccentric sisters who run the charming establishment took her dog for a walk, leading him across the side of the road instead of for a brisk walk through the accommodation's seventeen acres of woodland because of a bear warning. With wild animals such as those roaming casually outside our door, we thought we'd drive to a nearby restaurant before returning to the lodge's upper deck to enjoy the bottle of wine and the magnificent views as the sun descended behind the Cumberland plateau.

A cup of tea and a fry-up is the best way to start a day of golf-ball searching, and although Julia apologized for having to cook bacon the American way (so it's like plastic), no breakfasts come better than the ones dished up at the Wildwood Lodge. We departed Jamestown at just after nine for the Saturday leg of the Yard Sale, a day which we assumed would be the most popular so far.

Despite being the headquarters and focal point of the Yard Sale, Jamestown was a bit of a letdown on the sale front and we continued making good progress through the small towns of Grimsley and Clarkrange before arriving in Crossville, 35 miles to the south of Jamestown. We'd already passed 195 yard sales. In Crossville there was a sale of substantial size, one where we thought we could rummage for purchases, and as soon as we arrived, I dragged Bec towards a long wooden table covered in Nixon badges from his presidential campaign under which sat a tub of golf balls. There, amongst hundreds of white counterparts, glistening like a star at the top of a Christmas tree, was an orange golf ball. I could hardly contain my excitement, and quickly rescued him from amongst his inferior bedfellows.

'How much for this?' I asked, trying to contain my joy.

'For what?'

'That!' I bellowed, pointing at the luminous beacon of hope and all that is good in the world in my hand.

'One ball? Is that it?' he replied, not realizing what I was willing to pay for it and how I had searched endlessly for it as if one orange golf ball was my Atlantis. 'Just take it,' he snapped.

Bonus.

As we strolled past other pitches, including the first Nazi-related stand which included a swastika flag which could be ours for as little as ten dollars, Bec was left having to think of another item to find. 'Does that mean I'm one-nil down then?' she asked.

'I'm afraid so,' I replied.

'I'm never gonna find any Washington crockery. It's a good job you didn't say Lincoln – that would be almost impossible.'

'Actually, with their politics and the way they feel towards his presidency down here, there are probably some commemorative plates celebrating the day he was shot.'

Crossville was the first city in which travelling the equivalent of Bournemouth to Edinburgh following a seemingly endless procession of yard sales began to feel a little uncomfortable. Guns and other dangerous weapons had been prevalent since the outset, but in the middle of Tennessee quirky John Deere coasters and baseball cards were displaced by ultraconservative articles such as regimental SS clothing and a 'COLORED WAITING ROOM' sign, a vulgar memento from a shameful era in America's past.

Still, it was handy for presidential plates, and Bec managed to locate a French dish depicting the US president signing some sort of treaty. With the scores now tied at one all, it was time to choose a second challenge item. I had to locate something showing the English flag while Bec had the more straightforward task of hunting for a Superman mirror (the type where the character takes up more room on the mirror's surface than your reflection does, rendering it entirely useless).

We had been instructed by our friend Kerry Regan to bring her back the most 'gash'* present we could. In Pikeville we found it. As I was wondering whether to

* 'Gash' in the sense of inane, stupid or rubbish, not the vulgar term for a vagina.

purchase her a trophy which she could use to pretend she had been named St Claire County Council Student of the Year, Bec was parting with a dollar for a Whirlpool Corporation belt buckle (the world's leading manufacturer of washing machines and other major home appliances).

As expected, Saturday had been the busiest day on the Yard Sale trail. We may have only covered just over a hundred miles, but we had passed a staggering 452 sales. With the same distance left to cover on the final day of the event, we were confident that with an early start (and most sales being either cancelled or put off until the afternoon owing to religious commitments), we had more than enough time to reach Gadsden, set up our own stall, and make a profit. At six, we pulled into a Quality Inn on the outskirts of the southern Tennessean border town of Chattanooga, a city made famous in song by Glenn Miller (ask your gran).

Lookout Mountain overlooks Chattanooga to the north and the Georgian border to the south. Its main attraction, the Ruby Falls, is a 145-foot underground waterfall which was formed more than two hundred million years ago. It's an ideal place to have a morning off from yard sales. Named after the wife of Leo Lambert, who discovered the natural phenomenon in 1928, the falls are now a tourist staple in Chattanooga and nearby Rock City.

I don't normally visit tourist attractions or accompany tour groups whilst I'm abroad. The times I have done so, I seem to end up less informed than I would have liked, as I get quite easily annoyed by the strangers whose company I am in. In 2005, Bateman and I toured Hearst Castle, the palatial mansion once owned by newspaper tycoon William Randolph Hearst, as a morally healthy escape from our frivolous law-breaking. The 90,000-square-foot estate was magnificent, and immaculate throughout. Roman baths with tiles inspired by Italian mausoleums and swimming pools surrounded by statues of Greek gods exuded an air of opulence and extraordinary extravagance. But the tour was utterly ruined by the American contingent of the group who found it necessary to yell 'Wow!' and 'Gee whizz!' after each and every fact about the house. Two years before that, I had taken a flight to the Grand Canyon and had to view the prodigious gorge while sitting next to two guys from Alabama who, after boarding the plane and telling me in great detail who they were and where they were from, continued to irritate the Native American pilot by asking him if he lived in a teepee and whether or not the tour company offered night flights over the canyon. Night flights?

Entrance to the Ruby Falls looked busy. Very busy in fact. Bec and I found a parking space in the second over-flow lot and joined the back of a very long line of camera-wielding tourists. After twenty minutes and two short shuffles forward, word had reached our part of the queue that it could be anything up to two hours before we could see the falls and that it cost fifteen dollars . . . each.

'Stuff this!' I said, rather too loudly. 'I'm off.'

'You can buy five Tic-Tac-Putts for that kind of money,' Bec observed. We'd both seen Wookey Hole anyway.

We jumped into our car and continued up Lookout Mountain and across the border into Georgia, a state which hosted just a 40-mile link of the route before the yard sales continued into Alabama. The yard sales now began to feature in places where there seemed to be no population at all, at roadsides where there was no house or building in sight. Every few miles a lay-by would be occupied by a pick-up truck with a large table covered in 'goods', on the side of roads which hadn't been quite as badly signposted since the crockery episode in Oregon.

After losing our way on a couple of occasions, at noon we made our way across the border and into Alabama. We hoped the mass of departing congregations would now be swapping prayers and hymns for purchasing whims. Unfortunately, crossing the border meant we had entered a new time zone. It was eleven a.m., when the majority of church services were just beginning. As more and more inadequate stalls passed by our windows, my attention was drawn away from what was outside and focused more on what was happening inside the car and, more specifically, what was on the radio. In all my time in America, the only interruptions I'd experienced on music stations were the hilarious local adverts with a tacky jingle and small print uttered at incomprehensible speed. As we crossed into Alabama, I found certain words were being edited out of songs broadcast, even though I wasn't listening to R&B or rap, in which the only lyrics which could be broadcast at such an early hour would be 'hoe' as long as it was describing an agricultural implement. I was tuned into a popular and contemporary hits station. A simple line such as 'Closing the god-damn door' taken from a song by Panic at the Disco left a silence between 'the' and 'damn'; and even the Sean Kingston song 'Beautiful' had been totally rewritten so the word 'suicidal' was replaced with 'in denial' and 'crime' was phased out. It was all very surreal. Didn't improve the song much either.

At a junction of two roads, just outside the last town of any significant size before Gadsden, we decided we would scour the stalls as a last-ditch attempt to buy some goods to sell on further down the road. It wasn't a large-scale sale, nor was it one with much choice. It did, however, have a ten-dollar Davy Crockett-style hat for me, and a fifteen-dollar John Deere tractor assembly kit which I'm sure Bec bought just because it meant wasting my money instead of her own.

When we finally entered Gadsden, we felt a massive sense of relief. Not only had we completed the Yard Sale route with enough time to spare, but we were finally in a city of substance and civility, where people conversed on street corners and in shop doorways instead of whilst leaning on the side of a gate. Negotiating the final turn of the Yard Sale route, my eyes were drawn to the Noccalula Falls, Gadsden's 250-acre public park. Instead of the botanical gardens or the 90-foot waterfall situated nearby, my eye was focused on its car park and the sign that informed me that Gadsden's yard sale, the 'FIRST AND LAST', was just 200 yards away and featured over 150 vendors. Checking that I still had my NASCAR rug and Tic-Tac-Putt safely on the back seat, we pulled into the car park to decide how to begin trying to sell the goods. It wouldn't be easy. It was already two in the afternoon and although surely no one would be able to resist the temptation of hitting golf balls into a moulded-plastic base, we had no stall and no idea how to obtain one. Our best hope was to ask a salesman nicely if we could use part of his/her table – he or she could keep whatever profit we'd make and everybody would be happy. Clutching the game, rug and wearing a coonskin cap with the tail hanging down my neck, we prepared for action.

We needn't have bothered. An hour before our arrival, a storm had passed over Gadsden and all but five of the vendors had packed up and left, taking with them every potential customer and leaving a desolate and rain-sodden car park in their wake.

9

A Britt Abroad

When Bec and I arrived in Kansas City, Missouri, the last thing I wanted to do was drive. The four days of constant yard sales, added to the fact that I'd had to leave my beloved Tic-Tac-Putt in Alabama, hadn't put me in the best of moods. Bec was still finding varnish in my hair and tiny pieces of duct tape in places you wouldn't imagine, and I had managed to flood one of Birmingham airport's departure gates with burning hot coffee when I accidentally pushed the wrong button on the industrial-sized coffee machine, which looked more like the control panel of a submarine. As we boarded our plane from an opposite gate ten minutes later, the coffee shop assistant was still combating the uncontrollable flow of brown liquid armed with just a mop, placing 'WET FLOOR' signs on the tiled floor and gesturing his disbelief with constant shrugs of the shoulders. Nothing was going to cheer me up in Kansas City.

Because it was cheaper to fly to Missouri, we were

going to drive the 300 miles north to Mason City, Iowa. The only car the rental company had remaining was another Chrysler PT Cruiser. While it could handle straight roads pretty well, it was practically incapable of negotiating any sort of curve or turn. Turning the wheel and waiting for the vehicle to steer in the desired direction was a process as long and drawn out as tacking an eighteenth-century sloop. Still, roads in Iowa and Missouri are mostly flat and straight, so there wouldn't be a great need for turning left or right (sorry, port or starboard).

'Welcome to Iowa – Fields of Opportunity' reads the sign on the border. After travelling for an hour deeper into the state and witnessing not a single undulation nor the minutest change in the contours of our featureless surroundings, just plain 'Fields' seemed a more accurate slogan.

After a drive lasting over four hours, we arrived with great relief at our motel in Mason City, Iowa: a convenient distance from our next festival, and two hours south of Minneapolis airport where, to be honest, we should have flown in the first place. Stepping out of the motel's pool following a refreshing post-drive swim, we made our way to the nearby farming town of Britt.

Like all of its surrounding settlements, Britt isn't anything special. Its tiny population of two thousand residents is in slow decline, the town stands on the junction of two highways perpendicular to each other (boxed in by further roads – so as not to ruin the patchwork quilt-like design of Iowa) and, according to city-data.com, it's home to two registered sex offenders. (Just thought I'd mention it.) With almost a third of the town's economy generated by revenue from the transportation industry and farming, it comes as no surprise that the local landmark is two huge grain silos, situated by the side of the main train line on which the town was founded. And it's because of those antiquated train tracks that we were in Britt in the first place.

There may not be a station as such but Britt stands on one of the few train lines still in use in America today and the town witnesses freight passing daily on its way to Chicago, Nebraska and other destinations along the famous Union Pacific and Santa Fe railways. Following the introduction of the railroad, towns situated near the tracks attracted vagrant workers who had used the freight carriages as free transportation. These people became known as hoboes, and the town of Britt celebrates their rich heritage annually.

In 1899, three of Britt's energetic men, Thos. A. Way, T. A. Potter and W. E. Bradford, proposed to do something different to show the world that their sleepy farming town was capable of doing anything the larger cities could. The three men succeeded in bringing the National Hobo Convention, which had been held in Chicago's Market Street for some time, to Britt the following year. By all accounts, the festivities received mixed reviews. Britt wanted attention and with hundreds of young residents dressing themselves in torn clothes and fake blackened eyes, ragtime music, horse races and journalists who descended on the town from as far away as St Louis and Philadelphia, that's exactly what it got. Tensions arose, however, between convention-goers and the 'real' hoboes who attended the turn-of-the-century event and are reported to have become disillusioned with the festivities and saw the spectators' choice of attire as 'blatant exploitation of their brethren'.

Although Britt had gained a notable reputation as a 'hobo town' the community didn't host another convention for more than thirty years. Only when the county fair died did Britt decide to observe Hobo Days as an anniversary. In 1933, at the peak of the Great Depression, the first annual convention was held, and when the date was moved to a Saturday in 1971, a total of 25,000 people took to the streets of Britt in celebration.

According to earlier research that I conducted into the Hobo Convention, Britt claimed that 2007 would see the 107th annual event. And that's where I have a bit of a problem. I don't wish to seem picky, but 107 isn't even within a reasonable margin of error. For starters (as you will be well aware if you have been paying attention), the convention wasn't 'annual' until 1933, and there was just one hobo celebration before that. Since then, it has been held every year with the exception of 1941–45 (when America finally decided to join the Second World War). By my calculations, that made 2007 the 71st Annual Hobo Days. Not bad, but still not 107.

As Bec showed no interest whatsoever in my calculations, we pulled into one of the dozens of available parking spaces on the side of what looked like abandoned streets to visit the Chamber of Commerce, whose officials would, I was sure, be very excited by my findings. The chamber was nothing like any I'd been in before. For starters there was no one there and, what's more, it was situated in the far corner of a shoe shop. A large, mild-mannered gentleman, who, if he'd sported a beard, would have made an exceptional Father Christmas look-alike, stood behind the counter and must have noticed us loitering.

'Can I help you?' he asked.

'We were just after some information about the Hobo Convention,' Bec replied.

'I can tell you all you need to know.'

Bill Eckels was the owner of the Cobbler Shoppe, a small main-street business specializing in footwear and clothing. I had never met a cobbler in my life before venturing to the States; now Bill was the second in under a month. He noticed we were from the UK almost immediately and began to tell us of his family's Scottish roots, before informing us that his grandfather staked everything he owned in a bet that he could outrun a horse and cart in a 200-yard race. His grandfather won and the Eckels family has remained in the area ever since. After ten minutes or so, we realized that although Bill had spoken at great length about the history of his family and of the town, not a single word of it related to the Hobo Convention.

'The Hobo Convention?' he asked, after I mentioned it to him again. 'I'm not quite sure. I've never been.'

Hobo Days doesn't officially begin until the lighting of the Jungle Fire at seven p.m. on the Thursday. With several hours to spare, Bec and I visited the Hobo Museum just a block away from the Cobbler Shoppe to garner some information about life as a hobo, as I was sure that not all freight-train riders were an adorable German shepherd that would cleverly foil an assassination plot before boarding a conveniently placed box car without a word of thanks from his temporary master to the tune of 'Maybe Tomorrow' by Terry Bush.*

The Hobo Museum is located in Britt's disused cinema and, although it is no bigger than a village hall, it contains the most extensive range of hobo artefacts in the world. In the foyer, above a Christmas tree and a list of famous hoboes – which included folk singer Burl Ives, Winthrop Rockefeller and Clark Gable – an important message adorns the entrance to the main display room and serves as an admonition to all who fail to distinguish between hoboes and the homeless. 'A hobo is someone who travels for work, a tramp travels but will not work, a bum neither travels or works' – a poignant, if not grammatically incorrect, definition of a hobo.

Because of the building's previous use, the entire display area stood on a gentle slope. Each table was propped up on several books and one wall was a good six feet taller than its opposite partition. Despite not having shown a film since 1975, the museum has an hour-long documentary which plays on a loop on a small television screen at the back. As the titles rolled, Bec and I settled down and watched with interest.

There isn't a definite explanation as to why the workers became known as hoboes, but it's commonly thought that they began working as farmhands and the term derived from the words 'hoe boys'. At the height of the Great Depression, and with no prospects at home, many decided to leave in the hope that there would be work for them elsewhere. Embarking on a freight train was an illegal but free way to get there.

---

* I apologize to people who have never seen a single episode of *The Littlest Hobo* and didn't get the reference.

Life as a hobo was a bitter struggle. Boarding and alighting from moving carriages was extremely danger-ous, not to say life-threatening, and when safely back on the ground the men and women still needed to evade capture by the railroad companies' own security staff, whose members were notoriously heavy-handed. For safety, the hobocs banded together, and a sense of brotherhood was formed amongst travellers, and camps began to spring up by the sides of the railroad. These were called 'jungles' and were a safe haven where weary hoboes could stop for something to eat or wash their torn clothes before catching a train to a new destination. Maltreated and scorned by society, they were sustained by their sense of camaraderie. The immeasurable hard-ships they faced was a fee they were prepared to pay for a life of freedom.

The documentary *Riding the Rails* was as touching as it was informative. It not only relayed the facts about hoboes, but focused on the stories of half a dozen Americans who had lived such a life. When asked to think back on their experiences and if they would ride a box car today, one of them, Clarence Lee, gazed forlornly into the camera as if in a trance before tears fell from his eyes. 'No, I don't want to ride one today. That was days though, good gracious.'

Just before seven, we made our way to Britt's own Hobo Jungle, an area to the side of the tracks complete with box car, picnic tables and kitchen area used by the hoboes. It was open to the public for the duration of the weekend to give festival-goers a chance to meet and talk with them about riding the rails and listen to some of the best storytellers in the country. As soon as we arrived, we realized that the 2007 Hobo Convention was to be an event of great significance, reflection and mourning.

Maurice W. Graham rode the freight trains at the tender age of fourteen during the Great Depression and first came to Britt in 1971. Owing to his fondness for the older engines, Graham became known as 'Steam Train Maury' and was a favourite among the hobo community. Maury was crowned Hobo King five times and was honoured with the title of 'Grand Patriarch of the Hoboes' at the 2004 convention. Just three months after Britt's 2006 Hobo Days, Maury 'caught the westbound' after suffering a stroke at his home in Ohio, leaving behind two daughters and his wife of sixty-nine years. To Britt and the hobo community, Maury's death was a considerable loss. The 2007 event was dedicated to the memory of the hobo to whom the rest looked for guidance and wisdom. The town certainly won't forget him – the road on which Bec and I parked adjacent to the jungle has been renamed 'Steam Train Way'.

By seven, a small crowd had assembled and were sitting on two three-row bleachers overlooking a specially constructed fire, which looked more like a half-completed game of Jenga. Karl Teller, known as Redbird Express and dressed in a cap and a garage-attendant shirt, looking more like a truck driver than a traditional hobo, began proceedings by welcoming everybody to the 2007 Hobo Convention. Following salutes to the four winds (a sign of appreciation for what the separate breezes bring with them, involving a one-armed gesture that's a cross between a one-armed zombie impression and a Nazi salute), the ceremonial fire was lit and ashes from other hobo conventions held in the past year were asked to be added to the flames. A dozen or so people approached the fire, tipping the contents of their specially made urns (ranging from jewellery boxes, miniature vases and a metal flask to a Sour Cream and Onion Pringles tube) on to the fire as a symbolic gesture of fellowship.

In a tribute to his memory, Steam Train's widow, Wanda, paid homage to his brethren and handed out several awards, announcing that Slo Freight Ben, a three-time former queen just four years shy of her hundredth birthday, was to be honoured as Hobo Queen for Life. As she was pushed in her wheelchair by her daughter Carol, Slo Freight (real name Benita Sankey) embraced her friend. Jokes were made about the time when, with no ride and eager to attend the convention, Slo Freight, then an octogenarian, began to cycle to Britt from her home 126 miles away.

It soon became the turn of the hoboes to entertain the crowd. At first it seemed as if participants were only allowed to enter if they had some sort of novelty act. First up was a young girl by the name of Angie Dirtyfeet who was spurred on by her mother, Minneapolis Jewel, a candidate for the 2007 Hobo Queen, who was apparently attempting to gain an early advantage by parading her daughter as a future Barbra Streisand. Liberty Justice finished the evening's proceedings and serenaded the audience with some traditional hobo folk tunes. With a guitar on his lap and a hobo beside him (who bore a striking resemblance to ZZ Top's Billy Gibbons) plucking a string bass to form a two-piece orchestra, Liberty's gimmick was the constant gusts of air from an oxygen tank at his feet which made a strange musical accompaniment after every line he sang.

On Friday afternoon, Britt's town centre was bursting with life and was a completely different scene from what we had witnessed the previous day. Adults inspected a multitude of sidewalk stands selling anything from hobo gifts to candy floss, whilst children raced around the streets and enjoyed the dozen or so attractions, including an inflatable bungee-run just yards from the Cobbler Shoppe's front door. We decided to go in and try again to talk with a representative of the chamber. As usual, no chamber member was there and so we chatted to Bill once more about the weekend's crowning ceremony.

'The crowning ceremony?' he said. 'I don't know. I've never been.'

The list of past Convention Kings and Queens acts as a useful who's who of Britt's dynasty, and with past royalty including names such as the Pennsylvania Kid, Ramblin' Rudy and Luther the Jet Gett, the roll of honour reads more like a card from an evening of amateur wrestling. In Britt's municipal centre, just across the street from an attraction in which students were attempting to soak a classmate by hitting a target and triggering a mechanism which would drop them into the drink, local artist Leanne Castillo had her art on display.

Sixty-five people have been dubbed Hobo King since Charles Noe was crowned in 1900, and the art on display featured paintings of every single one. Placed in chronological order from the first or only time they were bestowed with the title, it was a fascinating insight into the look and appearance of a hobo and a way of putting a face to the name. As I expected, images of the late Steam Train Maury dominated the gallery with miniature pictures of the patriarch available for three dollars. Although there is no set dress code for a hobo, with his long, white and wise-looking beard and tired face, Maury seemed to typify the look. Facial hair is almost a permanent fixture on a hobo and some sort of headwear appears to be obligatory, as it's meant to say something about the wearer. Denim or dungarees appeared in nearly every picture and some hoboes were proudly flaunting a staff – not only to be used as an aid to walking but also as the personal symbol of an experienced traveller.

With a few hours to spare before a hobo poetry reading, we visited one of the local bars on the main street. Despite its quirky name, J & D's Hob Nob has nothing to do with biscuits made from rolled oats, and is just like any small-town bar in America (with the exception of their Christmas decorations being up in August). It was dark, there were neon signs advertising different brands of 'Lite' beer, and country music was blasting out of the speakers. What was remarkable about the bar was that there were just as many hoboes in the bar during that afternoon than there had been in the jungle during the lighting of the ceremonial fire the previous day. Some were talking of old times and laughing with fellow travellers they hadn't seen since the 2006 convention, whilst others sat quietly reading a paper or simply slept, their heads dropping to their chests.

At four, we made our way towards Steam Train Way and the Hobo Jungle for an afternoon of poetry reading.

Joining the small crowd that had assembled to listen to the poignant words, it became obvious to us that the most important item required for a poetry reading was a milk crate. Upturned, the plastic box helped whoever recited the text to adopt the official poetry-reading pose, a position in which every reader soon became comfortable. Slamming his right leg on to the base of the crate, resting the book on the bend in his leg and leaning towards the crowd, Redbird Express began the event by reading some verse from a book of hobo poetry. Many other feet took to the crate, including the chairperson of the Hobo Foundation as well as a man who attempted to recite an entire lengthy poem from memory. The piece took much longer than it should have done owing to constant 'No, hang on's and pointing his finger on each beat as a way of jogging his memory.

Following an hour of poetry, Bec and I had the chance to meet some hobo royalty. Dressed in a pair of brown shorts, blue Hawaiian shirt and a baseball cap worn backwards, the medallion-wielding 2006 Hobo King approached us and shook our hands.

'Hi, I'm the king,' he said.

His name was Iowegian Rick and if anyone had travelled to the convention by way of freight train that year, it was likely to be him. With a greying goatee beard, long, greasy hair and not a great many teeth, Rick looked as if he was telling the truth when he said that he had spent the last year travelling the country – for the most part by freight train.

'We've travelled all the way from England,' said Bec.

'And you, my dear, are an English rose,' he replied, kissing Bec on the hand.

No wonder he won the title last year; maybe he should change his name to Slick Rick.

'You gonna run for king again?' I asked.

'Oh, no,' he laughed. 'Being king is too much responsibility and I'm not into that.'

After asking Bec if she would dance with him at the post-coronation ceremony the next night, he returned to the Hobo Jungle slowly with a limp in his walk.

Saturday was the final and most important day of the weekend's festivities. Not only would there be a morning parade through the streets of Britt, but a new king and queen would be crowned in a ceremony in the afternoon. The cavalcade of floats began in the west of the city at the local high school and made its way past us almost immediately. Like the parade I'd seen before in Elko, where local businesses and organizations threw candy to the audience, Britt's was nothing special. In fact the only significant difference was that although just as many horses were used in the hour-long procession, the roads didn't end up resembling an urban cesspool.

For lunch we made our way to Mary Jo's Hobo House, a café opposite the museum which prides itself, as the name suggests, on being a great supporter of the hobo culture. Once inside, the strain placed on the café due to the demands of the day had resulted in the menu containing just two items: Sloppy Joe or a salad. Minneapolis Jewel and her husband Tuck were often parading through the bar with placards and sandwich boards in a last-ditch attempt to gain a few additional votes for their claim to become the 2007 Hobo King and Queen. For me, their rudimentary campaign was wasted. As far as I was concerned, his sign, 'VOTE TUCK FOR KING OF HOBO'S', which included an incorrect use of an apostrophe, was more than enough reason to turn my nose up at his candidature and not offer him any support when it came to the all-important voting.

By noon, many of the audience members for the ceremony had gathered in the city park for the handing out of free mulligan stew, a dish which was prepared by hoboes in camps and jungles since as early as the turn of the twentieth century. According to the local newspaper, the *Britt News Tribune*, this year's mulligan stew giveaway consisted of 450 lbs of beef, 900 lbs of potatoes, 250 lbs of carrots, 300 lbs of cabbage, 35 lbs of peppers, 100 lbs of turnips, 150 lbs of parsnips, and 24 gallons of mixed vegetables. It would serve approximately five thousand people. It came in a little handy tub and tasted pleasant, similar to a beef casserole.

As the microphone bellowed into action, Bec and I climbed aboard the back seat of a stand with direct view of the bandstand in which the crowning would take place, armed with cushions we had bought from a nearby Dollar General. We were sitting next to Come On Pat, the 1996 Hobo Queen and a lady after whom Dexy's Midnight Runners came remarkably close to unwittingly naming a UK number one hit single. Her king that year had been Liberty Justice, and hush descended on the city park when he placed his oxygen tank by his feet and began to sing the national anthem. Although it was the umpteenth occasion during the summer that I had to endure the song, it was the first time that the rendition had me entertained and I enjoyed every second. With the constant jets of air entering his nostrils and resounding through all four of the city park's speakers, it sounded as if 'The Star Spangled Banner' was being performed as a duet by Johnny Cash and Darth Vadar.

Dozens of hoboes sat patiently in the bandstand whilst arrangements were made for the opening speeches. Bec and I felt like commentators with the former queen as our expert guest. I started by asking Come On Pat whom her money was on.

'Oh, Minneapolis Jewel will be queen,' she answered confidently.

As an update on the fund-raising for the new Hobo Museum was being announced by the founder of the Hobo Foundation, I opened a notebook and attempted, to the best of my abilities, to make a note of what happened next.

The 1997 king, Frog, approached the microphone and recited a poem about how industrial America was both founded on and built by the hoboes of the country. (By the way, his name stands for 'Friends Rely on God'; he's not called Frog because he only has one leg and presumably has to hop everywhere.) Adman, the 2004 king, lauded Slo Freight Ben and her presence at yet another Hobo Convention. Minneapolis Jewel, who you could tell wasn't the patient and quiet type, took to the stage and awarded 1994 king, Iowa Blackie, with a whoopee cushion, before Roadhog USA, dressed in American flag braces, praised Britt as being 'the friendliest place on earth'. Another past king, Luther the Jet Gett, made a speech which involved a DVD of Disney's *High School Musical* and a 1937 Johnny Lomax song which had something to do with a canal. Finally the present queen, Ms

Charlotte, spoke at length about her time as hobo royalty, and said that now she had worn the crown after years of failed bids, there was good reason to step down.

It was only then that I realized that the speeches, poem-reciting and general time-wasting antics had nothing to do with the naming of a king and queen. Britt mayor James Nelson announced the rules for hoboes claiming candidature for the prize.

To become king, a man has to be a legitimate rail-rider, either now or in the past. This is decided by a committee that screens each entrant and asks him a series of questions to ensure the validity of his candidature. To win the crown of Hobo Queen, a woman doesn't necessarily have to have ridden a freight train, but must be familiar to the hobo community and recognized as a worthy contender by the screening panel. Goodness knows who the members of this screening panel were, but it appeared as if seven contenders had qualified (or were the only people who had thrown their names into the ring) for the final stage. Much like the Film Festival in Corvallis, where judging was based on the very fair and simplistic voting system of the power of the clap, each potential royal had two minutes to wow the crowd before the applause separated the regal from mere peasants.

A hobo who went by the name of Green Card George was first up. His chief selling point was that he had been off drink and drugs for over two years. He finished his couple of minutes with a song and the words 'God bless Britt'.

Inkman, otherwise known as Tommy from the Railroad (Tommy Maras to his postman), decided to use his two minutes to recite a poem he had written. I'm not sure what it was called but it began as a poignant reminder of how Uncle Sam had treated hoboes, and was a definite crowd-pleaser. 'A hobo is someone who builds palaces and lives in shacks,' he said. 'Built America but is denied the vote, builds factories and is then denied work in them.' The poem continued with some pretty terrible comparative analogies including something to do with building cars and pushing wheelbarrows.

Next on the stage was Tuck, husband of Minneapolis Jewel, who was nervous when put in front of a microphone. He simply spoke about the pride he would feel in becoming king and that he would celebrate the victory with all of his fellow hoboes.

The last hobo who stood in their way was Liberty Justice, the only entrant who had won the title before. He opted for the American way of doing speeches: praising troops and saying things like 'God Bless America'. He ended with the line: 'You can all be hoboes; you don't have to ride the tracks.'

For me, the winner was Inkman, and the crowd's applause seemed to indicate it would be a close call between him and Liberty Justice. The judges appeared from their vantage points and convened in front of the bandstand. It was obvious they had chosen the winner. However, we wouldn't find out who it was until after the queens had stated their claim to the crown.

As far as I was concerned a hobo called Lady Sonshine had the crown in the bag. According to her speech, 2007 was the fourth straight year she had entered the competition, and if her emotional words 'I am already a queen in the hearts of the hoboes and that's good enough for me' wasn't going to gain her the crown, the rendition of a folk song based on the life and memory of Steam Train Maury she had performed earlier in the day would do the trick. Apart from Crash, a girl who looked about fifteen years old, the only person who stood between Lady Sonshine and her date with destiny was the charismatic and (literally) larger than life Minneapolis Jewel. She had already won the title in 1986, 1991 and 1997, and was once again throwing her hat into the ring, a symbolic gesture that came true when she did in fact throw her hat into the crowd. Thankfully, her speech was as short as her husband's. 'I do believe in hoboes. I do, I do, I do,' she shouted before placing the microphone back on to its stand. The audience applauded the three entrants and the judges made their decision.

As a similar test in Corvallis proved, voting by applause is not an accurate way to elevate someone to a position of power. The ovations which followed Inkman and Liberty Justice were far more prolonged than the clapping Tuck received. But because a previous winner of Hobo King hadn't won the title since 1981, I was utterly convinced that Inkman would leave Britt with the crown. As for the queens, Lady Sonshine had it in the bag, and I'm sure that even Steam Train was staring down at her from a giant box car in the sky. Only an idiot would have voted against her.

'And the 2007 King of the Hoboes is . . .'

What the Tuck!?

Tuck had won the crown. Now anything was possible. It became clear that the 'sporadically placed judges' had probably been positioned in Chicago, at our motel, and on Tuck's lap.

Thankfully, the judges were proved to have been paying attention when Lady Sonshine was named as Tuck's queen, defeating Minneapolis Jewel in two run-offs for the title. Tuck and Lady Sonshine were crowned in the Britt sunshine, having an upturned tin cut into the shape of a crown placed upon their newly regal pates.

In the evening, we made our way into the Hobo Jungle for the post-coronation party, the last time that the hoboes would be together in Britt until next year. A storm to the north of the town had buried the jungle beneath a dark and menacing cloud cover, and the lightning which illuminated the night sky as often as different chords were struck during the evening's entertainment created a scintillating natural backdrop. As king, it was Tuck's duty to place the first log on the ceremonial fire. In doing so, he not only managed to create a plume of smoke that covered half the crowd, but caused many near the fire to jump up and brush burning charcoal off their clothes.

The evening followed a similar pattern to the convention's opening night. Liberty Justice entertained us with a series of hobo folk songs and many other guests followed, adding their own voices to the closing of the convention. By popular demand, Lady Sonshine, accompanied by Serenity, repeated the Steam Train Maury song which had won her the title of queen, and followed it with a stirring version of 'Where Have All the Flowers Gone?'

By Monday morning, Britt had returned to its sleepy existence, and the only remnant of what the town had just experienced were the discarded signs which welcomed visitors to the 107th Hobo Convention. At the end of the final evening and thinking we wouldn't see him again, Bec and I had posted a card through the back door of the Cobbler Shoppe to thank Bill for all his help during our stay. Stalling for time before we had to make the four-hour journey to Kansas City, we entered the Cobbler Shoppe for the last time to say our goodbyes in person.

'I was wondering who sent the card,' he said, pleased to see us. 'I was guessing it was from you guys.'

Bill showed us to his workshop where he was busy mending a customer's boot. Using a type of glue which had an olfactory potency equal to that of chloroform, Bill demonstrated his work. I was genuinely interested in the repair of a heel and tried to ask questions, but with the fumes from the glue clogging my sinuses, I most probably looked like a kid who was feigning enthusiasm after discovering he was the victim of mistaken identity by the producers of *Jim'll Fix It*, but was still going to make the most of his free day with a cobbler.

On the return drive to Kansas City, I had plenty of time to evaluate the weekend's event and the oddities which both Bec and I had witnessed. To be honest, I wasn't sure what to think. Since the weekend, I've read many accounts of other hobo conventions held around the country and found that opinion of Britt is divided. For years there have been conflicts between the town leaders and the Hobo Foundation, and many hoboes have been driven away, not wanting to get mixed up in politics. The Hobo Cemetery in the town is proof that many of the brethren wish for Britt to be their final stop, and although the true hobo is now a rarity, that is no reason to forget them and the contribution they made to the country.

Following the recent deaths of Steam Train and Slo Freight Ben (who sadly 'caught the westbound' a month after the convention), the ranks of the true hobo, one who rides the rails in search of work, were even more depleted. The way of life is in fast decline – a fact no one at the convention tries to deny. Instead, it seems as if the emphasis has shifted to a celebration of a moral way of living one's life, and Hobo Days now acts as a window through which audiences can view a past American culture of unique spirit and kinship all too distant from today's world. Perhaps my only previous knowledge of such a life, gleaned from watching countless episodes of *The Littlest Hobo* as a child, wasn't that far from the truth after all.

Maybe Britt should take a new approach and hold a Cobbler Convention every year. I already know who would attend – although I'm not sure which of the two would have to be crowned Cobbler Queen. In the end, the only thing I was sure about was that during the entire four days of stories, songs, poems and general revelry, none of us saw a single freight train passing by.

10

Captive Audience

I love the British Broadcasting Corporation. If you ask me, the licence fee is worth every penny. Not only do we receive countless hours of broadcasting (for which certain programmes alone are worth the fee), but the discerning Brit is treated to an overwhelming choice of eight television stations, ten national and a multitude of local radio networks, a constantly updated internet site, and an interactive television service. Best of all, there are no adverts. The latter in itself is worth paying thirty-seven pence a day for. Programmes aren't constantly interrupted by someone trying to interest me in a loan, no one asks if I've had an accident at work and want to claim compensation, and there are no jingles or cheesy melodies subconsciously cementing a telephone number into my brain. As a public service broadcaster, its role has always been to 'educate, inform, and entertain', and, as a result, its weekly schedule remains impartial and broadcasts a wide range of programming to cater for the needs of a nation.

American television is very different. It has always tended to annoy me, and on the final leg of our journey in Oklahoma City, where we had checked in early into our motel and had a chance to watch hours of what it had to offer, that annoyance peaked. The major networks (with the exception of PBS, which broadcasts intellectual programmes and British sitcoms from the 1970s) tend to have a similar line-up every night: a couple of terrible sitcoms (the ones based in a big house with a moral dilemma to solve) will be followed by a reality show, the news and then a chat show. I'm not saying some good hasn't come out of American television in the past, but with daily line-ups that don't do anything to educate or inform the viewer, it's no wonder that the majority of people I have spoken to in America couldn't locate England on a map, and don't realize that basketball is actually crap.

I don't know why I've ranted on about this for so long. The thing that tipped me over the edge in Oklahoma City was the references to Asian automobile companies during radio and television commercials. 'Hyundai' was suddenly pronounced 'Hon-day', 'Mazda' was 'Moz-da', and 'Nissan' became 'Nee-son'. Goodness knows what they'd do with Mitsubishi.

I'd now spent exactly two months on American soil, yet only on arriving in Oklahoma did it seem, for the first time, that we were truly in a foreign country. Nothing seemed quite right. The restaurant at which we ate an afternoon meal was a cross between a diner and a motor-way service station gift shop. Sitting behind us was a guy who looked as if he had followed us there from the

Hobo Convention, and our lazy-eyed waitress was shocked to discover that we weren't Russian. Following the meal, when Bec and I awaited the bill, our waitress returned and began some light-hearted small talk.

'So, how long you guys here for?' she asked.

'Oh, we're only here for tonight and Thursday,' I replied. 'What's there to do here?'

'Frontier City down the road is pretty cool. It's only open at weekends though,' she replied. 'I'm free on Thursday.'

Was she making a pass at either Bec or me? Did she really think that we were in the habit of inviting waitresses on day excursions with us? We quickly paid the bill and scarpered, leaving a healthy tip for the waitress whose dreams of spending a day with us had been suddenly dashed.

In the hope of finding something to do, Bec and I headed for downtown and, in particular, Oklahoma City's entertainment district. Once an area of abandoned warehouses, Bricktown is now the social heart of the city. It's full of vibrant bars, sporting facilities and theatres. Modern day structures blend beautifully with the carefully restored older buildings and a canal winds its way picturesquely between them.

Just a few blocks north of Bricktown stands the Oklahoma City National Memorial, a vivid reminder that a murderous act of terrorism is unfortunately what the city is most famous for. At the time, the 1995 bombing of the Alfred P. Murrah Federal Building was the deadliest terrorist attack on American soil, injuring over 800 people and claiming the lives of 168 others. Today, a three-acre memorial commemorating the fateful day is to be found on the site where the federal building once stood. Twin bronze archways stand at either end of a thin sheet of water, known as the 'Reflecting Pool'. Each is inscribed with a time: 9:01 on the east gate represents the final minute of peace, while on the opposite arch 9:03 signifies the time at which recovery began. On the banks of the memorial, the pool is overlooked by the 'Empty Chairs', 168 glass and bronze chairs set out in nine rows enumerating the loss of life and signifying on which of the building's nine floors each person lost his or her life. Each seat is meant to symbolize the empty chair at their families' dinner table and is engraved with the name of the victim, with unborn babies featuring on the seat of their mother and nineteen smaller chairs representing the children who died in the blast.

Returning to Bricktown, we queued to buy a ticket to watch the minor league Oklahoma Redhawks play at the thirteen-thousand-seat AT&T Brickyard Ballpark. Since Bec didn't want to sit through an entire game, we changed our minds and went to watch a few innings from possibly the best seats in the house, which had a commanding view overlooking the entire stadium: the front seats of our rental car on the eighth level of a multi-storey car park.

We drove 100 miles from Oklahoma City to the strangely named town of Okmulgee. Although it lies an hour north of our destination McAlester, it had the closest motel with a vacancy.

The historic city of McAlester, population of just under twenty thousand, is the largest city in the Native American Choctaw community and is home, according to the 'WELCOME TO MCALESTER' sign, to 'COWBOYS AND ITALIANS'. In the nineteenth century, the city became popular with Italians who came to work in the coal mines, and an act in 1907 joined McAlester with South McAlester to form one municipality. More recently, the city was the location for the trial of Terry Nichols for his role in the Oklahoma City bombing, and just seven months before our arrival, McAlester experienced a major ice storm which left many parts of the city without water and electricity for a week. Damage in rural areas was described in the local newspaper as 'looking like 1,400 tornadoes came through'.

In the summer, ice is just something you dream of when the temperature pushes the mercury to 100 °F. To take its mind off the sweltering heat, the city is proud to host the Oklahoma State Prison Rodeo – an event not only contested by regular professional cowboys, but also by inmates from the local and state-wide penitentiaries, and the largest rodeo in the world to be held behind the walls of a jail. The 67th Annual Prison Rodeo was set to be one of the biggest yet, as not only were there a record number of entrants for the three-day spectacle, but it coincided with Oklahoma's centennial. It's an event that is only thirty-three years younger than the state itself. To learn more about the event and the history of McAlester, Bec and I went in search of the building which was fast becoming our first port of call in any town: the Chamber of Commerce.

Set in an old nursing home, the clerks at the McAlester Chamber of Commerce not only had our tickets for the two shows, but were more than well informed about the event and the town. Along with hundreds of IPRA

(International Pro Rodeo Association) riders, inmates from eleven correctional centres from all over Oklahoma would compete over the three days. For only the second year, two of the jails in contention were all-female. They would be competing under the same rules and riding on the same crazed ranch animals as their male counterparts. To seek further information, I picked up a few pamphlets and browsed posters and newspaper clippings about the event.

'If watching a bull skewer a paedophile isn't reason enough to vacation in Oklahoma, then nothing is,' gleefully claimed one thrill-seeking article. Yet I had seen many earlier reports on the internet that claimed the event treated animals badly and that the Prison Rodeo was simply 'state-sponsored cruelty'. I couldn't possibly comment on something which I hadn't witnessed for myself, and my only concern was that the event would be like the three-hour rodeo I once watched with my dad in Cheyenne in 1997. I was bored to tears.

The Oklahoma State Penitentiary is a formidable and uncompromising place. It is a solid, towering, beige edifice that shows no evidence of its age. Iron-clad windows, above which rifle-bearing wardens overlook the jail's perimeter from the dozen turrets 50 feet above the ground, are a forbidding addition to the structure's impregnable façade. Prior to Oklahoma achieving statehood in 1907, all felons sentenced to jail here were sent to Kansas at a cost of twenty-five cents per day, but following the state's admission to the union, McAlester was chosen as the site for the penitentiary. When $850,000 had been approved, construction began in 1908 and inmates who had been originally sent to Kansas returned to Oklahoma and set about building their own future cells and jail blocks.

All the buildings that were built then, with the exception of the New Cellhouse, still stand today, and by the looks of the outside haven't seen a lick of paint since. The New Cellhouse was destroyed in 1976 after the most costly riot in American history on 27 July 1973, when thirty million dollars' worth of damage was caused to the building. Five years after the riot, a federal court found that conditions within the penitentiary were unconstitutional and additional buildings were built. Today, only hardened criminals are incarcerated within the walls of the Oklahoma Correction Center. It's home to medium-security prisoners as well as the jail's newest addition, 'H Unit', where the main prisoners are held. Here murderers, rapists, kidnappers and armed robbers live alongside one another in a maximum security unit which provides disciplinary segregation cells, death row and the lethal injection chamber, where since 1976 eighty-three men have drawn their final breath. Between 1915 and 2008, 167 prisoners have been killed there: eighty-two by electrocution, eighty-four by lethal injection and one by hanging. Currently, seventy-five prisoners await death in the penitentiary, one of whom is named Richard Smith.

Surrounded by the rather prosaically named Perimeter Road, the west side of the correctional centre is slightly more inviting. Colour is used on the walls for the first time. Between two turrets painted red, white and blue, which look as if they were built from giant Lego bricks, which have been forcibly prised together, stands a giant gateway below which a drawbridge and moat wouldn't have looked out of place. Because a simple walk through the gateway would lead us behind the walls of a maximum-security prison, yards away from convicted felons, two wardens armed with shot-guns and rifles were poised atop each of the turrets, and several uniformed men and women were positioned in front of the entrance. We approached the gateway to begin the rigmarole of questions and body searches and discovered just how stringent the security was.

'Any tobacco or knives?' asked one young woman.

'No,' I replied.

'OK. In ya go.'

The rodeo area is an impressive sight. Purpose built to stage the annual event, the fourteen-thousand-capacity arena is made up of proper seating at the very front and concrete blue- and red-painted terraces overlooking them. At the far eastern end, huddled behind the chutes in two caged areas of the seating, stood the male and female inmates who would be taking to the animals later in the evening.

Country and western music filled the arena in preparation for the start of the rodeo. I don't know about you, but I find country and western music to be pretty repetitive. I have nothing against it, but because of the melodic and lyrical similarity between songs, I find it incredibly difficult to recognize when one song ends and another begins – as I may have complained before. I did notice that a great way to start a song would be with the line: 'I was heading down to [insert Tulsa, Memphis, Nashville, Austin or similar city name here].' Subsequent verses can be filled quite effortlessly with words such as 'whiskey', 'jukebox', 'beer' or 'pick-up truck'. With a guitar or banjo as a stringed instrument accompaniment, you'll be on to a winner.

While preparations were still being made by the event's organizers, many in the arena were already on horseback and parading around the perimeter, throwing objects into the crowd. Believing it to be free food or a helpful gift of some sort, I stood up and raised my arms to suggest I wanted whatever they were handing out. Unfortunately, the riders turned out to be members of 'God's P.O.S.S.E.', an evangelical organization whose members are people who work within the Criminal Justice System, and what they were handing out were free copies of the Bible.

Finally, the MC flicked the microphone on, and welcomed the seven-thousand-strong crowd to McAlester, to Oklahoma and to the world's biggest behind-the-walls rodeo. A group of people known as the Canadian Valley Rangerettes, an all-female equestrian drill team, stormed into the ring clad in red, white and blue and wielding American flags. They raced through the arena, throwing dirt into the air as they weaved and slalomed their way through each other with brilliantly timed equine choreography to the tune of 'America the Beautiful'. Following this, a quick tribute to Jim Shoulders, a rodeo legend who passed away two months before, was announced. Alas, having thought we had escaped a national anthem after enduring 'America the Beautiful', country and western performer Jarrod Birmingham took to the microphone and the inevitable followed.

I was one of the lucky ones. Being seated on a chair next to some railings, I could place my hands in my pockets and lean against the iron bars until we could sit back down again. Just three seats to my left, a teenager had noticed my rather lax posture and adopted a similar stance. Noticing this, his mother quickly took her hand away from her heart and clipped him around the ear for his insubordination before returning to her reverential pose. By now it was eight thirty, so at least we knew what time we could arrive for the following day's show without having to endure the preliminary patriotism.

The whole event was split into fourteen separate units, four of which would be contested by the professional rodeo; and there were three unique events which you wouldn't see anywhere else. The first of these was the 'Mad Scramble', where all of the chutes are opened and the arena explodes with wild bulls, broncos and inmates determined to stay mounted – a perfect show starter guaranteed to get the audience excited.

And it certainly did.

No sooner had the chutes opened, Soson Anderson, a female inmate from the Mabel Bassett Correctional Center (in for four separate counts of shooting with the intent to kill),* was thrown into the air like a rag doll. During the ensuing mêlée, a team of medics rushed to her aid whilst trying to avoid a similar fate themselves. As the frantic spectacle came to an end and the beasts returned to their pens, Soson was strapped to a stretcher and became the first of many people to leave the arena supine.

---

* It didn't state what the inmates were in for in the programme, but the Oklahoma Department of Corrections' online offender search is most useful.

After the pros had shown the crowd how to leap on to steers from the back of a horse, wrestle them to the ground and tie their legs together and with (apparently) double knots, the spectators were introduced to one of the rounds for which the Oklahoma Prison Rodeo is famous.

'Bull Poker', as it's known, has little to do with royal flushes or straight faces; it's more like musical chairs, albeit a more brutal version of the game. Basically, a garden table is placed 20 feet from the door of a chute and five men circle it until a selected track of music stops. When silence descends on the arena, each participant sits in the seat closest to them and a 2,000-pound angry bull is released from the table's adjacent pen. The last inmate to remain in his chair leaves with a cash prize and presumably excrement in his pants. The crowd rises from their seats at the announcement of Bull Poker, excited by the prospect of an inmate or two leaving the arena on a stretcher or a bull's horns.

When the music had stopped and the inmates had taken their positions, the MC's voice shrieked in anticipation as the chute door swung open and a bovine tank on steroids emerged. It charged straight for the table. Immediately, the man positioned closest to the bull, whose back was facing the mammal, darted out of the way. The beast lowered its head and for the tiniest of nanoseconds, the belligerent beast seemed to have disappeared beneath several feet of garden furniture. Immediately after, before the bull emerged, the white table was destroyed, snapped clean in half by the beast's upward thrust, which sent fragments of plastic and inmates into the night sky. After only a matter of seconds, a 'winner' was declared. On the ground a nervous wreck of a man cowered on an upturned chair, holding its base in fearful determination, looking more like a victim of a gritty hostage siege. Bull Poker is definitely one of the crowd's favourites; so much so in fact, that after consulting the programme I saw another round of inmate-goring was due later in the evening.

If an inmate being impaled by a ton of aggressive cattle isn't your cup of tea, a gentleman dressed as a clown who hides in barrels to protect him from the animals may brighten your evening. If at any point in the proceedings the crowd seems unimpressed or bored, Ron Hunter, with painted face and extravagant clothing, is on hand to drum up support and interest from the audience by cracking a joke instead of a rib. The high school principal's career as 'rodeo clown' began in 1985 after he commented that the current entertainer was horrible. Dared to try it himself, he took over the role and has been at the Oklahoma State Penitentiary Prison Rodeo ever since. For the most part, he completes his duties very well, and although a great deal of his material is rehearsed with the MC, you can tell he is pretty quick-witted. During a quiet moment between two events, owing to a microphone on the clown's attire, the audience gets to listen in to a conversation between Ron and one of the inmates.

'Can I use all of the arena?' the inmate asks.

'Sure you can,' he replies. 'Just make sure you stop at the gate!'

Following a severe round of bareback riding, in which inmates attempt to remain on the back of a wild horse for eight seconds whilst being bounced fiercely by the animal's constant bucking to remove his unwanted passenger, the animals are put to use again in the 'Inmate Wild Horse Race'.

For my money, this is the best event. Six 'broncs' (one for each of the three-person teams) are released from the respective correctional centre's chute. As it kicks and storms off in any direction it chooses, it is the job of the team not only to catch and place a saddle on the beast, but one member must also mount the horse and ride it across the finish line located at the halfway point of the arena, 100 feet from the pens. Because six teams take to the task each time, a sudden skirmish envelops the arena, and the action is almost impossible to follow with just one set of eyes. As one team are busy shooing their horse into a corner in order to saddle it, showing an equal measure of calmness and frantic panic, another gang of inmates race by, chasing their horse in an attempt to save one of their number who has hold of the beast and is being dragged unceremoniously across the arena floor. Back at the chutes, the Lexington Correctional Center team call for medical assistance after witnessing one of their members fall to the ground following a flurry of kicking from their subject. Finally, following ten minutes of non-stop cowboy consternation in the face of equine malevolence and frenzied calcitrations, the crowd cheers as the home team bring their horse across the line. The audience return to their seats, short of breath and still reeling from what they've witnessed. They don't have a great deal of time in which to recuperate; once all of the horses have been captured and sent to the back, it's the turn of the remaining five correctional centres to try their hand at the event.

Another round of Bull Poker is announced and the crowd rise from their seats, cameras at the ready, to witness a bull run straight past the table, saving the lives and limbs of the participants and making every one of the inmates an instant winner.

With the crowd becoming impatient and baying for blood following an unimpressive inmate bull ride and an IRPA event involving cowgirls riding their horses around three upturned barrels arranged in a cloverleaf pattern, they are finally introduced to the event which the majority see as being worth the entrance fee on its own.

It's called 'Money the Hard Way' and the premise couldn't be simpler. Every inmate enters the arena and each has the same task: to rescue a pouch with a hundred dollars in it. That sum may not sound a great deal, but when you realize that it's the equivalent of four months' pay to an imprisoned hardened criminal, you can see it's certainly 'big money' to them. The only problem is that the elusive pouch is tied between the horns of a 3,000-pound Brahma bull. As they take to the sandy arena floor, the hundred or so inmates wait patiently for the chute to open, with the brave prisoners edging nearer to the door and the majority hanging back, wanting no part of the action. The pen opens, a raging, angered bull flies out into the arena and the song 'I Fought the Law' blares out of the penitentiary's public-address system. A dozen inmates surround the bull, and amongst the jumble of arms and legs reaching across the head of the beast, bodies are tossed into the air or shunted to the ground as the bull forces his way through the convicts. As several step aside, a group of opportunists ambush the creature, with one managing to dislodge the pouch, which falls to the ground. Other prisoners trail the bull before realizing that the pouch has already been removed and the money won. The crowd congratulate the victor on a job well done, but through their smiles and cheers, an undercurrent of disappointment is detectable due to the brevity of the event. As the crowd flood to the exits following 'Money the Hard Way', the convicts who still have a round of bull riding do so to a depleted audience.

As Bec and I reached our car, the show was still continuing on the inside, and the organizers were more than likely kicking themselves for featuring Money the Hard Way as their penultimate event.

Bec and I discussed the event whilst attempting to leave the penitentiary with the procession of other vehicles, already anticipating Saturday's rodeo and another chance to see an epic battle between wild ranch animal and convicted felon. We were so engrossed that in an attempt to leave the growing queue of slow traffic, I joined a road which went under, but did not join, the main highway out of the town before coming to an end after a mile and a half. It wasn't a completely wasted detour, however. Because the road was so quiet, we witnessed our first ever armadillo in the wild: a nine-banded armadillo to be precise, whose pale taupe, bony armoured shell and long tail were illuminated beautifully by my rental car's headlights just moments before I ran over it.*

---

* Don't worry – it's probably still alive. Surely all of that armour can protect it from a 4-wheel drive vehicle travelling at 50 mph.

*

The next day, we arrived in McAlester having passed dozens of signs informing us that Jesus would be returning (one of which stated that 'HE IS COMING HERE AND YOU'D BETTER BE READY'). Now, this may be true, but if the Lord had chosen Oklahoma as a setting for the second coming he was surely taking the piss and had selected McAlester for ironic purposes only. Maybe I'm wrong and he does have a sense of humour after all.

We arrived in the main street just in time for the start of yet another town parade. This time, the townspeople were out in force to witness a parade honouring the Prison Rodeo. In a clothes shop, just off the main parade route, Bec and I got talking to two of the assistants about the rodeo and its unsavoury participants.

'Are you going tonight?' asked one.

'Yes,' Bec replied. 'We went last night too.'

'I do like the Prison Rodeo. My favourite participant is in it again this year,' said the other.

'What's he in for?' I asked.

'Murder,' she replied breezily. 'He stabbed his girlfriend seventeen times.'

Bec and I stared at each other in disbelief before the assistant noticed the looks on our faces. 'Oh! That was a long time ago,' she continued. 'He's a lovely guy really.'

Outside, the parade passed without a single hitch. Only a minimal amount of horse shit littered the street. My personal highlights were the arrival of the catchily named 'Little Miss District 12', and the appearance of the McAlester Scottish Rite Freemasonry members, who took to the streets in fraternal caps behind the wheels of miniature cars, weaving in and out of each other's path and generally looking like a bunch of secret-handshake simpletons.

The day's schedule of events was to be kicked off by Jarrod Birmingham, the country and western singer who had earlier scuppered my attempts at attending a non-national anthem event. As he took to the stage, welcomed to McAlester by the local mayor, rainfall the like of which I've never experienced hit the city. People darted away through fast-forming puddles to shelter beneath shop awnings or in cafés. Jarrod and his entourage fled the stage. The heavens didn't just open that day, they appeared to have been severely ram-raided.

Bec and I rushed to a nearby coffee shop for shelter, where we bought a single coffee and kept spitting swigs we had taken back into the mug while waiting for the torrential downpour to subside. After thirty minutes, we ventured back on to the soggy streets to survey the scene. Drainage covers gargled under the gallons of water which rushed down the kerbs. In the main street, downpipes and loose guttering spewed water on to the already sodden ground, leaving the entire place devoid of revellers and stands. Fortunately, neither the organizing team nor Jarrod Birmingham were anywhere in sight.

At eight fifteen, we made our way to the penitentiary for the second and final rodeo of the weekend. Realizing it would take at least five minutes to get there, and a further quarter of an hour to walk from our car, make our way through the rigorous security checks and locate our seats, we believed we had timed it perfectly to miss the patriotic annoyances. The first thing I noticed as we stepped into a field which acted as a parking lot for the rodeo was that a helicopter was circling the penitentiary, shining a bright light down on the building. Either this was for dramatic effect during the early stages of the weekend's most popular show, or someone had escaped.

Just as we entered, some young girls approached me and asked if we would like to purchase a programme. As I displayed the copy I had bought the previous day, the arena was suddenly hushed to a deathly silence as 'O say, can you see . . .' echoed through the terraces.

Everyone around us stood as if anchored in position by the words of a song, and even the guards on their prospective lookouts put down their guns to adopt the reverent, motionless position. If the prisoners had any sense, they would abandon their fifteen-year tunnelling plans and simply escape during the anthem. From what I could make out, as long as the lyrics are being blurted out, any American within earshot is rooted to the spot as if suddenly paralysed from the hair down. With one arm affixed to their chests, the guards wouldn't be great shots either.

The final show promised to be a messy affair. Owing to the downpour earlier in the day, the arena's sandy, dirty surface had become a treacherous quagmire, and with the exception of some inmates returning to the stands looking as if they'd spent the afternoon being trampled into a soggy rugby field in northern Wales, the majority of rounds passed without highlight. The Mad Scramble was injury-free and the Bull Poker followed a similar path to the unsuccessful round which featured in Friday's show. Such was the drought of death-defying action and meagreness of inmate injuries, the guy behind us dozed off and was slowly dripping his soft drink on to the floor.

Suddenly, the crowd burst into life. Daniel Liles, an inmate of the Oklahoma State Penitentiary and, in the crowd's eyes, a home town hero, was introduced.

'He's a veteran,' shouted the MC. 'Give it up for Daniel Liles. It's his fourteenth straight year at the Prison Rodeo!'

The crowd gave Liles a standing ovation for his years of service to the event. At the same time, I sat down and thought that if he was able to attend a prison rodeo for so many consecutive years, what on earth was he in for?*

His bareback-riding attempt came to a disappointing end as he didn't last the eight seconds required to register an official score. As a result, he jumped up, slammed his fist to the ground and looked crestfallen – but probably not a fraction as inconsolable as the family of his victim.

A further round of the Wild Horse Race was followed by the final Bull Poker – a dull affair by the previous evening's standards, since the table remained intact and the bull simply ploughed mercilessly through only half of the contestants. The gentleman who had nodded off woke just in time to save the last sip of his drink. The earlier downpour had dampened the ground to such a degree that the IRPA Barrel Racing title would be won by a rider who had taken to the course during Friday's dry conditions.

* First degree murder and 'injury to a public building' (whatever that means). Liles and his brother murdered Joe Yarborough in a motel room in Oklahoma City before disposing of the body in the South Canadian River in August 1982. Standing ovation, anyone?

Failing to learn from their mistakes, the organizers stuck with their plan to stage Money the Hard Way as the penultimate event, resulting in an eager crowd rattling their car keys in anticipation of a quick win and an immediate mass exodus. As the surviving masses took to the arena floor, the bull was released and was quickly surrounded by enthusiastic inmates. Luckily for the members of the audience and the longevity of the event, the Brahma broke free from the pack and evaded an early attempt on its hundred-dollar pouch. The beast ran to the opposite end of the arena, more than fifty yards from the nearest felon, and I could sense trepidation spreading through the crowd and the anxious contestants. It turned and faced the hundred-strong pack and as a dozen inmates stepped away from the main bulk of the mob towards the bull, now scuffing its hoof ready to charge, everyone's keys were placed firmly back in their pockets. Fuelled by both adrenalin and stupidity, a convict made a dash for the animal. He changed his mind midway through his assault, but too late. As a timely reminder to the other felons, the man was skewered by the behemoth's right horn and sent hurtling over twelve feet into the night sky before returning to the muddy arena floor in a heap. Half a dozen inmates rushed past their fellow prisoner without any concern for his wellbeing, eyes fixed firmly on the prize. As they set upon the bull, two were tossed violently to the ground. One of the remaining contestants escaped a savage lunge as another made a last-ditch attempt at the pouch as he fell to the ground. He swiped at the pouch and managed to grab it. Then he sprinted to safety, raising the pouch aloft and bringing the crowd to their feet in a standing ovation, an applause that continued while many members of the audience made a swift move towards the gate after a sudden reappearance of their car keys.

And that, in a muddy field surrounding a maximum-security penitentiary, was that, the end of a memorable journey of American oddities and delights. Only minutes ago, Bec and I had been witnessing murderers and rapists being shoved, shunted, lanced and launched by a feverish array of bovine adversaries. In two months I had jumped in a pit of mud, won a film festival, bared my bottom to hundreds of commuters and been killed by a Native American on five separate occasions. Now all that awaited me was the prospect of home. The phrase 'polar opposites' sprang to mind.

Once again, I'd had to compete against the summer temperatures that hit the US, and as I boarded my plane at Oklahoma airport, I promised myself that if I ever returned to America it would be in the spring or autumn when heat didn't have to be constantly battled.

I just didn't know how soon that would be.

At home, I realized that the only event I missed out on, the World's Largest Machine Gun Shoot in Kentucky, is held biannually. It was to be staged next in mid-October. Bending my credit card to breaking point, I booked two seats on a flight to Cincinnati. I had one specific travelling partner in mind.

11

Going Out with a Bang

'Shit. I've lost my passport.'

'What do you mean you've lost your passport?'

'I mean, I've lost my passport.'

We hadn't even set foot outside my front door and Bateman was already showing the credentials which made him such a joy – and nuisance – to travel with.

'Where did you last see it?' I asked.

'In the pub last night. Do you reckon they're open?'

'At half five in the morning? Probably not.'

Fortunately, my local is a bed and breakfast, so someone was available to unlock the front door and allow Bateman to retrieve his passport so we could begin the five-hour drive to Gatwick.

It was cheaper to fly to Cincinnati than Louisville. We took a flight via Detroit, a sparkling new airport that tries rather too hard to impress. A giant fountain stands at the entrance and beneath the numerous check-in desks and luggage carousels is a concourse which links each terminal to the remainder of the airport. It must be an epileptic's nightmare: at the bottom of a long escalator, a hallway approximately 100 yards long with pedestrian conveyor belts at either side uses colourful lights and a soundtrack similar to the shower scene in *Psycho* to brighten the travellers' commute, creating an atmosphere similar to a hospital's multi-sensory room for children with severe mental disabilities. Reaching the end of the psychedelic corridor, past a lady who had fainted, we made our way to customs. This meant having to complete another Visa Waiver Departure/ Arrival form, which would have to be presented during an additional meeting with whatever insolent megalomaniac was waiting for us on border patrol.

In the light of Bateman's outstanding speeding fine, I decided to be completely truthful on my form and so ticked the box marked 'business' under 'reason for travel'. Bateman simply opted for 'vacation' and hoped an American criminal record wasn't revealed during his light interrogation. As we made our way through the terminal, we joked that if the worst came to the worst he could spend a few days at the airport whilst I went and shot some guns. It soon transpired, however, that it was I who was destined for trouble.

I was chaperoned to booth 26, where Mike, an austere-looking chap with a haircut which suggested that, much to his displeasure, he had been drafted into immigration having just completed his spell of frontline fighting in Iraq, was waiting for me.

Mike had already disposed of one senior citizen and spent twenty minutes questioning a Brazilian, before calling for a colleague and his Alsatian to take him to a nearby room for further interrogation, when it was my turn to approach the booth.

'Good afternoon,' I said with an overwhelming sense of merriment.

'Hey.'

'How are you?' I asked.

'What brings you to America . . .' He consulted my form. '. . . Mr Smith?' His tone, his glare, his whole bearing when questioning me made my innocent presence in the USA seem incredibly suspect.

'Well, it may sound strange,' I replied, 'but I'm going to a Machine Gun Shoot in Louisville.'

'A Machine Gun Shoot, hey?' He pointed at his own handgun in its holster. 'Why?'

'Well, I'm writing a book about strange events in America, and seeing as we don't have them readily available in England, I thought this was ideal.'

'There a company paying you to do this?' he asked.

'Well, sort of. I wrote a book for them a couple of years ago and they stupidly asked me to write another.'

He looked up at me, clutching my passport in his hands. 'What was your first book about?'

Shit. The worst question he could have possibly asked. It was time to not lie, necessarily, but withhold certain aspects of the truth.

'Oh, I just travelled around America – a bit like this actually.'

'Oh yeah?'

'Yeah.'

'Doing what?'

'Oh, nothing special.'

'What though?'

'I kind of went around America breaking strange laws.'

Mike stopped, looked up at me again and placed the rubber stamp at arm's length. 'Breaking laws?' he asked. 'You didn't evoke any interest from the police, did you?'

'Only in Chicago,' I replied. 'We were almost held at gunpoint. Funny story, actually.'

What on earth was I doing? The simple answer was 'No.' Instead, I was regaling Mike with the story of the time Bateman and I were mistaken for bad-ass gangsters following the slowest and least exciting police chase in history.

'Right, sir, you're going to have to go to booth thirty-two.' He completely interrupted me, just at the best bit of the story when one of the Chicago cops, upon hearing that we were from England, leant his head through the window and shouted, 'G'day!'

'What for?' I asked. 'There's nothing wrong, is there?'

'You're a Smith. We get a lot of you so we have to check that you are who you say you are.'

Further interrogation followed, and this time I simply kept my mouth shut and was allowed passage into America, joining a queue of people waiting to hand over their declaration of customs forms. As Bateman and I discussed my lengthy immigration process, Mike halted his queue of tourists, departed his booth and walked purposefully in my direction.

'Mr Smith!' he shouted. 'You know you said you came over here for some sort of crime spree a couple of years ago? You weren't actually arrested or cautioned for any violation, were you?'

'No,' I replied. 'But Bateman was stopped for

speeding and didn't pay his fine in Wyoming.' (Of course I didn't say that – I'd learnt my lesson as soon as Mike's eyes viewed the tick next to the word 'business').

'Oh, OK then. Enjoy your holiday,' Mike replied, eyeing me with suspicion before making his slow retreat to his booth and awaiting arrivals on an Air France flight from Paris.

Upon our late arrival into Cincinnati, we checked into one of the nearest motels to the airport, remembering to stay well clear of the infamous Budget Host. We arose early, intending to make the most of our short time in the States, and started the 100-mile drive south to Louisville, to attend the opening day of the World's Largest Machine Gun Shoot.

Our rental car, a silver Dodge Charger, was the first convertible I'd ever been given by a hire company – perfect for summer travel (if you ignore its steering inefficiencies) but not so great if you happen to be in Kentucky in October, when temperatures aren't at their peak and lowering the top to the wind chill isn't advisable. When we finally arrived at our motel in Louisville, it was too early to check in, so I approached the desk to ask two questions. One I was sure they could answer with considerable ease, whilst the other was rather more taxing – especially for an American. The helpful clerks knew straight away the nearest and best place where Bateman and I could buy breakfast, but, as I predicted, struggled when asked if there was anywhere in the city that would be showing the Rugby World Cup; a sporting competition which took some explaining to the members of staff because of the word 'world'. It took more than ten minutes to make them understand that unlike baseball's 'World Series', the Rugby World Cup actually involves nations from all over the planet taking part and therefore actually justifies the inclusion of the word 'world' in its title.

When I had first booked my flight to Louisville, England's national rugby team were in a terrible state. They had underachieved at the Six Nations tournament and had lost all three of their World Cup warm-ups; even the Welsh had beaten us. A 36–0 thrashing in an earlier group game at the hands of South Africa left me sad but confident that by the time I flew to America, on the weekend that coincided with the semi-finals of the tournament, England would have already been eliminated.

Trust England. A scintillating display against the Australians a week before our departure had landed the team a clash with France for a place in the final, and somehow we had to fit watching the match into our hectic three-day schedule.

Other than having a rather amusing name, the Knob Creek Gun Range was once a military munitions test range and is conveniently located on the very edge of the Fort Knox Military Reservation, a major United States Army post, and famously home to the US Gold Bullion Depository. The fortified vault holds over 140 million ounces of gold, and although the public aren't allowed inside, your average Joe need not be too worried. If you have witnessed the opening title sequence to *Disney's DuckTales,* in which Scrooge McDuck dives into a huge pile of gold coins, you'll be able to imagine the vault. It's probably very similar.

The biannual shoot is open to members as well as the general public and as a result the range, set in a region surrounded by nothing but forests, has a great deal of space devoted to parking. Such is the popularity of the event that from the lower parking lot (or field as it is commonly known), you could see dozens of people carrying an array of different firearms, clad in all manner of sub-military attire including bomber jackets, body warmers and protective goggles, waiting patiently at the far end of the field for a yellow school bus to transport them the 800 yards to the main entrance.

Tickets to the event cost a paltry ten dollars per person per day and only five dollars for shooters below the age of twelve. Yes, you read correctly, *shooters* under the age of twelve. Whilst queuing to purchase an entrance wristband, I was offered a 'Rudy Giuliani' badge at the same moment I noticed a poster mocking the politics of Hillary Clinton. With Kentucky being a deeply Republican area, the NRA-endorsed notice warned that 'her' in the White House meant a return to a Bill Clinton-style administration, in which he lobbied for both the Brady Bill and the Assault Weapons Ban – two major pieces of gun-control legislation he signed in an attempt to make America a safer society.

How dare he do such a thing!

Once in, it became clear that the Machine Gun Shoot was an eclectic mix of my past experiences. The people and their love of guns evoked memories of the Custer's Last Stand Reenactment I had attended with Rod and Bob in Montana. The buying of weaponry and assorted paraphernalia, coupled with the politics and opinions of the attendees, were a chilling reminder of the atmosphere at both the World's Longest Yard Sale and the Redneck Games.

Although we were already positioned by the main range, where shooters had booked firing lanes months in advance to guarantee themselves a spot at the event, the only shots that could be heard were those of people taking part in shooting competitions on the two lower ranges. With the short break in firing about to come to an end, Bateman and I headed for a nearby stand in search of some cheap ear defenders.

'Where you from?' asked the gentleman from behind his little counter.

'England,' we replied.

'What you after?'

'Some ear defenders, please.'

'They're all there,' he said, pointing at a heap of varying designs ranging from plugs on string to the standard building-site ear defenders that wrap around the top of your head.

'It always this busy here at the shoot?' I asked as he proffered a stuffed monkey wearing a cape with the words 'Knob Creek 2008' written on it in my direction.

'Oh, no,' he replied. 'By tomorrow, you won't be able to move.'

In the end we each opted for a set of ear defenders similar in size and shape to little Walkman headphones stylish in the late 1980s. Before we could rip them from their packets, the warning that a ten-minute shoot was about to begin was sounded, and all hell broke loose. No sooner had one bullet broken free of its chamber than a barrage of ammunition was unleashed into the range, sending tremors through the ground as a maelstrom of deafening crashes, bangs and explosions created a wall of sound which thundered towards me in an unrelenting onslaught. Dust and smoke covered the shooting area in a fine haze, then the blast created by the firing of a monolithic cannon at the far side of the field reverberated through my legs, engulfing the crowd in a plume of smoke. As more ammunition rained down on the refrigerators, old cars and metal drums which the organizers had placed as targets, causing untold damage, the hundreds of detonations created such an overwhelmingly loud noise that I could no longer hear the helicopter which had hovered above my head ever since the seemingly eternal racket began. Next, an M4 assault rifle added to the din as it dismissed its cartridges in blisteringly quick succession. Empty shells flew out, streaming down the back of the gentleman to its left in a waterfall of lead. Without even a momentary break for silence since it started, the firing reached its conclusion, with a cacophonic crescendo of further ear-splitting blasts and eruptions. An almost perfect silence followed, and the smell of gunpowder lingered in the air. The throng of exhausted spectators began to remove their protective headwear or fingers from their ears and survey the torn and battered field. Bateman and I were shattered by this baptism – literally – of fire.

Because it was only the opening afternoon of the three-day event, we decided to use the Friday to explore the wonders of the Machine Gun Shoot. We would not be parting with our money until later on in the weekend. On the lower range, a field which was perhaps half the size of the main range, people waited patiently in line to try their hand at pulling the trigger of firearms which could be hired for as little as twenty dollars. This was also the location of the 'Jungle Walk', a competition in which each entrant was handed a semi-automatic sub-machine gun and had to fire at a series of targets in the quickest time possible. With the Jungle Walk fully booked until the following day, Bateman and I decided it was best if we left the Knob Creek Gun Range and used the remainder of the day to grab something to eat and find a bar which would guarantee us the viewing of Saturday's all-important rugby tie.

Owing to his job as a person who beats up unruly northern people (otherwise known as a doorman at one of Newquay's nightclubs), Bateman constantly demands protein. If he isn't drinking one of those obscene milk shakes, then he is in desperate need of chicken. The poultry requirements of a person of Bateman's stature add up to an entire battery farm. Ignoring the fact that it's a huge conglomerate with the wealth of a small European nation, a Wal-Mart delicatessen proved man enough to fulfil Bateman's dietary desires. Upon return-ing to our motel, the meal I provided had almost satisfied his appetite, and though he soon started whining for yet another meal, the moaning came to an end when (thankfully) he fell asleep at only six in the evening.

Creeping out of the room, I left our accommodation on Bardstown Road in search of Molly Malone's Irish Pub, down in the heart of Louisville's entertainment district, where I had been told by the clerk at the motel's front desk that I would have the best chance of watching the game.

My journey on Bardstown Road, in the direction of

Louisville's downtown area, went well, and the number of bars that passed my car window raised my hopes of the match being broadcast somewhere in the vicinity. My progress was abruptly halted by a police barricade, dozens of cops and several squad cars surrounding a man in a blood-stained boiler suit holding a large kitchen knife in his right hand. As ordered by one of the officers, I immediately took an alternative route and found a place to park on a side street several blocks away, before taking to the streets on foot to see what was going on.

Just as I left the car, an explosion like a gunshot resonated through the narrow alleys. Running back towards the barricades through a commotion of sirens and whistles, I passed a child who had seemingly suffered a bullet wound to the stomach and had slumped on to his mother's lap. No one seemed to care. Pedestrians simply walked by without batting an eyelid, or quietly positioned themselves on the kerb away from the boy.

And they were right to do so.

As a hearse approached the top of the hill, followed by a group of teenagers in the long, mournful ghost masks made famous by the series of *Scream* films, it soon became apparent that no crime had been committed and there wasn't a knife-wielding maniac on the loose. In actual fact, the streets had been closed off because of a staging of Caulfield's Halloween Parade. And why not? After all, it was October the 12th.

In my search for Molly Malone's, I made my way through numerous Freddy Kruegers, Jason Voorheeses, and more demonic and gruesome characters including the chainsaw-wielding Leatherface from *The Texas Chainsaw Massacre* and *Big Brother*'s Jade Goody (just kidding – mass murders are one thing, but that's just taking it too far. Children were at this event!). Eventually, I made it to the Irish bar. My hopes of them showing the match rose even higher when I saw it was directly next door to the Celtic Center, a gift shop selling Irish merchandise, which advertised the international rugby tournament.

Bateman and I were in luck. Molly Malone's *would* be broadcasting the match. Unfortunately, it wouldn't be shown live. Instead it was to be broadcast twenty-four hours after the game, at exactly the time that Bateman and I would be at Cincinnati airport awaiting our flight home.

Live sport shown a day after it took place? Is there any sense in the idea?

Sitting outside their business, the owners of the Celtic Center didn't know of anywhere in the entire city that would be showing the titanic clash. Defeated, I made my way back to the car trying not to dance to 'Ghostbusters' as Ray Parker Jr's 1984 hit blared out of the speakers of a passing 1959 Cadillac ambulance, decorated perfectly to match the vehicle used in the film.

Bateman was still fast asleep in a now pitch-black motel room and so I made my way to the front desk. With the help of Terence on reception, a copy of the local Yellow Pages, a Louisville entertainment tourist guide and his laptop, we spent over an hour contacting sports bars, restaurants, nightclubs and even out-of-state gambling establishments in a bid to find somewhere that would be showing the World Cup rugby. To make matters worse, the match happened to kick off at exactly the same time as an American football game between the Universities of Kentucky and Louisiana (a sport similar to rugby but much softer, owing to the players' need for helmets, padding and an abundance of protective clothing).

After numerous phone calls and Google searches, we finally found a drinking establishment that would be showing the game live: Molly Malone's. And not the one on Bardstown Road either. In fact it was Molly Malone's Irish Pub of Covington, 100 miles northeast of Louisville, who stated proudly that they were the only pub in the entire state of Kentucky that would be showing the game live.

When Bateman woke up, I told him about the bar and where it was and we planned the following day with military precision. We would have breakfast at eight and arrive at the Machine Gun Shoot an hour later to ensure ourselves an early slot on the Jungle Walk. At one in the afternoon, we would drive to Covington, watch the rugby from three until five, and return to Knob Creek a little before seven so as not to miss the highlight of the weekend: the Night Shoot. Barring extra time or a mechanical breakdown, it was a foolproof plan.

If I'd asked Terence for a wake-up call, then Bateman and I would probably have woken up before nine thirty and wouldn't have arrived at the Machine Gun Shoot ninety minutes later than planned. Thinking this may have ruined our chances of taking part in the Jungle Walk, we rapidly paced past the cannon and machine guns on the main field and down on to the lower range.

A huge queue, snaking its way up the path, waited in line to hire random firearms from vendors on the range, and the Jungle Walk had several people skulking around the sign-up desk. Kevin, dressed in camouflage jacket, cap and jeans, looked up at me as I approached him.

'Hiya,' I said. 'I was just wondering when the next available time is for the Jungle Walk.'

'Well, next slot is gonna be around two thirty,' he replied.

'Ah. That's a bit of a problem for us, you see. We have to leave at one. Neither of us is going to win either so can you possibly sort something out?'

Kevin ran his hand across his clipboard while stroking his beard with the other. 'I'll tell you what I'll do,' he said. 'You sign up and pay now, and when you get back, we'll sort something out. To save more time, my buddy's doing a safety talk and taking questions on the course if you wanna listen.'

I signed our names on to the bottom of the list and joined a father and son who had taken up their positions for the safety briefing. I was still close enough to Kevin, however, to catch the strangest response I had ever heard from someone discovering my name. I'm used to people calling me 'Dick' or commenting on how common Smith is as a surname, but Kevin's comment was unique.

'Richard Smith, huh?' he said in bewilderment. 'Sounds more like a disease.'

I've never been very good at paying attention to or following orders – perhaps that's the reason why during a charity parachute jump, after spending two weekends training how to perform the perfect descent, I ended up bungling out of the plane in a downward spiral before pulling on the wrong toggles and landing in a heap almost half a mile away from the airfield. The Jungle Walk briefing was the same. I tried to listen intently to the man, but even though I knew I would be handling a dangerous weapon later, my mind kept drifting off on to trivial matters such as the power cables positioned behind the man and the wart on the left side of his neck. As a result, all I could remember was that they wouldn't tell us where the targets were and there was a certain time when we were prohibited from shooting. I think. It may have been when we had to shoot non-stop.

We didn't want to join any queue for firearms which could result in us missing the match, so we decided it was best if we simply browsed the aisles of Knob Creek's military gun show. In all honesty, the sale wasn't too dissimilar to some of the gun stands I had seen in the southern states during the World's Longest Yard Sale. There were exotic night-vision scopes and even grenades, which both had eye-watering price tags attached, and the usual SS uniforms and Nazi accoutrements made an unwelcome return to the tabletops, as well as a T-shirt Bateman wanted to buy with the words 'GIVE WAR A CHANCE! HAPPINESS IS A MUSHROOM CLOUD' emblazoned atop a smiling face and a nuclear explosion. I searched in vain for a souvenir, but either the objects were too expensive or I didn't actually know what they were. Anyway, there was almost nothing I could have bought which customs wouldn't question me about the moment I returned home.

At one exactly, we left the range amid another wild ten-minute blitzkrieg from the automatic weapons (including cannon fire). This time a Gatling gun joined the fray, which showered the range in a turf-uplifting, tumultuous salvo of aggression. Hopping back into the Dodge, we set off for Covington, leaving behind the conservative and religious beliefs of the Machine Gun Shoot. The only conversion we were hoping to be part of would be one that had just left the boot of Jonny Wilkinson.

Just a mile from the Ohio border, overlooking both the Cincinnati skyline and the beautiful John A. Roebling Suspension Bridge, was Molly Malone's. Downstairs, the bar was well lit and the atmosphere was gentle and genial as friends settled down to watch the American football tie. As rugby fans, we were shown the staircase to the uppermost extremities of the pub's three storeys. Enveloped in a musky smell and a mix of Australian, French and English supporters (as well as a couple of Americans who had probably wandered in by mistake), we approached the bar, ordered a couple of drinks and paid twenty dollars each for the privilege of watching the match.

It was tense and cagey, but in the end, the 200-mile journey combined with the overpriced drinks and extortionate viewing fee didn't matter an iota. A last-minute drop goal 4,000 miles away in Paris saw half of the room on its feet and England's progression to the final.

'Right, you drive. I'm gonna carry on drinking,' demanded Bateman as he headed into a nearby gas station's shop and I filled the tank.

Over 100 miles and 6 cans for Bateman later, we arrived back at Knob Creek. By now, the day had entered the twilight hour and neither of us was overly keen on taking part in the Jungle Walk. Bateman simply wanted to continue his private celebrations and I was only too happy to join in. We found Kevin and told him that we believed the conditions were too dark and that we would like our money back.

'Are you sure?' he asked. 'We can do it in this light, you know.'

'Are you sure?' I asked in my turn, hoping to stall him so the light faded even further.

'Yeah. We'll give it a go!' he quipped.

'Thing is,' I replied, 'England won, and my friend is pretty drunk.' Bateman wasn't drunk at all, actually, and nor was I hopeful this would work. I imagined that even if I said he was paralytic, Kevin would still hand us an Uzi.

But he groaned in disappointment. 'Oh, here's your money back then.'

With the money securely in my wallet, Bateman and I made our way back up to the main range for the Night Shoot, Knob Creek's weekend highlight. There was no set time when the Night Shoot would take place, and the brochure I was handed on arrival stated simply that it would be staged at some point between five and ten. I'm no genius but I was pretty sure that something called a 'Night Shoot' would more than likely have to occur after it got dark.

A crowd of maybe a thousand people had gathered behind the range and on the roof of a building that over-looked it. As Bateman and I took to the roof, we jostled for position amongst a throng of people who must have drawn a similar Night-Shoot-had-to-happen-at-night conclusion to my own. Several pick-up trucks appeared on the range to arrange metal drums and attach pyrotechnical charges to the objects in the field. Twenty minutes of general fannying about followed, the audience grew impatient and rumours that 'it would start any minute now' circulated a number of times.

As a helicopter circled overhead, I was reminded why the Night Shoot hadn't already begun. All weekend, raffle tickets had been sold to visitors to the Machine Gun Shoot, with the first prize being a trip in a helicopter to fire the opening few shots of the Night Shoot. As the chopper hovered above the range, short, infrequent gunshots could be heard which, compared to the earlier rumbles which emanated from the range, sounded as if the shooter was aiming at the targets with a spud gun. After a couple of minutes, the helicopter banked to its left, pointed its nose to the ground, and disappeared over the trees. At that precise moment, all manner of camera and video equipment was turned on and focused on the darkness in front.

A quick crackle from the right of the range was shortly followed by a bombardment of bullets. Being the Night Shoot, tracers were allowed and the range immediately lit up with beautiful technicolour explosions, as if a firework factory had suffered a terrorist attack. A series of the metal drums' charges were detonated and half a dozen plumes of flame filled the night sky, illuminating the entire range.

As further explosions filled the air, tracers haloed the field like a belligerent rainbow, and the unrelenting din made the siege of Stalingrad look more like a Sunday school outing. It lasted ten interminable minutes until the final single shot was fired, like a solitary clap following a round of applause. The crowd around me stood in awe and disbelief. Bateman and I quickly headed for the gate.

An early shower the following morning helped to clear the hangover that had enveloped every sensory part of my body, yet even after I had eaten breakfast and restored lost fluids, something didn't seem quite right. I was missing something. My wallet and phone were both on top of the television, and the car keys were on the floor . . .

It was Bateman's bed. It hadn't been slept in.

I wasn't worried. Bateman had done this to me once before in a strange town named Grand Island in Nebraska, which was neither grand nor an island. That day he had disappeared after some potations and had arrived back at the motel a little after noon. I imagined he would do the same this time round, as I tried to cast my memory back to the hazy details of the night before.

I distinctly remembered visiting several bars on the road where the Halloween parade was held. I was offered a free lift home when the final bar on our post-victory celebration bar crawl closed its doors, and I didn't think returning to the motel at three thirty a.m. was too bad. Bateman disagreed and the last I saw of him was when he was getting into a car with four complete strangers.

Phew! At least that meant he was going to be fine.

An hour passed and there was no sign of him. At noon, I visited the local Wal-Mart and bought a sandwich for lunch, before returning to the motel to check out and to ask if any of the staff had seen or heard from him. They hadn't, and so I did what any good friend in a similar situation would have done: I looked for him in a place he definitely wouldn't be. I made my way to the Knob Creek Gun Range for the final day of the Machine Gun Shoot.

Either the majority of people had already had their fix of gunfire earlier in the weekend, or had slipped into the same mysterious vortex where Bateman had disappeared, because compared to the Saturday, Knob Creek on Sunday was like a ghost town. The main range was still unleashing hell, but few people were perusing the aisles of guns for sale, and, more importantly, the queue which had made its way up the bank away from the rental range the day before was totally non-existent. With no queue, two days of witnessing constant gunfire and the Jungle Walk reimbursement money burning a hole in my pocket, it was about time that I tried my own hand at pulling one of the triggers and added to the noise levels.

Above the sign-up desk was a large list of types of weapon and how much each gun and a certain number of rounds would cost. As a person who thought an M4 magazine was a publication for motorway enthusiasts, the display might as well have been written in hieroglyphics for all I could understand. I tried to make sense of the 'BAR-20 rnd mag', 'M249 Minimi – 50 rnd belt' and other nonsensical abbreviations, but finally opted for the only weapon I had heard of.

'I'll have a go with the Grenade Launcher,' I said.

'You do know it only shoots fake grenades with paint

inside, don't you?' replied Brad, who stood in front of an armoury of weapons.

'Does it?' I replied. 'In that case I'll go for the AK-47.'

In actual fact it was an AK Valmet, the Finnish version of the terrorists' favourite, and a gun which made Brad quote from the Quentin Tarantino movie *Jackie Brown*. 'AK-47,' he chuckled. 'The very best there is. When you absolutely, positively got to kill every motherfucker in the room.'

I nestled the butt of the assault rifle into my right shoulder. Brad positioned my legs so most of the pressure was on my back leg before asking me if I wanted the gun to fire single shots or to be placed into automatic mode.

'I'll start off with singles please,' I replied.

I squeezed the trigger gently with my finger. The tip of the rifle rose swiftly into the air as a bang echoed through the range, sending a slight twinge into my shoulder and leaving a rather impressive-looking hole in a car door over 50 yards away. Another shot into the car door followed before I repositioned myself and aimed at a refrigerator. Gaining confidence after a couple of shots into the ground, I asked Brad to switch the beast into automatic mode and let loose with the remainder of the magazine. I tightened my grip as the rifle reacted like a wild animal in my arms. It began to shoot wherever it chose, and the magazine emptied abruptly after just a couple of seconds of shooting into the air. I wasn't surprised at the brevity of its automatic display – the Valmet can discharge an impressive seven hundred bullets a minute.

Feeling the need for further unnecessary destruction

of white goods and old vehicle parts, I threw another forty dollars in Brad's direction and selected another gun from the rack, pointing at a gun that reminded me of the A-Team. The tainted green hunk of metal was a Heckler and Koch G3, an automatic battle rifle first built by the West Germans a decade after the conclusion of the Second World War. It was about the same length as the AK, but was a bulkier and firmer piece of weaponry, weighing at least 10 pounds. It felt cumbersome in my hands. I opted again to begin with single shots, but it felt awkward, because I'd forgotten what to do with my legs. If Saturday's queue had suddenly reappeared, filling the alleys with tens of dozens of marksmen, it would have been pretty obvious to any passer-by just which one of us was English.

Taking suggestions as to what I should shoot at from some spectators, Brad advised that I should finish the round off in automatic mode. With just a twenty-round magazine placed into the gun in the first place, the remainder of the bullets took what seemed like a little squeeze's worth to use up. Goodness knows how much the Night Shoot and regular bursts of artillery costs the owners of the guns. The seconds I'd spent with the G3 and the AK were one of the most exhilarating experiences in my life, and it was certainly the quickest eighty dollars I'd ever spent.

The short time I'd spent with Brad and the other gun-obsessed chauvinists reminded me that although I was enjoying myself, I was doing so on my own. Bateman was still missing so I returned to the motel where I expected he would be waiting for our trip to the airport.

He wasn't.

It was serious now. It was half two in the afternoon, and our flight left Cincinnati airport, a good hour and a half's drive away, in just over four hours' time. Goodness knows what had happened to him.

Unfortunately, I have a transatlantic touch of death about me. Whenever I travel to America, someone very well known seems to die. When I first visited the States in 1997, Gianni Versace was murdered the very day I arrived, and ever since that date I've suffered similar experiences. In 1999 Jill Dando, Oliver Reed and Alf Ramsey completed a hat trick of heaven-bounds in just the space of a week; and even when I spent just four days in Las Vegas a few days before my twenty-first birthday, 1966 World Cup final commentator Kenneth Wolstenholme and Dudley Moore passed on. The death of CBS anchor Peter Jennings occurred when Bateman and I were touring the nation on a frivolous crime spree in 2005, and Mike 'Frank Butcher' Reid had kicked the bucket a day after our hopes had been sunk in Heber Springs' Cardboard Boat Race. Perhaps I should just stay at home in future and not jeopardize the lives of celebrities by clearing customs at American airports.

The only reason I point out this strange peculiarity is that as far as I knew, no one well known had died since my arrival in Cincinnati three days ago. Perhaps in a cruel twist of fate the Grim Reaper had Bateman in his sights this time round. What's worse was that if he really was dead, I'd probably be the investigating detectives' prime suspect.

At three, I had waited as long as I could and with the risk of missing our flights and the money I had spent on them, I packed both of our bags into the boot of the

Dodge and made my way to Cincinnati, hoping that Bateman had somehow sponged a lift to the terminal from whoever he had spent the previous night with.

At a little before five, I had checked in, proceeded through the relevant security checks and settled down in the departure lounge in front of an NFL game between the Dallas Cowboys and the New England Patriots, occasionally glancing over my shoulder in the vain hope that Bateman would appear behind me. Suddenly my name was announced on the airport's public address system, with a message to contact my nearest airline operative.

As I searched the various gates and corridors for a member of staff, I was reminded of the only other time my name had been announced at an airport. It was in Alicante when I had just finished watching England play Switzerland in the 2004 European Football Championships with my friend Max Dennis. I was a little the worse for wear and after the announcement was made that I was the only passenger not to have boarded the craft, I reached the gate with seconds to spare and eventually fell asleep in the toilet. I don't care what you say about aeroplane lavatories, the fact that they are cramped is a positive bonus. With me sitting on the toilet and my head in the sink, I could have lost any bodily fluid from any orifice during the flight home and it would have been collected with no mess or fuss.

Eventually, I found an appropriate representative and was handed a number to call. It was the number of the Emergency Room at Louisville's University Hospital. As I rushed to the nearest payphone to check on my friend, my hand was shaking, terrified of what I would hear.

As it turned out, Bateman's life wasn't in any sort of danger at all. In the late morning, he had been found asleep in the grounds of one of Louisville's universities by several members of an American Football team, who needed his body moved in order to begin their arranged fixture, and who had promptly summoned a police officer. After spending the early hours at a basketball player's party in the suburbs, Bateman had been dropped off at the motel by the same people who had offered him a lift when I last saw him. Unfortunately, it turned out to be one of the other two Quality Inns in Louisville. Bateman set off on foot in search of the right hostelry, but soon gave in and collapsed. Since the motel's room key was Bateman's only possession, the policeman had no choice but to take him to hospital, where the nurses rang the only number on the key card, which put them through to the local branch of Domino's Pizza.

Whatever thoughts I had of returning to Louisville to pick him up were soon dismissed when it turned out that he didn't have his passport and that according to the nurses who had treated him, all Bateman was suffering from was a severe hangover. And anyway, Bateman had always complained about the short length of our stay. Now he had the chance to experience Louisville for a little bit longer, albeit from a hospital bed, on his own, with no money. Still, a holiday's a holiday.

Stepping aboard Northwest Airlines Flight 32 from Detroit to London I had my final gulp of American life. There would be no more late additions to the plan and the concrete runway beneath me would be the final piece of US soil I would see. I had visited America almost half a dozen times before, and if this was the last time I would see the country, I was glad that this was how it had been done: an eighty-day journey of wonder, bewilderment and sometimes shameful scenes, through the heart of both the country and its people. After visiting almost a dozen events and festivals, meeting an array of different characters and making new friends, it dawned on me that I was suddenly on my own. Still, maybe this final experience wasn't one worth sharing. The movies on show weren't exactly Oscar winners, and the screaming child three rows behind me had me wishing that I had somehow smuggled the Valmet into my hand luggage.

Epilogue

Bateman made it back to the UK two days later wearing the very same clothes as when he was found, having found his passport and booked a flight home.

Upon our return, Antony and I each found a cheque for seventy-five dollars on our doorsteps from the Hardin Chamber of Commerce for our work in the Custer's Last Stand Reenactment.

Sadly, Antony's grandmother, Elizabeth Luke, passed away peacefully on 3 November 2007, aged sixty-four, after a brave battle with her illness.

Acknowledgements

There are several people who I'd like to thank and without whom the book would have been drab, mundane and prosaic (OK then, even more so). With the exception of immigration officers and people who steal global positioning systems from police officers in Massachusetts, I seem to have an uncanny knack of meeting the kindest and most generous Americans each and every time I set foot on to their fair land. In every instance, I am in need of some sort of assistance or aid, and, without a prompt or gentle hinting, they react with unrelenting benevolence, like a flock of natives to a beached whale. Not least deserved of a mention are the Beatties, whose skills in cooking and open-arm Montanan welcoming made Camp Wishah-Kudah-WunWun a home from home when Antony and I were starting out on our journey. June and Rod were the perfect hosts, and with the exception of bruising my shoulder, the pair made living in a field in the middle of the Montanan wilderness as comfortable as it possibly could be. Also a big thank you to Bob Port and his lovely wife Jill who, along with Rick Williams and his wife Pam, made our entire visit to the camp a lively and enjoyable one.

Also, a lot of appreciation goes to Mark Broconi and his wife Aleks who not only kept Antony and I sane at the Mooning of Amtrak, but can also now categorize themselves along with such locations as Long Beach and the Pacific Ocean as the only positive things about Los Angeles. The evening Antony and I spent with them was one of the most enlightening and pleasurable get-togethers I have experienced whilst stateside; and although I have somehow misplaced it since my return to the UK, I remain eternally grateful for the 'Yardhouse' hooded top Aleks bought me. I have since more than returned the compliment and bought them each a pasty when they kindly took a 300-mile detour out of the British leg of their European vacation to visit me in Cornwall just before Christmas.

The kind deeds of Jeremy of the Yamaha and Honda dealership in Little Rock shouldn't go unnoticed and nor should the helpful staff of Riverside Box Supply, who provided us with cardboard, which in no part con-tributed to our dramatic boat-building disaster. That was completely our fault. I would also like to thank Betty Seder, Ruble Upchurch, Walter Page, Gale Reed and all of the other clerks and managers of the Chambers of Commerce I visited whose names I didn't manage to learn, but whose assistance and information were equally of great help.

The week Antony and I spent in Corvallis was one of

the most comfortable and fulfilling few days of the entire journey, and this was in no small part because of the hospitality of Mary Jeanne Reynales and her husband Dave. Thanks also to Andy Foster, Bill and Michele Powell, Peter Platt, the rest of the *Fall from Grace* crew; and thanks to the Turd for being such a worthy adversary. We really appreciated all of the gang's generosity to a couple of useless Brits who, it was quickly discovered, were useless both in front of and behind the camera.

A big thank you to Bill Eckels of the Cobbler Shoppe who acted as Britt's replacement Chamber of Commerce clerk, but whose knowledge of the National Hobo Convention was vastly inferior to his proficiency at cobbling.

Finally, special thanks to Antony, Bec and Bateman for their companionship, and to my agent, Rebecca Winfield, and British and American editors Katie Espiner and Lindsey Moore for allowing me to do something I enjoy so very much, and for ensuring that the book was delivered on time.

Thanks once again to everyone, and I apologize in advance to anyone whom I may have accidentally forgotten. And I'm sure Antony would like to echo my sentiments and would do so if he was still with us. But he's back in Cheltenham.

Л 15 – 20   15
            15 45
            10
            5
30   35 – 40
50 – 55